A DOZEN DOCTORS

Autobiographic Sketches

EDITED BY DWIGHT J. INGLE

THE UNIVERSITY OF CHICAGO PRESS
CHICAGO & LONDON

Library of Congress Catalog Card Number: 63-20908

THE UNIVERSITY OF CHICAGO PRESS, CHICAGO & LONDON
The University of Toronto Press, Toronto 5, Canada

Originally published in PERSPECTIVES IN BIOLOGY AND MEDICINE

Published 1963. Composed and printed by THE UNIVERSITY OF CHICAGO PRESS, *Chicago, Illinois, U.S.A.*

Preface

The autobiographic sketches collected into this volume are by great men in biology and medicine. Some of these men spent their lives in the laboratory and some at the bedside. Each one of them was a great teacher.

Most students of biology and medicine today are not motivated to study contemporary history. There are so many facts for the instructor to teach and there is so much for the student to learn that each guides his life in the classroom by whatever seems likely to be required by standardized examinations. And yet, if the student is more a lamp to be lighted than a vessel to be filled, he needs and will be responsive to the beauty and excitement of the processes of life and death.

The human side of history is told best by the people who had roles in it. All the men who wrote these stories lived during the same periods of great discovery, contemporary with us, but each has something unique to say. The personal side of each story will give the reader something which will clothe scientific facts with interesting perspectives on how discoveries are made and how gifted men can, when they cleave to the way of the intellect, achieve the stature of which they are capable.

Five of these twelve doctors became Nobel Laureates. Sir Henry Dale and Otto Loewi together received the prize in 1936 "for their discoveries relating to the chemical transmission of nerve impulses." W. R. Hess in 1949 shared the award "for his discovery of the functional organization of the interbrain as a co-ordinator of the activities of the internal organs." In 1943 George von Hevesy received it "for his work on the use of isotopes as tracer elements in researches on chemical processes." George Hoyt Whipple shared the award with two others in 1944 "for their discoveries concerning liver therapy against anaemias."

Perspectives in Biology and Medicine originally invited and published these brief autobiographies. The journal's readers appreciated them so warmly that they are now presented in this permanent form because of the inspiration, insight, and information that they have to offer to the wide audience of people aware of the impact that scientific thought and thinkers have on our modern world.

DWIGHT J. INGLE

Contents

SIR HENRY DALE,

O.M., G.B.E., F.R.C.P., F.R.S.

Some Fifty Years in British Medical Science

I was a Londoner by birth and early schooling. I have, indeed, lived for all my life in London, except for nine years of study in Cambridge, three of them at school and then six at the University, as a scholar and a research student of Trinity College from 1894 to 1900. Even before I entered the University I believe that my interests had been given a certain bias toward the natural sciences, especially toward biology, and even physiology, by my good fortune in encountering, while still at school, teachers who had some special knowledge of those subjects and gifts for transmitting some of their own enthusiasms.

However that may be, Cambridge University, at the time of my entry in 1894, was a center of stimulating progress in physiology, as it has, indeed, continued to be. Michael Foster was then still the Professor of Physiology and, of the brilliant group of those who had been his early Cambridge pupils, W. H. Gaskell and J. N. Langley were still active there. Our first contact as students with Gaskell was through his remarkable course of advanced lectures, which remain in my memory as the most stimulating and inspiring of all that I ever heard. They dealt largely with physiological problems to which his own researches had contributed, and gave us the lasting impression of research in physiology as something supremely worth doing. It seemed also, as he vividly recalled his own experiences, that anybody with even a moderate faculty of ingenuity and enterprise ought to be able to try his hand at such research. Those were days, of course, long before the electronic elaboration of physiological techniques. Langley had no such gift of inspiration as a lecturer. He was deeply engaged, however, in collaboration with H. K. Anderson, in the researches which were to disentangle, in an

Sir Henry Dale, acknowledged dean of experimental medicine in Great Britain, has at one time or another been awarded all the high honors of his profession. His present retirement post is Consultant to The Wellcome Trust, London, created by the will of the late Sir Henry Wellcome.

imposing sequence, the details of Gaskell's "involuntary" nervous system, for which Langley was later to introduce the term "autonomic." Even as students, we could hardly fail to receive some impression, from the knowledge that original work of such exquisitely patient accuracy was actually in progress, in the department where we were studying. Before I had finished my student course, with physiology as my special subject for the final examination, I think that I had made up my mind to try to find an opportunity to try my hand at research in physiology. As it happened, one of the very few research studentships which existed in those days, the Coutts-Trotter Studentship at Trinity College, became unexpectedly available just when I was ready to apply for it, in 1898, through the departure from Cambridge of Ernest Rutherford on his appointment to the Professorship of Physics at the McGill University, Montreal. I was able, therefore, to spend the next two years as an apprentice to physiological research, under Professor Langley's critical supervision. During those two years I did two pieces of work at Langley's direct suggestion, gaining useful experience of methods required for the investigation of a nerve supply, and demonstrating, I hope, that I had no morbid intolerance of the drudgery which accurate research usually involves. I also gave myself the pleasure of pursuing independently some ideas of my own, about a possible common basis for the galvanotactic reactions of Infusoria, and the chemotactic attractions exhibited by the same organisms to acid or alkali. I am sure that my equipment in physics, for such an undertaking, was lamentably defective; but I enjoyed the experience immensely, and W. B. Hardy, when he read my account of what I had been doing, not only expressed great interest, but strongly urged me to make plans to stay in Cambridge and go on with the work.

Care for my future, however, made me decide to complete the medical course, which I had been neglecting, and I entered St. Bartholomew's Hospital, London, in October, 1900. Clinical studies, as then conceived, appeared to require, not merely an abrupt breach with the physiological ideas so recently predominant in my interests, but even an acceptance of tradition and empiricism as providing the essential basis of knowledge for use at the bedside, almost to the exclusion of experimental evidence. Two years later I had to make another decision. I was offered, on the one hand, a house-physicianship—and should have been glad to have a year of experience and responsibility in practical medicine. On the other hand, an opportunity was presented for a further period of research in physiology. The George Henry Lewes Studentship, another of the few research emoluments of those days, fell vacant just then; but somebody else would certainly be holding it a year later, if I allowed the chance of applying for it to pass.

I was really faced with the choice of a career; and though I judged that one devoted to teaching and research in physiology would be more speculative than one in clinical medicine, I found it the more attractive, as being more congenial to my own experience of the kind of thing which I seemed to be able to do most easily. Accordingly I applied for and obtained the studentship, and was glad to find that Professor Starling was able to give me the use of a room in the department of physiology, in University College, London. The housing of such departments in those days, whether in Cambridge or in London, seems in retrospect to have been miserably inadequate, by comparison with the relative wealth of both space and equipment, which have now come to be regarded as natural and necessary. The laboratory at University College, however, had not only an impressive history in connection with the development of physiology in England, even from the days of William Sharpey, but was still growing rapidly in fame through the co-operative researches of Ernest Starling and his brother-in-law, William Bayliss, who formed a remarkable combination, complementary to each other in several respects. When I entered their department, they had recently discovered secretin, and were busily engaged in exploiting the new range of problems which its action made available to research. Starling offered me the opportunity of examining the histological changes produced in the pancreas by prolonged stimulation with secretin. Histological technique was never a strong point in my equipment; and no knowledge was available then, either of the part played by other factors, both neural and hormonal, in the secretion of the specific enzymes of the pancreatic juice, or of any of the now familiar stains, specific for the cells of the islets of Langerhans. My inexperience misled me into interpreting certain changes which I observed, in terms of Laguesse's conception, now almost forgotten, of a reciprocal metaplasia between the cells of the acini and those of the islets, in the course of development. I worked hard on this subject for a year and, under kindly and encouraging pressure from Starling, wrote a long paper about my observations, which the Royal Society published in its *Philosophical Transactions*. I never had any clear confidence, however, in my own interpretations of these findings. It did not surprise me, therefore, to find that they were soon to be completely outdated and discredited, by later and really convincing evidence about the cytology and the functions of the islets; but I think that this experience, even as emphasizing for me the proper method of conducting an investigation, and the proper criteria of significance in appraising its results, was not without its educational value.

I spent the later months of my tenure of the Lewes Studentship in Paul Ehrlich's Institute in Frankfurt. I was not there long enough to adapt myself so fully to Ehrlich's exclamatory method of expounding his ideas, as to be able to get any substantial investigation even under way. My appreciation, however, of what I gained, from even so brief an opportunity of daily contact with a man of his rare and many-sided genius, grew steadily with the years; and it has, indeed, continued to grow, with the part which I have recently taken in promoting the publication, still in progress, of a complete edition of Ehrlich's widely significant, though not very voluminous, scientific writings.

Returning to London, I found that another appointment, affording opportunity for research with a part-time teaching obligation, was falling vacant in the department of physiology at University College. It was the "Sharpey Studentship," which still exists, and would now rank, I suppose, with a Readership in an English, or an Associate Professorship in an American university. Its stipend then was £150 per annum, on which, at that time, an unmarried man could just manage to live frugally in London. I thought that I ought to get one foot, as it were, on the ladder of academic promotion. I therefore applied for the studentship, and was appointed; but the only immediate result was to give me the whole responsibility for the departmental teaching during the summer term.

Toward the end of that term an approach was made to me, with regard to an opportunity of an entirely different and then unfamiliar kind. The late Henry S. Wellcome had become the sole proprietor of the pharmaceutical business of Burroughs Wellcome and Company, which he and a fellow American, Silas K. Burroughs, had founded in London in 1880. Wellcome had established, in 1894, research laboratories in the southern suburbs of London, which he had named "The Wellcome Physiological Research Laboratories." There was something of a pioneering character, in those days, in this creation of laboratories with serious research in view, in connection with a British pharmaceutical business. And it appeared, in fact, that little had been done in these laboratories during the first decade of their existence, then ending in 1904, beyond the successful production of the diphtheria antitoxin, and of certain other immunological remedies. Now, however, Wellcome was anxious that they should begin to provide a more direct justification for the title which he had chosen for them; he wished them now to embark, indeed, on a program of genuine research, which was to extend, at least, into the general field of physiology, in which pharmacology was naturally to be included. The friends, to whom I mentioned this approach to me, were almost unanimous in advising me to have nothing to do with it: I should be selling my scientific birthright, they seemed to think, for a mess of commercial pottage. I had a frank talk with Mr. Wellcome, however, who convinced me that he was, at least, sincere in his desire to have research of general importance and permanent value done in his laboratories, and that, if I accepted the appointment which he offered, it was not his intention that I should be under pressure to produce results of direct and immediately obvious advantage to his business. I determined to give the opportunity a trial, and, although I found it necessary in the early stages to stand firmly, from time to time, on what seemed to me to be matters of important principle, I never had serious or lasting reason to regret the change which I had made.

I have described elsewhere (1), in an introductory chapter to a selection from my published papers and lectures, how Mr. Wellcome himself had suggested to me, very modestly, that I should try to throw light on the previously obscure pharmacology of ergot; and how, though my compliance with this suggestion had been neither eager nor hopeful, it furnished me, through a most remarkable succession of accidents and coincidences, with a series of clues, leading to my participation in nearly all the more interesting researches with which I was thereafter to be connected, during the remainder of my ten years' stay in the Wellcome Laboratories, and, subsequently, during the twenty-eight further years which I spent as a member of the staff, and eventually as the Director, of the National Institute for Medical Research. There is no need to repeat this history in detail. I may just mention ergotoxine and what came to be called its "sympatholytic" action, bringing me into closer contact with the work of my friend T. R. Elliott, and his brilliantly precocious suggestion, as early as 1904, of a chemical transmission, by epinephrine, of the effects of sympathetic nerve impulses; the oxytocic action of extracts from the neurohypophysis; pressor amines and sympathomimetic actions, including the very closely mimetic action of *nor*-adrenaline; histamine, with the relation of its effects to allergic reactions, its natural occurrence, distribution, and physiological significance in the animal body; and acetylcholine, with actions suggesting the chemical transmission of other nervous effects, further preparing the way for Otto Loewi's epoch-making demonstration of such transmission, and for the later extension of the direct evidence for it to ganglionic synapses and voluntary neuromuscular junctions. I had come upon the "pointers" to all these developments incidentally to the study of ergot; and when at long last, in 1935, more than thirty years after I had started my own unsuccessful quest for it, an ergot alkaloid really justifying its obstetrical reputation was discovered, almost simultaneously in several different laboratories, and given at least as many different names (ergometrine, ergobasine, ergostetrine, ergonovine, etc.), I still had the privilege of watching, at close quarters, the leading contribution which colleagues of my own made to this ultimate success.

It will be seen that both the main appointments which I held had offered me, in theory, whole-time opportunities for research. In neither case was any regular, or formal, teaching duty involved; but the support which I had received, first from industry and later from the national funds, had naturally implied other obligations than that of carrying out researches of my own free selection. The biological standardization of drugs had figured early among these; and I had soon become skeptical of the serious value of many of the perfunctory tests which were currently in use and cited to justify claims to such "standardization." The outbreak of World War I, only a month after I had joined the service of the Medical Research Committee (now Council), threw immediately upon me the obligation to apply such tests for maximal toxicity as were then current, to control the quality of the new preparations of salvarsan and its derivatives, the production of which had been made urgent by the sudden stoppage of supply from the original German sources. The experience greatly deepened my distrust of casually adopted criteria of this kind; but the pressure of wartime duties made impossible any serious research with a view to improvement of the situation. Incidentally, it was the threat of my complete submersion, by the veritable flood of demands then being made upon my attention, which brought Alfred Newton Richards hurrying across the Atlantic in 1917, to help me to keep alive some part of my own research program by his invaluable co-operation; and this began for me a scientific and personal friendship which I continue greatly to prize. It gave me a special satisfaction to be able, in World War II, at the beginning of 1942, to pay a return visit of co-operation to my friend Richards in Washington, on this occasion in connection with his high administrative responsibility for wartime medical researches in the United States. And, in the same connection, I must, with very deep gratitude, acknowledge that this was only one of many occasions, on which I have had the privilege of visiting the United States and Canada, usually both on a single journey, in response to friendly invitations, and always with the result of making and renewing most valued friendships. In a number of such cases I have been fulfilling engagements to deliver lectures, of which I may specially mention the Herter Lectures in 1919 and the Dohme Lectures in 1929, both at Baltimore; the Harvey Lecture and the William H. Welch Lectures in New York in 1919 and 1937; the Pilgrim Trust Lecture in Philadelphia in 1946; and the Tisdale Lectures, at a series of the Canadian universities, on my way home from New Zealand, in 1950—my seventy-fifth year. I have been recalling the occasions of these transatlantic visits, and have so far remembered eighteen, between 1919 and 1957, without feeling quite certain that I may not have forgotten one; even if I have not, it seems to work out at an average of nearly one in every two years! And I cannot begin to estimate the happiness and the stimulus which I have gained from these frequent contacts with American and Canadian Colleagues and friends, in their own countries, and with many of them in my own as well.

When the components of the National Institute for Medical Research, scattered during the war, had been assembled in the Hampstead building which was to be its home for the next thirty years, a succession of largely independent events seemed to conspire to make the problems of biological standardization, especially of the new kinds of remedies, an official preoccupation for me, at both national and international levels. Such matters were, indeed, for many years, to make a claim on time and thought which I would willingly have given to more fundamental, but not, I think, more important research activities. I had for years felt a special responsibility for the pituitary posterior-lobe extract, then being widely used in obstetrics for an action which I had first observed. Obviously, for such a purpose, the activity of the many different extracts being offered could not safely vary beyond relatively narrow limits. Yet my then colleague J. H. Burn and I had found that the activity of the extracts on sale in Britain alone, and with similar recommendations of dosage, varied over a range of 1 to 80. The dosage of insulin presented an equally urgent problem. I was sent officially to Toronto in 1922 with another colleague, the late H. W. Dudley, to report on the claim for this great and then new discovery; and, on our return, I had to assist the Medical Research Council in arranging for the controlled production of insulin in Britain. This brought very directly to my notice, the ineffectiveness of the methods then available for measuring and indicating the activity of a remedy so valuable and, at the same time, so potentially dangerous with inaccurate dosage. There was already a competition between different "units" put forward from different countries, with no known relation to one another, each of them based on the absolute determination of an end-point reaction in a different animal species, and none of them having any adequate statistical basis for the evaluation even of its own results. A position, evidently, with which only international action could adequately deal.

I must allow myself a further digression to recall that this contact with the insulin problem marked also the beginning of another of those enduring friendships, which have meant so much to me, both scientifically and personally. Even on my first visit to Toronto, an understanding seemed to grow naturally with the junior partner in the historic insulin enterprise, Charles H. Best, that he would come over to work with me as soon as he had completed his medical qualification. So I was to find myself, in due course, working with Best on the detailed mechanism of the action of insulin—my only adventure, I think, into problems of metabolism—and, at a later visit, on what was, for me, the less novel ground of the natural occurrence of histamine, in the different organs of the body.

The real initiative, leading to my connection with the creation of an international basis for biological standardization, came from the late Dr. Thorwald Madsen, of Copenhagen, who had preceded me by a few years as a visiting worker under Paul Ehrlich. Madsen, who had become the first chairman of the Health Committee of the then new League of Nations, had been impressed by the importance of securing international recognition of the antitoxic serum standards, and the units of antitoxic activity based upon them, for which most of the world had, before the war, been dependent upon Ehrlich and his Frankfurt Institute, but for the further preservation and issue of which an international center seemed now to be very desirable;

Madsen's own State Serum Institute in Copenhagen appearing, further, to be naturally indicated for this function. Madsen was the chairman, in 1921, of a first international conference, at which the main subject of discussion was the adoption of the Ehrlich standard and unit for diphtheria antitoxin. Then, early in 1923, he discussed with me the possibility of international agreements concerning biological standards for other remedies than the immunological ones, and asked me to take the initiative in this further direction. Ehrlich's discipline, and daily contact for many subsequent years with the accurate standardization of sera by his methods, had left me with a firm conviction, that the only proper basis for the biological standardization of any kind of remedy must be the provision of a stable standard substance, in terms of which the value of a unit of activity could be permanently defined, while free scope would be left for the improvement by research of the biological tests to be used in making comparisons with it. And, in fact, after a rather vigorous clash of interests and opinions at an initial conference in Edinburgh, in 1923, I had the satisfaction of seeing international agreements concluded, at a second conference, at Geneva, in 1925, accepting as stable material standards, for insulin and the pituitary posterior lobe, preparations which had been put forward respectively by my own colleague Dudley and by Carl Voegtlin of Washington, and further defining, for all time and for all the world, the specific activities contained in exact weights of these substances, as representing the units of insulin and of post-pituitary extract. The same principle of stable standards was then readily applied, with appropriate modifications, to drugs of the digitalis series, to salvarsan and its derivatives and analogues, and, eventually, to the vitamins and the still expanding series of the hormones, and, most recently, to the antibiotics. At the British National Institute for Medical Research a special department, initially and for many years under the expert and devoted directorship of the late Sir Percival Hartley, then became responsible for preparing and providing all these biological standards, and for making them available for all international, as well as for the British national requirements. During World War II, while Copenhagen was occupied by the German army, our British department was able to take over the responsibility for the international distribution of the serum standards also.

Another and most important contribution to the application of these biological standards was made by the introduction of sound statistical principles into the application of those methods which are dependent on the determination of a "lethal dose," or, more generally, of what my former colleague, Professor J. H. Gaddum, has termed a "quantal response." To this development I can claim to have given no more than a sympathetic encouragement, based upon my own experience of the statistical inadequacy of the methods which had earlier been in use for many of such determinations. I found cause for great satisfaction, therefore, in the valuable initiative taken in tackling this problem by the late J. W. Trevan, who had then succeeded me in the pharmacological aspect of my functions at the Wellcome Laboratories, and by J. H. Gaddum, when he was still my colleague at the National Institute.

This concern with the biological standards, both national and international, was only one of the responsibilities which I came to acquire, outside the main current of my own special research interests. In 1925 I became one of the secretaries of the ancient Royal Society of London, and retained the position till 1935. It gave me the opportunity of making many personal and scientific contacts with the distinguished company of the Fellows, and with other contributors to the biological aspects, especially, of the society's *Proceedings*. The position entailed a fairly heavy editorial responsibility, among a number of others for the general benefit of the society; but, though it was full of such varied interests, my tenure of it did not add to my freedom for research. In 1928, the Medical Research Council, by appointing me the first director, made me formally responsible to them for the general policy and administration of the National Institute for Medical Research. Till then my official position had been only that of the head of its department of biochemistry and pharmacology, although it must be admitted that, with the generous good will and understanding of my colleagues who had charge of the other departments, a prominent share of the initiative and responsibility for actions in the interest of the institute as a whole, which had to be taken by one or another of us, had for years been passing into my hands. My new appointment was, accordingly, to some extent, an official recognition of what had been happening without it; nevertheless, it did inevitably entail some further encroachment on freedom for my own researches.

Altogether, indeed, from 1925 onward, I had come to hold so many administrative duties, some connected with and others extraneous to my main research appointment, that it became clear that, even with the unselfish collaboration of a succession of distinguished colleagues and visitors,

I could only do even moderate justice to my own primary research obligations, by a conscientious neglect of the more general responsibilities which I had been unable to refuse.

Under such conditions, I succeeded, through the generous consideration of my immediate co-workers, in maintaining an active interest, and even some personal participation, in the researches which were in progress in my department, up to about 1938. This was a period during which, from about 1933 onward, the chemical transmission story was undergoing a rapid extension, at the hands of the brilliant group then working close to me. It was, I suppose, the work which had thus been issuing from my laboratory which the Stockholm Committee had chiefly in mind, when, in 1936, they honored me by the award of a Nobel Prize, jointly with Otto Loewi, whose friendship and scientific comradeship I had also enjoyed, in spite of the breach of our contacts by World War I, ever since we first met in Starling's laboratory, in 1903.

In 1938, however, most of my remaining time and energy began to be claimed by the detailed planning of the new National Institute for Medical Research, now at Mill Hill. The building of this was begun in 1939, but by 1941 it had reached a stage at which its further progress was interrupted, by requisition for a purpose which Authority then regarded as more urgent than medical research for the needs of war. Thus it came about that the eventual redesigning of its interior, took place to its very great advantage under my successor, Sir Charles Harington, who was able to incorporate in its equipment many of the great scientific advances which the demands of war had even accelerated.

I had retired from the National Institute in 1942, war conditions having extended my appointment there for two years beyond its normal limits. Meanwhile, in the autumn of 1940, I had received what any British scientist must regard as the supreme honor of election as president of the Royal Society of London. My five years' tenure of that office, all years of war except for a few final months, were naturally bereft of most of the society's normal functions, and of all those relating it to a wider public. The position brought me, on the other hand, more than a full measure of advisory duties of a secret nature, including service on, and from 1942 the chairmanship of, a small, highly confidential Scientific Advisory Committee to the War Cabinet. In 1942 I had further accepted the resident directorship of the Royal Institution of Great Britain, which had become vacant through the death of Sir William Bragg. This gave me the responsibility for keeping the educational and research activities of that institution alive, though at a much reduced level, during the war years; but it gave me also the privilege of occupying, during those same years, a residence of great dignity and imposing scientific history, within easy access of the Royal Society and of the main offices of the government.

With the end of the war, I found myself appropriately, at the age of seventy, in retirement from what had been my main duties and interests. I found, however, and still find, plenty to occupy me, as the chairman of a board of five trustees appointed under the will of Sir Henry Wellcome. The position was in many ways analogous to that of the Carlsberg Foundation in Copenhagen; the Wellcome trustees inherited all the shares in the business of which Henry Wellcome had been the sole proprietor, and their main duty is to spend the dividends which they receive, on the support of researches which contribute to the advancement of medical knowledge, and on the creation or endowment of research museums and libraries of the history of medicine. The activities of this trust, in thus supporting medical science and scholarship, were beginning to become fully effective at about the time when my other appointments were coming to a natural end. And I have thus been able, in the years of waning energy, still to maintain some contact with progress in a wide range of the medical sciences, though now only from the side of promotion.

This reminiscent account of my scientific life has naturally quickened in me a certain feeling of nostalgia for the earlier days of personal participation in research. Taken as a whole, however, the memories thus aroused have been proud and happy ones, reminding me of the many distinguished colleagues with whom it has been my great privilege to work and to form lasting friendships. The long and close collaboration with the late George Barger ended when he became Professor of Medical Chemistry at Edinburgh, in 1919. With the late Sir Patrick Laidlaw I had such happy associations at two stages, when he worked with me on physiological problems in the Wellcome Laboratories, and again, some ten years later, when he became a pioneer and leader in researches on virology, dog distemper, and human influenza, at the National Institute at Hampstead, till his premature death in 1940. Of my immediate research colleagues at the institute, members of the staff of my own department there, the late Charles H. Kellaway left to become director of the Walter and Eliza Institute at Melbourne, Australia. On his return to England to become research director to the Wellcome Foundation, Kellaway was succeeded at the Hall Institute by Sir F. Macfarlane Burnet, who had also spent two years at the National Institute in Hampstead. Charles (now Sir Charles) Lovatt Evans left me to occupy what had once been Starling's chair of physiology at University College, London, and, in due course, G. L. (now Sir Lindor) Brown left to succeed Lovatt Evans in that chair, and has now, at two removes from me, become also the biological secretary of the Royal Society; while J. H. Burn and J. H. Gaddum are now professors of pharmacology in Oxford and Edinburgh, respectively. F. C. MacIntosh is professor of physiology at McGill University, Montreal, and my own former department at the Institute, now at Mill Hill, is now led by Wilhelm Feldberg. Of the trans-atlantic visitors, with whom I have had the privilege of working directly, in addition to those already mentioned, two have become Nobel Laureates—in 1944 Herbert Gasser, who has also been director of the Rockefeller Institute, and Dickinson Richards in 1956; while Walter Bauer is now professor of Medicine in the Harvard Medical School, at the Massachusetts General Hospital, Boston, and A. McGehee Harvey in the Johns Hopkins Medical School, Baltimore; and of course there are many others who could be included, and from other countries.

I am conscious of a glow of pride, as I recall the opportunities which I have enjoyed, of work and friendship with so many men of such high distinction, and in so many departments of the medical sciences. And I am sincerely grateful for the invitation to record these happy memories.

REFERENCES

1. H. H. Dale. Adventures in physiology. London: Pergamon Press, 1953.

FRANK ALEXANDER HARTMAN, PH.D.

Biology as a Career

A Welshman who conducted Sunday religious services on occasion and a German woman who could shoot squirrels for the table and handle tools as well as a man brought up a family in Illinois in the early days. They were parents of my father. Two children of English extraction grew up on the shores of Lake Sunapee, New Hampshire—one a girl of a family of thirteen, and the other a boy belonging to the Sprague clan. Upon maturity they were married and migrated west finally settling as farmers in Gibbon, Nebraska. These were the parents of my mother.

It was in Gibbon my father and mother met and were married, and I was born there December 4, 1883. During the early years of my life we moved to Lincoln, Nebraska, and I entered grammar school at nine years of age. My mother, having been a teacher, taught me previously.

My summers were spent with my grandparents in Gibbon until I was in my teens. These were among the happiest times of my life. I fished for bull heads and sunfish in Wood River, roamed the prairies, and hunted for birds' nests along the Platte River. A neighbor taught me to stuff birds and mammals, so I proceeded to make a collection. I kept live hawks, owls, ground squirrels, and lizards, thereby learning much about their habits. With regret I returned each autumn to the city and was struck by its smoke and drabness.

On the farm I also learned the nature of hard work by cultivating corn, haying or stacking bundles, and threshing grain ten hours a day. However, there was still time to explore the countryside. My grandmother in Gibbon grew many flowering plants in a large outdoor garden and in a bay win-

Dr. Hartman, Research Professor Emeritus, Department of Physiology, Ohio State University, worked his way through college as the beginning of a distinguished career studying the adrenal glands and diseases related to them. He shares the credit for the first preparation of biologically active extracts of the adrenal cortex and for demonstrating qualitatively different kinds of biologic activity in the adrenal cortex.

dow indoors. These plants were of great interest, showing a variety which supplemented the wild forms in the field.

During the depression of 1893 my father became a railway postal clerk, and in 1894 we moved to Kansas City. The Missouri and Kaw Rivers and their bluffs and bottomland gave new vistas for roaming and seeking specimens during my spare time, although the summers in Nebraska continued to be as thrilling as ever. I became increasingly devoted to biology, reading all the books available on natural history and collecting birds and other specimens. Books like Bates's *Natural History of the Amazon* were especially stimulating. I also learned the use of tools in my father's carpenter shop.

When I entered high school I took Latin and Greek as well as all the sciences offered, influenced by my father, who, although never able to finish college, had sound ideas on education and had read a great deal. Participation in the activities of the science club confirmed my determination to follow some field of science. Excursions to investigate the invertebrate fossils in the limestone outcroppings around Kansas City introduced me to paleontology. I helped the chemistry instructor prepare material for class, thus gaining the opportunity of learning more than the average member of the class. By filling all my vacant periods with extra subjects, I was able to finish in three and one-half years.

Early in my high school course my parents suggested that I should teach country school after graduation before going on to college. However, I wished to continue immediately in college. In order to make this possible I carried the *Kansas City Star* during the last two years of high school and was able to save $300 toward my college expenses. In the autumn of 1902 I entered the University of Kansas, at Lawrence. Another student and I rented a small cottage two miles away in the country and set up housekeeping. In order to save expense I had canned 100 quarts of tomatoes during the summer.

As a freshman I enrolled in an evolution course for juniors and seniors given by Professor Francis Huntington Snow, who had recently retired from the chancellorship of the university. He asked me, "What is your game?" since I would receive no credit. Naturally I wanted to take the course because of his reputation in biology; credit was immaterial. That first year was a busy one, my spare time being spent in collecting trips around Lawrence. I tried cross-country running, at which I did fairly well, but decided that it required too much energy needed for more important things. I recall coming across in the hills southwest of Lawrence a beautiful snake stretched out sunning itself in an opening in the woods. I quietly walked up to it and took it by the nape of the neck. It was new to me but looked like a poisonous form. I pried its mouth open but saw no fangs. Just then a crow flew up in a tree close by. While still holding the snake and my gun in one hand, I pulled the trigger with the other. The noise irritated the snake, so to reassure myself I opened its mouth again, and lo! the fangs were now lowered in plain sight. Needless to say, it was taken care of immediately. This snake turned out to be a copperhead, twenty-nine inches long.

At the end of the school year flooding of the Kaw River delayed my return to Kansas City. While waiting for the flood to subside I volunteered to help in the vertebrate paleontology museum. This experience was followed by part-time employment at the museum when I returned in the fall. My job was to clean and catalog fossils at the rate of fifteen cents an hour (later raised to twenty-five cents). This enabled me to meet part of my expenses until graduation.

I took most of the courses offered in botany and zoölogy and also German and French. Although I could afford few extracurricular activities, I found time to sing in the glee club and to be active in the Snow Literary Society. My participation in athletics was limited to lacrosse in my senior year. I remember our coach, Dr. James Naismith (the inventor of basketball), trying to straighten my nose, damaged during a mixup after the ball. This attempt in the field with a couple of sticks was unsuccessful because the bones were broken. A trip to the doctor's office, where steel instruments were available, was necessary.

Among my teachers was Professor W. H. Carruth, who led one to appreciate German literature. Perhaps the clearest teacher that I had was William Chase Stevens, professor of botany, but the man with the greatest influence was Clarence Erwin McClung, professor of zoölogy. Although not an especially good teacher, Professor McClung fostered research at an early stage. If a student developed an idea which he wished to investigate, Professor McClung gave him every encouragement. In this way many began problems before going far with course work and before their knowledge of the field might discourage experiment. The spirit of adventure is often dulled by too much course work and is sometimes entirely lost. Moreover, formal courses leave little time for research. Many of Professor McClung's students continued in zoölogy or related fields as a career because of this early experience.

Before graduation I had tried experiments with cultures of protozoa, thinking that since all the life activities were embodied in a single cell these forms should be ideal for studying the functions of life. However, because all functions are located in a single cell, the problem is more difficult there than in higher forms with specialization. I also studied the habits of the lizards and amphibians of Kansas.

I was privileged to accompany Professor McClung, Roy G. Hoskins, and others on an expedition to western Kansas during the summer of 1904. We collected fossil fishes and mosasaur bones from the Cretaceous chalk beds as well as grasshoppers for cytological study. Roy Hoskins and I preceded the others by a few days and established camp. He was a cheerful companion, singing frequently and doing the cooking. When the biscuits he cooked over buffalo chips turned out to be too hard for our consumption, they proved excellent to throw at jackrabbits. We obtained much valuable material both fossil and recent. I well remember collecting the proboscis of a new species of *Protosphyrina*, an ancient fish.

I was graduated in 1905, three years after entering the university, and continued in graduate work the next year. Work for my thesis was on the spermatogenesis of the grasshopper, *Schistocerca americana*. Professor McClung had discovered that the chromosomes of some western grasshoppers were unusually well suited for such study because of their size.

I left the university during the middle of the school year to take a job in the high school at Beardstown, Illinois, as teacher of science. This was a railroad town on the Illinois River; a place where the superintendent of schools, when he wanted to instal manual training, was told that the boys could obtain their experience in the shops. The school board also prohibited the teaching of evolution. In the spring Miss Anna Botsford, a school teacher in Lawrence, Kansas, and I were married. The next summer was spent in graduate work at the University of Kansas, and in the fall I accepted a position in biology at the high school in Wichita, Kansas. I held this appointment for two years, finishing my master's degree which, however, was not granted until 1909.

My next opportunity arose in 1908 at Seattle, where I taught biology at Broadway and Queen Anne High Schools for six years. My next goal was the Ph.D. degree. With two children and a wife, that took planning. However, a great variety of opportunities for field work in the new environment was not to be ignored.

Excursions into the Olympic and Cascade Mountains with students, trips along the beaches of Puget Sound, two summers among the islands near the Canadian border, one being at the Friday Harbor Biological Station, broadened my outlook.

Since the University of Washington did not offer the doctor's degree in zoölogy, I thought of going elsewhere. Paleontology being a major field of interest during my undergraduate days, I considered going to the University of Chicago for this degree. I realized that the opportunities for research in the field of paleontology were very limited. About this time two developments decided my course of action. Roy G. Hoskins, who was studying for his Ph.D. at Harvard, send word that I could obtain a fellowship with Dr. Walter B. Cannon. Also, the department of chemistry at the University of Washington was offering a Ph.D. degree for the first time. I finally decided to take the doctor's degree in physiological chemistry at Washington and then go into physiology with Dr. Cannon. Fortunately, a light teaching schedule at Queen Anne High School permitted me to spend considerable time at the University of Washington. My research problem was to determine the volatile substances in urine under Professor William M. Dehn. This eventually required processing 2,000 liters of urine. Dr. Dehn set a good example of application in research. He would leave the laboratory at 4:00 P.M. for a game of handball but would return after dinner to work in his laboratory.

I received my Ph.D. degree in June, 1914. In September of that year I reported to the Harvard Medical School, where I became Austin Teaching Fellow in physiology. Attendance at lectures and conducting a laboratory section for medical students quickly oriented me in the new field. This was my first experience in mammalian physiology.

Dr. Cannon's investigations on the movements in the digestive tract had led him to a study of the effects of epinephrine. He suggested that I determine the differential effects of this hormone on the vascular system. Study of various aspects of the question engaged me for the next five years. In searching the literature on the adrenal, I very soon began to realize, as had many others, that the most important function of this gland was still unknown. Although epinephrine was an extremely powerful substance, it would not replace the vital function of the adrenals when these glands were removed. Whenever fresh adrenals were available from a recently sacrificed animal, I began to experiment with them in a desultory fashion to see whether an active substance other than epinephrine could be obtained. I soon found that the presence of epinephrine in crude extracts interfered with direct testing.

In September, 1915, I accepted a position as lecturer in physiology at the University of Toronto. Here unexpected responsibility was thrust upon me. The war prevented Professor T. G. Brodie's returning from England until a full month after the university opened. In the meantime it fell to me to give all the courses in physiology, including lectures and laboratory work, my only assistant being a recently appointed fellow. Because of the war it was impossible to obtain the needed staff. This was valuable but strenuous experience. Upon Professor Brodie's return the pressure lessened but was still unusually high throughout the war. Although time available for research was limited, I again took up a study of epinephrine effects and began to investigate adrenal insufficiency in an attempt to find a satisfactory test for the adrenal cortical hormone, since it had been pretty well established by Wheeler and Vincent that it was the cortex which was essential to life. I also conducted experiments in connection with the war effort on the treatment of denervated muscle.

My experience with Professor Brodie was invaluable in that I learned many techniques as practiced by the British physiologists. During my last year at Toronto I also began to attend clinics with the medical students with the idea of finishing work for the medical degree in order to broaden my basis for teaching physiology. After several months of this I decided that it was more important to get on with research than to learn the art of medical practice.

When the war was over I became head of the department of physiology at the University of Buffalo. Here my teaching load was somewhat lighter, and I could do more research. I studied the effects of various stimuli on the release of epinephrine from the adrenal glands and began in earnest an attempt to obtain the adrenal cortical hormone. After much experimentation I decided that the only crucial test for the cortical hormone was its ability to replace the cortices in a completely adrenalectomized cat or dog. This test required many days or weeks because these animals survived from seven to ten days after adrenalectomy without treatment. The problem was to extract the hormone free from epinephrine since epinephrine, even in small animals, was toxic to the adrenalectomized animal. For some time my extracts were made from beef adrenal cortex separated from the medullary tissue by dissection. Even then some epinephrine was invariably present. After many trials, an epinephrine-free preparation was obtained by starting with an 0.8 per cent NaCl extract which was partially cleaned of protein by isoelectric precipitation and then saturated with NaCl. The precipitated globulin carried down with it an active substance which significantly prolonged the lives of adrenalectomized cats. After many years, this was the answer. On the assumption that there was only one hormone involved, I named it "cortin." This crude preparation increased the survival of adrenalectomized cats three- to fourfold. The results were published in 1927. Attempts to concentrate an active principle from the globulin precipitate were unsuccessful. Therefore, my group again turned to organic solvents, which we had used earlier—first ethyl ether because of its low boiling point and later ethyl alcohol.

We finally were able to produce a concentrated extract which could prolong the lives of adrenalectomized animals indefinitely.

The first trial of our adrenal cortical extract in the human occurred in 1930. A patient suffering from Addison's disease was brought to the hospital in shock (systolic blood pressure, 50 mm. Hg). Treatment for shock had little effect. Finally he was injected with our adrenal extract at frequent intervals. In a few hours he showed improvement. Since our supply of extract was very limited, it was impossible to give the patient as much extract as was required for a crisis, but he nevertheless showed remarkable recovery by the third day, when he ate his first meal, read, and talked with visitors. He improved steadily. Reduction in the amount of extract was always followed by relapse which disappeared upon resumption of adequate dosage. The patient survived for nearly eight months and then contracted bronchopneumonia. The necessary additional extract was not available and he soon succumbed.

Because of our limited facilities for preparing extract, we selected a few patients for study and carried out experiments on animals in order to discover the functions of what we then assumed to be one essential hormone.

Our observation of patients and experiments with animals convinced us that adrenal cortical extract had some influence on the central nervous system. The irritable state in Addison's disease is replaced by a state of calm under treatment. Adrenal extract also produced improvement in some cases of nervous fatigue neither definitely Addison's disease nor due to organic neurological change. A sense of well-being, even euphoria, replaced depression, the immediate effect being drowsiness and release of nervous tensions if present. These effects are not due to suggestion, because in Howard Liddell's experiments at Cornell with sheep in a state of neurosis due to overtaxing the nervous system by conditioned reflex experiments, there was marked improvement under adrenal extract therapy. This improvement persisted for more than three weeks after the last injection. Many years later the use of crystalline cortical hormone confirmed the effect on the nervous system in the human.

Our studies on the adrenal began to attract attention. We were awarded the gold medal of the American Medical Association, as well as other marks of recognition, and later received offers of much needed support for our research.

My activities were transferred to Ohio State University in 1934, where I became chairman of the department of physiology. Numerous students helped me in my experiments at Buffalo, among them K. A. Brownell, W. D. Pohle, and G. W. Thorn. Their collaboration continued at Columbus. Later, our studies contributed to a better understanding of Addison's disease and its treatment as well as the functions of the adrenal cortical hormones as determined by animal experiments.

In 1936, Kendall, Mason, Hoehn, and McKenzie reported isolation of the first pure compound which had the activity of adrenal cortical extract. In 1939 we published our observation that crude adrenal extract could be separated into two fractions, one causing sodium retention and the other maintaining adrenalectomized animals but with no influence on sodium retention. Some years after this (1953) a very potent sodium-retaining crystalline compound was isolated by Simpson, Tait, Wettstein, Neher, von Euw, and Reichstein, and Mattox, Mason, and Albert. In these and other studies we were aided by many investigators, especially L. A. Lewis, D. E. Smith, H. J. Spoor, and J. S. Thatcher.

Along the way, reports by others and our own observations emphasized the need for more comparative work on the adrenal gland, especially in light of more recent developments. So many studies were limited to a few common laboratory animals that it seemed that much valuable information might be obtained from comparative work on divergent wild forms. About 1940 I began a survey of the adrenal in forms ranging from the elasmobranchs to the primates, concentrating especially on wild birds since so little was known about them. Such a program fitted into our laboratory investigations, which on the adrenal are necessarily prolonged and interspersed with longer or shorter periods of little activity. I chose those periods to collect specimens in the field, which also gave much needed diversion in out-of-door exercise.

In order to find out whether season or climate played a role, I collected thyroids and adrenals of birds in various parts of the Western Hemisphere and at different times of the year. Specimens were obtained from the woods and fields around Columbus and the shores of Lake Erie and Buckeye Lake. In the spring and summer the shores and environs of Kezar Lake in Maine furnished material. During a late winter on Grand Isle in Louisiana I discovered that the brown pelican possessed very large adrenals. Careful study with Dr. R. A. Knouff showed that the adrenal of this bird contained cortical or inter-renal cells which are longer and more regular in arrangement than those of any other bird. This led to work with the Archbold Biological Station in Florida as a base. Here the opportunity to obtain other species from a great variety of habitats was presented. The prairies and lakes—especially Lake Okeechobee—the Big Cypress Swamp in the Everglades, Fisheating Creek, and the islands in the Gulf of Mexico furnished much new material for our survey.

This comparative study was continued in Woods Hole at the Marine Biological Laboratory, where we made a special study of elasmobranchs during several seasons. However, the most interesting and instructive of all field work was during six expeditions into the Republic of Panama. This work was conducted under the auspices of the Smithsonian Institution and the Gorgas Memorial Laboratory. The adrenals and thyroids from more than 360 species among 70 families of birds were collected, a large number from the tropics, enabling me to sample a wide variety ranging from hummingbirds to the king vulture. Mammals and reptiles were also collected. Near-sea-level habitats of Chagres Rio and its tributaries and the savannahs about La Jagua Rio furnished a great number of aquatic as well as terrestrial forms. In the Province of Chiriqui I worked at elevations of 4,000 to 7,000 feet above sea level, where mosquitoes are absent and the nights are cold, and where I frequently saw migrants from the north and encountered the quetzal, the most beautiful bird of all the Americas.

One of my most striking experiences was on Mount Copete. When walking up the steepest part of the trail, just ahead of me one of the pack horses with some of our equipment toppled over backward. I expected the packs to be smashed and the horse injured. Fortunately both horse and packs were unharmed.

In dissecting adrenals, the rather large differences in relative heart and skeletal muscle sizes (weights) led me to make a detailed study of these differences. It showed a direct relationship between relative weights and activity. Another incidental observation on hummingbird livers suggested a study of liver lipids among different bird groups.

Periodic work on these different problems enabled me to return with a fresh outlook to my main interest—learning all that I could about the adrenal.

When field work was in progress, our laboratory program conducted by my associates, especially Dr. Brownell, was being carried on. In these laboratory experiments we accidentally discovered evidence of a hormone which has yet to be isolated or identified. Enucleation of the adrenals of mice was followed by increased production of this hormone, called the "fat factor," up to a maximum at about nine days after operation. It differs from the gluconeogenic factor, which shows an increase to maximum at twenty-nine days after a similar operation. Three years later (1951) we demonstrated in dogs that the "fat factor" content in adrenal vein blood does not parallel the gluconeogenic factor content nor is it influenced by adrenocorticotropic hormone injection.

More recently our group has shown that the adrenal of dogs with experimental hypertension produces steroids not found in the adrenal vein blood of normal dogs.

The functions of the adrenal are more intriguing than ever before, not only in man and higher animals but in the whole animal kingdom. Work in the laboratory and in the field convinces me that our understanding of the endocrines—indeed, of all functional processes—is just beginning. A great opportunity lies before the investigator just starting his career.

More can be done to encourage students to choose biology as a career. Instruction should be in the hands of the scientist with the spark that kindles. Exposure to biology should and could begin in the early school years by observation and experiment. Reading and reciting are not enough. Field excursions and simple experiment can start at any time, the earlier the better. What one does for himself fires the curiosity and can lead to that spirit of investigation which we find in the dedicated scientist. Originality, wherever it is to be found, should be encouraged. It is the early years during the formative period when trends are most likely to be established. College work may do what earlier work failed to do, but to wait until obtaining the baccalaureate degree before embarking on research is like working on a treadmill before attempting to explore the world around one. Teachers should be leaders in the search for knowledge, not drill masters. Teacher and pupil should both be on the high road of experience, the latter being able to profit by a little guidance and example from a leader.

More than ever before, a student in the sciences should first obtain as broad an educational foundation as possible and then choose a field with a future in which he would rather work than anywhere else. Having chosen, continued devotion to some of the most important problems in this field should eventually be rewarding. With application, preparation, and perseverance as his watchwords, some measure of success is assured. Above and beyond this, the satisfaction of being a pioneer in the forefront of knowledge is one of the most satisfying experiences that comes to any man.

Too little work has been done by physiologists in the field to explore the possibilities of research in new forms. The common laboratory animals serve their purpose, but widely different wild forms can throw new light on fundamental problems. As biologists, some physiologists have become too narrow in their outlook by limiting their experimental material. Comparative physiology, which is well begun, is one of the great developments of the future.

The young investigator at the present time is fortunate in the new methods and new techniques available which enable one to work more accurately and accomplish results impossible before. Many more opportunities are offered for careers in science, and the support of research is increasing yearly. Although too much emphasis is placed on applied research to the neglect of the fundamental aspects, support of the latter is increasing also. Biological research has been somewhat slighted because of the great attraction of the physical sciences but it, too, will come to the fore when it is generally realized that the broader aspects of biology are closely bound to human welfare.

C. JUDSON HERRICK, PH.D.

Medical Teaching by a Non-Medical Specialist

The marvelous improvement in medical practice during the last fifty years is due in large measure to revolutionary changes in medical education, and the requirements of current practice have in turn set the pattern of the medical curriculum. This metamorphosis of American medical schools came slowly and tempestuously. I have observed this movement for nearly seventy years, first as a spectator and later as a participant, and this experience has given me firsthand information about one of its controversial features.

The training of physicians must be administered by those who know the requirements of good medical practice. The medical faculties, accordingly, have traditionally been drawn from the ranks of experienced practitioners, and the employment of teachers without medical training met strong opposition for obvious reasons. Because my appointment to a professorship in a medical faculty fifty years ago was one of the early instances of such use of specialists without medical training, I have been asked to report upon its practical operation as I saw it.

It has been my fortune (or misfortune) on several occasions to assume duties for which I was quite unprepared by reason of lack of native ability and/or adequate training. Some of these duties were imposed upon me by circumstances beyond my control; others were accepted as calculated risks by my own choice.

A typical illustration of the former came in 1918, when unforeseen exigencies of military service led to my assignment to the Army Medical Museum in Washington with unspecified duties. Shortly thereafter, when the resident pathologist was ordered overseas, my commanding officer,

Dr. Herrick was one of the great teacher-scientists of the University of Chicago—Professor of Neurology, Department of Anatomy. He was primarily interested in the anatomical basis of function, and his approach was comparative. His interests embraced all the things that man can do, hence, many of his writings were on psychology and philosophy. Dr. Herrick died January 29, 1960.

Colonel W. O. Owen, directed me to take over all Captain Cattell's duties.

"Very well, Sir," I replied. "You understand that I am not a pathologist."

"Perhaps you weren't yesterday. You are today."

So it happened that Major Herrick became a pathologist by executive order, although the Colonel was fully aware that the Major knew nothing about pathology. It was up to the Major to learn fast and to find pathologists who knew more than he did.

In contrast with such coercion, almost everybody has occasion once in a while to choose from among several possible courses of action the one that offers the best prospect of advantage in view of its requirements and his own fitness to satisfy them. If the most desirable opening is in an unfamiliar field, its selection may involve serious risk.

This was the problem with which I was confronted in 1907 when the invitation came to join the medical faculty of the University of Chicago, although I had no medical training or experience. To explain the nature of the risks involved for both members of the proposed contract, I will first sketch in outline my previous training and teaching experience.

A man in his eighty-ninth year has more experience in retrospect than in prospect. As this experience is reviewed, I realize that my education (which is not yet finished), from first to last, has consisted very largely in learning my own limitations and what to do about them. This involves adjustment to surroundings in such a way as to make the best possible use of native abilities and to compensate for deficiencies. From this it follows that accurate knowledge of the family history and of the environment in the early formative years is an indispensable part of any biography. These essential facts I have recorded in the biography of my brother Clarence (1), and only a few of the details need be mentioned here.

Our grandfather, Nathan Herrick, moved with his family from Stowe, Vermont, to the midwestern frontier in 1854, and our father, Henry Nathan Herrick, reared his family near or in Minneapolis, Minnesota, under pioneer conditions from 1858 to 1885. Clarence was born on June 22, 1858. Our father was pastor of the First Free Baptist Church of Minneapolis from 1866 to the end of 1871, and I was born in the parsonage on October 6, 1868. Father was obliged to resign his pastorate because

of failing health, and he then moved his family to a small outlying farm from which he had during previous years drawn most of the support for his family. Here his three boys grew up in a family circle meagerly supplied with the necessities for subsistence but rich in cultural aspirations and set in a farming community of rugged pioneers.

My formal schooling began in a one-room country schoolhouse, with a varied assortment of teachers, and ended with a Ph.D. in zoölogy from Columbia University. Along the way I blundered into a series of missteps which gave me valuable information about what not to plan to do with such mental furnishings as I had.

After completing nearly two years of the classical course at Denison University with a far from distinguished record, I realized that I was not cut out to be a linguist or a mathematician. In the tradition of the 1880's to "go scientific" was a confession of inferiority, but I was not willing to admit that I was a moron. Accordingly, I took the risk of transferring to the scientific course and making up my deficiencies in elementary science. Clarence at that time was professor of natural history at the University of Cincinnati, so naturally I moved to Cincinnati and under his teaching and guidance acquired a Bachelor of Science degree in 1891. After that I was on my own.

I knew that to get the Doctor's degree in zoölogy I would have to earn my way by teaching. Here again the going was rough. For one year in a secondary school I taught rhetoric, mechanical drawing, physical geography, and whatever else exigencies demanded. Then, at one jump into an institution about which I knew practically nothing, I landed as full professor in a small college in Kansas. Here I taught all the sciences in the curriculum, preparatory and collegiate, with no assistant. As the only occupant of a substantial science hall, I conducted classes (sometimes simultaneously) on three floors.

The next September I accepted a teaching fellowship to work again with my brother, who was then professor of zoölogy in Denison University. Three months after this appointment, Clarence was incapacitated by violent pulmonary hemorrhages, and there was no one to take his place. I was drafted to fill the gap, notwithstanding the fact that I was already registered as a student in two of the courses that I was expected to teach. It fell to me also to assume responsibility for the *Journal of Comparative Neurology*, founded by my brother three years previously. Thus at twenty-five years

of age, with the rank and salary of instructor in a small college, I became editor, publisher, and, incidentally, responsible for the large annual deficits of a technical scientific magazine still in precarious infancy. For these exacting duties I had no training or experience at all and had to feel my way along by trial and error—and the errors were appalling.

At thirty-one years of age I won the coveted Doctor's degree after meeting the minimum requirement of residence at Columbia. From 1897 until 1907 I was professor of zoölogy in Denison University. From my sixth year onward, the most important part of my education could not be listed in the curriculum of any school. These extracurricular influences in large part came from observation of my brother's interests and methods of work, supplemented by quickening of various other interests by the heterogeneous teaching experience. The latter activity showed me which of these interests it would be profitable for me to cultivate and what subjects should be left to others.

During the whole of this period, as just mentioned, the most important part of my education I got from my brother Clarence. He was a genius by genetic endowment, a born naturalist, and no obstacles or disasters, of which there were many, could divert him from this path. It is equally evident that I had no such obviously genetic aptitudes or dominant interests. I became a naturalist by a process of acculturation. A critical examination of these two careers shows how two children, born of the same parents and reared under similar environing conditions, could enter into a smoothly functioning partnership of scientific work, and this notwithstanding genetic endowments about as different as two brothers could be within the range of the normal. The abilities and limitations of the one in a measure compensated for those of the other. A third brother, William Howard, who practiced as United States deputy land surveyor, was another genetic anomaly. In this family three distinctive patterns resulted from the juggling of the genes, and there is no evidence known to me of a prototype of any one of them in the family history or collateral relatives. The actual use made of the diverse genetic endowments of these three brothers is open to inspection, and it is possible to distinguish the genetic and environmental factors with reasonable accuracy.

Of the other extracurricular influences which played a part in shaping the pattern of my scientific work, the names of Oliver S. Strong and George E. Coghill should first be mentioned. At the beginning of my program of

research in comparative neurology my brother advised me to start with the peripheral nervous system, that is, with an analysis of the nerves and their related end-organs. The primary function of the nervous system is to translate sensory experience into appropriate behavior. We should, then, first find out to what kinds of stimulation each species of animal is sensitive and then follow this analysis through to the organs of response.

Our knowledge of the exact composition of the peripheral nerves was so imperfect that such analysis of the central nervous system was impossible. At that time Oliver S. Strong (2) published an analysis of the nerves of the frog which set the pattern for an extensive series of studies on nerve components that continues until now and which came to be known abroad as the work of the "American school" of neurologists. I arranged, accordingly, to go to Columbia University, and during the year 1896–97 I sat vis-à-vis with Oliver at his work bench while beginning a dissertation on the nerve components of fishes. This was followed by a series of similar papers during the next ten years.

In the summer of 1900, while working for the United States Fish Commission at Woods Hole, Massachusetts, I first met George E. Coghill, who was then working with my brother Clarence in the University of New Mexico and who two years later published a dissertation (3) on the cranial nerves of the salamander, *Amblystoma.* Coghill's subsequent research had so profound an influence upon current movements in biology and physiological psychology, as well as upon my own life, that I have written (4) an account of his life and work.

While at Columbia I had another difficult choice to make. Candidates for the doctorate were required to select a secondary subject in a department other than that of their major choice. The department of anatomy was then housed directly across the hall from our zoölogical laboratory, and Professor G. S. Huntington graciously allowed a few graduate students in zoölogy to dissect specially prepared bodies under his personal direction. I very much wanted to take advantage of this rare privilege, and, if I had been able to foresee the events following 1907, I would undoubtedly have selected anatomy as the secondary subject.

On the other hand, neurology as I envisioned it is so intimately related with psychology (about which I knew very little) that when the opportunity came to spend two days a week in Professor Cattell's laboratory of experimental psychology I could not resist it. Although my lack of train-

ing in human anatomy later proved to be a very serious handicap, as I now look back I incline to think that, after all, I made the wiser choice. The acquisition of wider perspectives may be worth more in the upshot than details of factual knowledge.

My perspectives in general theory and especially in the natural philosophy of human nature have been broadened very little by study of the ancient classics but much more by wide and rather erratic readings in current biology, psychology, and philosophy. Probably the most significant of these sources are Charles Darwin, William James, John Dewey, George Santayana, Roy Wood Sellars, Charles Morris, C. S. Sherrington, Adolf Meyer, Robert M. Yerkes, and Henry Margenau. Clarence's influence on my mental development may be described as truly paternal—a one-to-one relationship. Those just mentioned and many others were related in a way more aptly described as "avuncular," to use the apt analogy suggested by my one-time student, H. M. Johnson.

My situation at Denison in 1907 was congenial. The teaching load was heavy, but I liked the work, and it was acceptable to both the students and the administration. The salary was small but adequate for the simple life in a little college town set in a farming community. There was little time or equipment for research, but a creditable output was possible, done for the most part while my colleagues were playing or asleep. It looked as if I had found a niche appropriate for my interests, aptitudes, and training.

This complacency was shattered by an invitation to become professor of neurology in the department of anatomy of the University of Chicago. The offer was attractive for many reasons, including a salary nearly double the maximum at Denison and the teaching limited to the area of my special interest and practically at the graduate level, for all medical students had at least two years of college work and many had the Bachelor's degree or equivalent. Ample time and equipment for research were assured, with the prospect of development of a practically autonomous graduate-school program of teaching and research in comparative neurology. At Denison I was a solitary worker, and personal contacts with other neurologists were only occasionally possible at the annual scientific meetings. The prospect of daily association with eminent leaders in my own and related fields was alluring.

There was, however, much to be said on the other side. First, was this

my kind of job? Up to that time I had set foot in a medical school only a few times, and of the requirements for clinical practice I knew practically nothing. Failure to make so radical a readjustment would be unfortunate for the students and disastrous for me. I did know, however, that the teaching of neuroanatomy in most medical schools was a tragic futility, and it seemed probable that my worst would be no worse than most of the current teaching of this subject.

There was a further complication arising from the historical background not only of my own training and experience but also of my wife's family history and interests, for she was born in Granville and lived in the tradition of Denison's most illustrious and beloved president. Her father, Samson Talbot, was president of Denison from 1863 until his death in 1873, and at that critical period he undoubtedly saved the life of the college.

The most serious feature of my dilemma was the question of my own health, which at that time was seriously impaired. I had seen the wreckage of my brother's career from overwork and frustration when he was younger than I then was. That year for the first time I had been given a competent assistant who relieved me of much of the drudgery. It would be possible at Denison to carry on in familiar grooves indefinitely without undue strain, and my position there would not be adversely affected if research had to be relaxed or abandoned. If, in view of my depleted reserves, the strain of readjustment in Chicago should result in disastrous failure of health, my wife and child would be left destitute, for the University of Chicago at that time had no provision for retiring allowances or widows' pensions. This obligation to my family was a crucial issue.

One evening while I was mulling over these considerations, my wife looked up and said, "Would you rather go to Chicago and burn out or stay here and rust out?" That settled it. The wife was a better sport than her husband. If she was willing to take the sporting chance, this was no time for me to vacillate. It is true that most teachers in colleges, as elsewhere, are hard and efficient workers who do not wear out before retirement. They certainly do not rust out. But I had examples before me of a few teachers who had died at the top in middle life, and the possibility that such a blight might befall me was disquieting.

The decision, once made, was never questioned or regretted. We knew the hazards involved and made plans accordingly. After our arrival in Chicago in September, 1907, we lived as simply and quietly as possible.

I devoted myself to the academic duties and rigorously eliminated all other obligations and distractions. The first year was a critical time, and the outcome was uncertain. The first two summers were spent quietly in Chicago in recuperation, and by the second year the readjustment was fairly under way, and the research program was well established.

Although I had taught comparative anatomy for more than a decade, my knowledge of human anatomy was so limited that it would have been appropriate, first of all, to make a complete dissection under the guidance of my colleagues. In view of the precarious state of my health, I did not dare to take the risk of this additional burden and so was obliged to do the best I could without it.

Before going on with this story it is necessary to outline a few features of the history of medical education in Chicago. The history of medicine and medical teaching in this country from the beginning to 1860 has been admirably summarized and documented by Norwood (5). After the Civil War, correction of the limitations and defects of the proprietary medical schools made slow progress until the publication of the Flexner report in 1910 (6), although there were some notable advances before that date.

The preceptor method of clinical teaching, which was in vogue until long after the Civil War and was the precursor of our present hospital training of interns, was supposed to accompany or follow a course of lectures at a medical college. Some of the foibles of this system can be illustrated by a typical incident.

Shortly after my arrival in Chicago I was invited to attend the meetings of the local neurological society, a small group of practicing neurologists. The dinner meetings were held in a downtown hotel. At my first attendance I found myself seated next to the venerable Dr. Moyer, on whose other side was the still more venerable Dr. Hall. Dr. Moyer chuckled as he told how he served with Dr. Hall as preceptor, stabling the horse, driving the buggy, and mixing pills, for more than the required two years and was impatiently waiting for the doctor's certificate of qualification for license to practice. Finally he mustered courage to ask the doctor if he thought the time had come for the certificate.

"Yes, of course. I'll write it now."

Whereupon Dr. Hall turned to his desk and wrote:

"This certifies that Harold N. Moyer has studied medicine under my direction for more than two years. I consider him qualified for a license to practice. His moral character is as good as that of the average medical student."

Young Moyer after reading the document was crestfallen.

"Is that the best you can do for me, doctor?"

"Humph! If you don't like it, write it yourself."

The candidate took the proffered pen and wrote:

"This certifies that Harold N. Moyer has studied medicine under my direction for more than two years. I consider him qualified for a license to practice. His moral character is as good as could be expected under the circumstances."

This document is probably now in the file of the Illinois state licensing bureau.

The slow transition to present methods of teaching and practice of medicine in Chicago has been described many times, and I need mention here only two of these works—Veith and McLean (7) and Irons (8). The details can be omitted now except for a few salient features.

One of the most notable of the reform movements was the opening in 1893 of the Johns Hopkins Medical School as an organic part of Johns Hopkins University and with university standards of teaching and research. Franklin P. Mall played a significant part in the organization of this project, insisting that human anatomy be taught as a science in its own right and not merely as an aid for acquiring technical skill in surgical and other practice.

In accordance with this principle, when the University of Chicago opened in 1892, its first faculty appropriately included Dr. Mall as professor of anatomy, Henry H. Donaldson, professor of neurology, and Jacques Loeb, assistant professor of physiology. Departments of pathology and bacteriology were added soon thereafter. All this was done before the university had a medical school or relation of any sort with a medical college or hospital. Thus the foundation was laid for the imposing structure which is now one of the university's major achievements. But it was only a foundation, and the building of the superstructure was long delayed.

The University of Chicago from its inception was committed to a program of medical teaching and research which differed radically from the conventional pattern. In view of the fact that successful medical practice

must be guided by adequate knowledge of the basic sciences and the refined technical methods involved, it was believed that the best way to accomplish this was to articulate the medical school with the scientific departments of the university as intimately as possible on the same campus and to organize the school in essentially the same way as the other university faculties. Each department should be staffed with members proficient in both teaching and research, so as to provide facilities for training leading to both the M.D. and the Ph.D. degrees. Improvement of clinical teaching would follow as a major objective. This would require that some, if not all, of the senior members of the preclinical departments should be specialists on full-time appointment with no other obligations.

The time was not ripe for so radical a movement, and many years elapsed before this ideal could be formulated in a workable pattern, but a beginning should be made and they made it. It was an experimental program from the first, and it still is. Some of the experiments were unsuccessful and had to be abandoned, but, in spite of these mistakes, a practicable program has been devised and is now working very well. Doubtless this pattern of organization and operation is not appropriate for all medical schools, but it has been in operation here long enough to prove its worth for the advancement of medical science and the preparation of a selected group of students for successful practice of high quality.

In the last decade of the nineteenth century, anatomy was generally taught by practicing surgeons. In many instances this teaching was well done as preparation for practice, but often it was pitifully inadequate. A few prominent anatomists organized the American Association of Anatomists in 1888, and their interests were well illustrated by the program of their seventh meeting, which I attended in December, 1894.

This was my first contact with a medical school. The meeting was in a little room at the College of Physicians and Surgeons on Fifty-ninth Street in New York. Dr. Dwight presided, with seventeen members present. The program was heavily weighted with anomalies from the dissecting room. One member presented a paper on the normal capacity of the human bladder as determined by the simple device of measuring the amount of discharge every time he felt the impulse to pass water.

When in 1892 Dr. Mall organized a department of anatomy in a university which had no medical school, it was, I repeat, with the avowed purpose of transforming human anatomy from a handmaid of medical

practice to a scientific discipline, with resulting improvement of practice. This he did in Chicago, although he held this professorship for only one year. Further progress was slow until L. F. Barker was made head of the department in 1899. He was succeeded by R. R. Bensley, who continued to develop Dr. Mall's program until in 1927 this department of anatomy was ranked by vote of American anatomists as the best in this country.

Rush Medical College was affiliated with the University of Chicago in 1898, and three years later all instruction of the two preclinical years was transferred to the university campus. It was difficult to find medical graduates qualified to meet university standards who were willing to make the financial and other sacrifices involved in full-time teaching appointments. Accordingly, the university continued the policy, inaugurated at the beginning, of employing non-medical specialists to fill many of these positions.

Those of us who lacked medical training had much to learn, and at first there were some failures to adjust theory to practice, but fortunately we were not too old to learn and so profited by our own mistakes. For the younger men this adjustment should not be difficult, but after middle age the hazards are greater. Despite these difficulties, this plan has actually worked so well that it is now in operation in medical schools generally. In 1952 the department of anatomy of a large medical school of a state university had a faculty of thirty-seven members, not one of whom had the M.D. degree, and the teaching there has been eminently satisfactory.

The addition of non-medical specialists has been extended into the clinical departments, as illustrated by the appointment of psychologists in some departments of psychiatry. The result is that in all good medical schools both clinical and preclinical departments are now organized on the assumption that an important function of the medical college is to contribute to the advancement of knowledge by adequately supported research. The outcome has not been the neglect and deterioration of practical training, as was at first feared by some, but, on the contrary, vast improvement of the graduates' qualification for practice.

It was during the transitional period that I became professor of neurology in the department of anatomy. The title, which I inherited from my predecessor, Dr. Donaldson, was appropriate for him, because, although he was not a medical doctor, he was head of an independent department

devoted primarily to research. But when this professorship was transferred to anatomy with responsibility for teaching medical students, the title was anomalous and confusing. In medical schools the professor of neurology is a practitioner of clinical neurology and/or neurosurgery. The confusion should have been avoided by changing the title to professor of neuroanatomy and so spared me the embarrassment of frequent calls by patients for medical treatment.

When the first- and second-year students of Rush Medical College were transferred to the university campus in 1901, many of them were unhappy about it and unco-operative. They were not interested in science but in practice, and they resented any exercise that had no obvious practical application. When they were taking Professor Lillie's course in embryology, they made noisy protests when required to study developing hens' eggs. "We are not going to practice obstetrics on hens," they wailed.

Six years later, when I began my apprenticeship as a medical teacher, it was inevitable that the approach to neuroanatomy should be from the standpoint of the comparative anatomist rather than that of the physician. The students were provided with dogfish for dissection of the nerves and brain in order to get a simplified picture of the basic structure of the nervous system. They carried away from the laboratory not only a nasty fishy odor that clung to their clothing for days but also a more persistent repugnance against any knowledge that was not derived from a human cadaver. And this was all that some of them carried from the dissection. This prejudice was mitigated somewhat when they found that the complicated structure of the internal ear and all its nervous connections could be easily and completely exposed in a clean dissection of a dogfish in less than two hours, a demonstration that cannot be made on a human dissection with equal clarity by any number of hours of painfully difficult work.

In the course of time the teachers acquired more skill in adapting the method and content of their courses to the clinical interests and aptitudes of the students, and the qualifications of students accepted for matriculation were raised to a higher standard. It soon became apparent to me that our students were a select group, competent, industrious, and dedicated to professional responsibility. Teaching them was a pleasant privilege, for it was a departmental policy that the senior members of the staff should personally conduct the elementary courses, not only in the lecture room but also by taking an active part in laboratory instruction.

Perhaps the best of my teaching in Chicago resulted from a request, made insistently from the department of psychology, for an introductory course on the nervous system open to students who lacked the scientific prerequisites for the medical course in neuroanatomy. To meet this demand, I announced a course open to all graduate students, with no prerequisites. It was immediately filled to capacity from all quarters of the campus—psychology, physiology, zoölogy, education, sociology, philosophy, divinity. Some of these had had no experience with science of any kind, others were as well trained in the basic sciences as the medical students.

Here was a group of mature and competent students who presented a fantastic pedagogical problem. The only practicable solution was to throw all pedagogical rules and conventions out the window. At the opening session I announced that this would be a go-as-you-please race. Attendance was optional, and there would be no formal quizzes, no final examination, and no grades reported except passing marks for those who qualified. There were only two requirements. First, that every member was to prepare a term paper on some subject of his own choice (subject to the instructor's approval) in which the literature of the topic chosen was surveyed and critically evaluated. The second requirement was that every member should make himself responsible for extracting from the course (the lectures, conferences, laboratory exercises, and reading) what was most pertinent to his own interest and program and submit a brief written report on this theme. Each member would be on his own and under no obligation to keep in step with anybody else.

The plan, or lack of plan, was successful beyond my expectation, because the students worked enthusiastically and to good purpose. There were practically no absences, and everybody got a passing mark because each of them got something of peculiar worth to himself. This was a pedagogical adventure for all of us, and we had a good time. In successive years the content and conduct of the course were never exactly repeated, and, because I felt free to experiment as I liked, I got more fun out of this course than from any other teaching in my forty years of experience. A more enduring and satisfying reward is the expressions of appreciation that continue to flow in from these loyal students.

In my advanced courses I was equally fortunate, for from the beginning I was associated with a group of graduate students and visiting scientists

of unusual qualifications. There were generally less than a half-dozen of these in residence at any one time, so that the seminars and conferences were intimate and the personal friendships then established are still the most highly prized fruits of the life of science. Some of these workers came from the far corners of the earth, and it warms the heart to receive their friendly greetings from day to day even now—letters from successful scientific workers scattered all over the United States and Canada, Europe, New Zealand, Japan, India, South America, and South Africa. Several of the most competent of these men came from China. The college training which they received there was excellent, but their knowledge of the English language left much to be desired. Notwithstanding this handicap and the difficulty of adjusting to our different pattern of culture, they proved themselves the peers of our American students, and their dissertations for the doctorate were as good as the best our laboratory produced.

The transfer from a small college to a medical school brought about as radical change in my research program as in teaching methods. My previous publications had dealt with the nervous system of fishes, and there was on hand a large collection of sectioned specimens awaiting further study. If this program were continued, early publication of a series of papers on brains of fishes could be expected. I felt, however, that enough had already been done in this field to show the appropriate methods and objectives insofar as methods then available permitted. It might be better for me and for the development of a systematic program of research in comparative neurology at the university to encourage others to continue the study of fishes and to devote my own efforts to an enterprise of wider scope.

The most distinctive and important part of the human brain is the cerebral cortex, and the functions of this cortex present the biggest problems of human neurology. Accordingly, I resolved to study the evolutionary development of this enigmatic structure, in the hope that it would yield useful information. It soon became evident that, in order to understand the cortex of any animal, we must know more about its relations with subcortical structures than we then did. In the human brain these relations are so complicated as to baffle analysis with methods then available. It would be better, then, to begin with study of brains more simply organized.

The salamanders and other primitive amphibians were selected for the

intensive study of this problem because their generalized brains are organized according to the same plan as the human brain, with the parts at a very low level of specialization. There is no superficial gray cortex in the cerebral hemispheres, although the areas in which differentiated cortex appears in the reptilian brain are clearly evident.

To discover the factors which may have led to cortical differentiation, the histological structure of the whole brain must be analyzed in detail. This analysis proved to be so difficult that most of my subsequent research has been devoted to this study. The salient features of this analysis were summarized in 1948 (9). My interpretation of the end-product of this evolutionary process, as seen in the human brain, is outlined in a recently published book (10).

Now one final comment on this survey of a life which has been rich in satisfactions found even in the many errors and failures as well as in some successes. I like this aphorism by Dr. Martin Gumpert, "You don't *grow* old. When you cease to grow you *are* old." As long as you can keep growing, life is a great adventure to be lived adventurously.

Having lived and worked for more than twenty years as emeritus, I can testify that congenial work is the best prescription for senility, although the pace, of course, must be slower with the passing of years. During the first ten years after retirement I was fortunately able to carry on the research program with no distractions except those of my own choice. Then, when the eyes could no longer tolerate work with the microscope, the next decade was devoted to systematizing my thinking on neurological and other matters in the general field of psychobiology.

The broader perspectives opened by this endeavor have advanced my educational program as never before. The years since retirement have been in some respects the happiest and most productive of my life. Four books and about fifty scientific articles have been published. Although the major problems of human personal and social adjustment still puzzle us, the co-operative efforts of workers in diverse fields have clarified the problems and pointed the way toward profitable lines of further search.

Even toward the end, when bodily weakness and other disabilities condemn one to the quiet life, when even the grasshopper becomes a burden, there are compensations. It is good to accept old age gracefully, and, if one can be gracious about it, then the joy of living is refined and enriched.

REFERENCES

1. C. J. Herrick. Tr. Am. Phil. Soc., **45**:1, 1955.
2. O. S. Strong. J. Morphol., **10**:101, 1895.
3. G. E. Coghill. J. Comp. Neurol., **12**:205, 1902.
4. C. J. Herrick. George Ellett Coghill, naturalist and philosopher. Chicago: University of Chicago Press, 1949.
5. W. F. Norwood. Medical education in the United States before the Civil War. Philadelphia: University of Pennsylvania Press, 1944.
6. A. Flexner. Medical education in the United States and Canada. Boston: D. B. Updike, Merrymount Press, 1910.
7. I. Veith and F. C. McLean. The University of Chicago Clinics and clinical departments, 1927–1952. Chicago: University of Chicago Press, 1952.
8. E. E. Irons. The story of Rush Medical College. Chicago: Board of Trustees of Rush Medical College, 1953.
9. C. J. Herrick. The brain of the tiger salamander, *Ambystoma tigrinum*. Chicago: University of Chicago Press, 1948.
10. ———. The evolution of human nature. Austin: University of Texas Press, 1956.

W. R. HESS, M.D.

From Medical Practice to Theoretical Medicine

Ancestry

I should like to begin this short sketch of my life with a few comments concerning my forebears. This will come as no surprise to readers interested in biology, who are well aware of the decisive influences one's inheritance has in the shaping of one's life. In my own case it is rather interesting, as two different folk-groups are represented in my pedigree. My father's ancestors belonged to the Alemanni, a Germanic tribe of the upper Rhine valley formerly under Roman control. In several expansive movements these peoples drove the Romans southward and over the Alps; they then occupied the now German-speaking region of northeastern Switzerland and are considered the principal ancestors of its present population. My mother's people came from the region of the former kingdom of Saxony where East European types were to be found along with the Nordic. This divergence between the maternal and paternal inheritance generally is of a certain genetic interest.

A rather broad range of trades and professions is to be found in my family tree. It includes farmers, craftsmen, and merchants as well as more distantly related clergymen and politicians who were rather gifted orators.

My father, a college teacher in physics, combined a remarkable sense of order with a teacher's talent. Although fundamentally a very serious man, he always retained a good sense of humor. My mother had an altogether happy and pleasant disposition, which stood in striking contrast to the rather sober mood and reserved attitude so characteristic of the inhabitants of eastern Switzerland at that time. It is no wonder that we had little contact with our neighbors, who looked upon us almost as strangers with dif-

Proffessor Hess started his scientific career in the field of hemodynamics. The main interest of his long career has been the organization of the vegetative functions, which led him to the study of the biological foundation of psychology. He occupied the Chair of Physiology, University of Zürich, at the time of his retirement. He continues to reside in Zürich, Switzerland.

ferent customs and social standards. My mother also had an unusually lively disposition. She bubbled over with energy—so much so, in fact, that she often had a hard time falling asleep. I, too, was to suffer from this difficulty throughout my life. I have always had to struggle to shut out the impressions and experiences of the day.

Early Environment

The editors who invited me to write a short autobiography encouraged me to include a psychological background to my life story. This is in keeping with modern autobiographic writing and means that the role played by the external environment in developing, shaping, and limiting an individual's inherited capabilities must not be overlooked.

My own childhood was provided with ample opportunities to become aware of nature at firsthand. My early curiosity about the world around me was stimulated and supported by my father. Even at the age of five, I used to explore the fields and meadows to collect plants, and every new specimen meant an exciting experience, for it was brought home and carefully classified with Father's help. Soon I had my herbarium and a collection of butterflies. As time went on, I became aware of the significance of the ecological setting, that is to say, of the specific interrelationship between flora and fauna. I could see, for example, that a particular species of caterpillar was always to be found on a certain plant. Such observations were unforgettable. Even much later I remembered the exact place where they had occurred. More and more it became clear that functional manifestations, such as the germination of a seed or the rapid sprouting of a shoot from a willow, were more apt to capture my mind than purely morphological features. Perhaps most fascinating to me was the observation of the metamorphosis from caterpillar to chrysalis to butterfly. I just couldn't get enough of nature. How beautiful were those solitary walks through fields and forests and along streams and rivers. By the time I entered elementary school I had thoroughly discovered the countryside surrounding my village.

Student Years

The phase in my life that did much to form my personality began with my entrance into the Gymnasium at the age of twelve. My father soon allowed me to visit his physics laboratory and to help out in setting up the

experiments for his classes. This early contact with classical physics was of great value to me in later life. It was during this time that I saw how the seemingly stationary processes in so-called static systems were in reality a system of antagonistic forces resulting in a dynamic equilibrium.

During my free time I used to make toys such as bows and arrows, sail boats, and airplanes from improvised materials to be found in and around the house. This did much to develop not only manual skills but also a certain practical sense and inventiveness. On the other hand, I had to overcome many difficulties with my studies. It was hard for me to remember isolated data which could not be associated with significant events. I also had trouble memorizing the vocabularies in Greek, Latin, and French. In short, in the linguistic subjects I was not a good student; I was poor also in composition. Throughout my life I have had difficulties in expressing my thoughts in writing. On the other hand, I have always been able to express myself clearly and convincingly in speaking. When involved in an interesting debate or discussion, the words flow freely. But when I try to put these same ideas on paper, I run into trouble, the sentences usually being too long and complicated. I have so often envied the writing skills of others.

The question naturally arises how it came about that someone like myself, whose true interests lie in natural science, should come to study medicine. I think that this can be attributed to the influence of our family doctor who treated me for pleurisy. This bout with tuberculosis cast the only shadow on my otherwise happy youth. Being very lively by temperament, it was all the harder for me to heed the warnings against overexerting myself.

I decided during the last semesters in the Gymnasium on the path I would take following graduation. The medical profession seemed to offer a course of training which would not be too severe in its demands. In addition, both seeing the application of science for the benefit of people and the doctor's role in the community appealed to me.

University life opened up new dimensions for an essentially small-town boy. First of all, I had to decide at which university I would study. My first choice was the University of Lausanne, located in the French-speaking area of Switzerland. There I would also have the opportunity of getting to know the essentially different traditions and customs of my fellow citizens who were of Roman descent. Following the first year, I took advantage of an opportunity to study for one semester in the capital city of Bern, where I was exposed to the well-functioning democracy of my country. I then went to Zürich, where I completed the preclinical courses in anatomy, histology, biochemistry, and physiology. The urge to travel—inherent in all youth—overcame me and I went to Berlin, at that time still under the Kaiser's rule. In addition to its famous clinics, Berlin had many interesting things to offer, such as museums, a zoölogical garden, an oceanarium, and an astronomical observatory. The countryside of Berlin, with its wide plains and open spaces, was especially interesting and novel for a Swiss accustomed to the hills and mountains of his country. Everything in the fields of art and theater was also at one's disposal. Despite all these varied possibilities, I remained faithful to my love for nature.

In 1903 I had an excellent opportunity to experience the sea in the German city of Kiel, whose harbor also served as a base for the German navy. How longingly my eyes followed the ships as they disappeared over the horizon into distant lands.

For me, the most unforgettable personality on the medical faculty of Kiel was the internist Quincke. He had the talent of presenting his cases in a very interesting way; I missed hardly any of his lectures. I also learned a great deal of surgery under Helferich, who was an excellent teacher, although to be sure an air of cynicism wafted through his lectures or demonstrations. The lectures in dermatology and venereology were excellent; the clinical case presentations were especially impressive, as more than adequate material was available from the port district.

Following the completion of my studies in Berlin, and after having devoted much time to personal scientific interests during the summer semester spent in Kiel, I returned to Switzerland. At the turn of the century, the length of study for doctors was ten semesters—that is, for an industrious student. Because I had devoted much time to my side interests, I felt that my prospects of passing the final examinations were rather poor. Nevertheless, I made up the classes I had missed in Berlin and Kiel by adhering to a rigid work schedule during the last two semesters in Zürich. I took no notes whatsoever, but gave my full attention to the lectures and demonstrations. For reading material, I consulted textbooks and atlases. This study procedure was supplemented with periodic discussions with my fellow students who were also preparing for final exams and who were informed about the "specialties" of the examiners. I successfully passed the examinations in 1905 and received the diploma bestowing the right to practice medicine in Switzerland.

Inklings of Research

Looking back on my days in medical school, I can still remember one incident which is worthy of mention. During a dissecting session in the Anatomical Institute in Zürich the instructor called our attention to an anomaly in the arterial blood supply of the foot. The arteria dorsalis pedis was not formed as a direct continuation of the arteria tibialis anterior as it usually is. Instead, a well-developed anastomosis with the arteria tibialis posterior was present. This fact, pointed out without further elaboration by the anatomist, interested me and I asked for an explanation. The teacher's answer that the anomaly was not at all infrequent did not satisfy my scientific curiosity. I finally gathered up enough courage and presented my own interpretation. It seemed clear to me that the differential resistance between the arteria tibialis anterior and posterior must be of considerable significance. The path with the least resistive drop in pressure carries the blood more effectively to the peripheral segments since it maintains the greater pressure reserves. It is this pressure reserve which procures blood for the vascular system of the foot via the anastomosis between two arterial branches. Thus, the above mentioned anomaly is a direct example of the relationship between hemodynamics and morphogenesis in the arterial system.

I can no longer remember the content of the discussion which followed in the dissecting room. In any event, the question remained open and arose again in Berlin in a different context. There I met W. Roux, the anatomist at the nearby University of Halle, who was the founder of the science of developmental mechanics. Because I was interested in the question, I was keen to learn the opinion of such a distinguished scientist, who had also worked on the problem of the relationship between hemodynamics and the morphological formation of the arterial tree with special reference to the angle of its branches. I therefore presented my ideas to him in the form of a letter and was very happy to receive a reply inviting me to Halle for a personal discussion. As a result, Roux suggested that the theory be published in the *Archiv für Entwicklungsmechanik*. It is understandable that my interest in scientific work received a strong stimulus. It led to a student's paper entitled "Eine mechanisch bedingte Gesetzmässigkeit im Bau des Blutgefässsystemes" ("A Mechanically Induced Conformity in the Structure of the Vascular System"). My concern with this problem led to further consequences, as the reader will discover later.

Choice of the place for my first internship was dictated by financial circumstances, which did not permit me to pursue a course of study in theoretical medicine, as I would have liked, following the completion of my training in 1905. From then on I had to earn my own living. My first assignment was a residency in the state hospital of my home canton rather than an unpaid position in a university clinic.

The department of surgery at the hospital was under the direction of Dr. Konrad Brunner, whose reputation extended beyond the borders of Switzerland. Retrospectively, I can see how much I profited from having worked in the well-disciplined team under Brunner. In addition to the routine daily chores, I came to understand and appreciate the skilled technique and high sense of responsibility of this great surgeon. Furthermore, I had the opportunity to see parts of the vascular system in vivo, which intensified my early interests in hemodynamics.

The relationship between the morphological organization of the vascular system and the flow characteristics of blood factors became more apparent in determining circulatory phenomena. I could also see that in practical medicine more attention was paid to the dynamic action of the heart pump than to peripheral factors such as the resistance and blood viscosity. The role of the latter was almost completely ignored, and therefore I decided to construct a convenient apparatus to measure blood viscosity for clinical usage. The problem was intriguing because the existing viscosimetric apparatus (e.g., Ostwald) applicable to so-called idealized fluids could not be used for measuring blood viscosity. Due to the coagulability of blood, the measurements would have to be completed within 2 to 3 minutes, and, for practical purposes, 1 to 2 drops of blood—as used in determining hemoglobin values—would have to suffice. In addition, it was desirable to develop a procedure which would allow the results to be read off directly, thereby avoiding calculations. How to construct an apparatus which could fulfil all these requirements occupied almost all my free time. I would concentrate on the problem especially during walks. After I had probed many varied constructions in my mind, a possible solution all at once occurred to me. It had the character of a sudden inspiration whereby the latent psychological tension becomes discharged. Unforeseen difficulties had to be overcome in order to actualize the mental concept into a practical, usable instrument. Much patience was required and modifications had to be made often to arrive at the goal.

At last the plan was fulfilled and measurements were made. The results and conclusions were published in a small treatise entitled "Viscosität des Blutes und Herzarbeit" ("Viscosity of the Blood and the Work of the Heart"). Dr. Konrad Brunner, my chief, who freely admitted that he had an inadequate knowledge of the problem, left the future of the work entirely in my hands. I therefore personally submitted the paper for publication in *Pflüger's Archiv für Physiologie*. I had to undergo a rather painful experience because of the authoritarian attitude then prevalent toward youthful scientists. Today, of course, the necessity and duty of promoting and encouraging young people in scientific research is well established. Pflüger wanted to know under whose direction the work had been carried out. Upon explaining to him that it had been done entirely on my own, he rejected the paper without comment. Fortunately for me, a member of the Zürich medical faculty who heard of the situation interested himself on my behalf. It was Professor Zangger who took over the printing of the work in *Vierteljahresschrift der Zürcher Naturforschenden Gesellschaft*.

The main finding in the paper was the demonstration that the viscosity of the blood varies with the number of circulating erythrocytes, which is one of the factors that may influence peripheral resistance. It further suggested that decreased viscosity of the blood can lead to turbulence and may be responsible for the so-called anemic heart murmur.

In the following years the science of viscosimetry of blood plasma and serum expanded considerably and, in combination with refractometry, it became possible to differentiate the albumin and globulin fractions in plasma or serum. An increasing clinical interest in blood viscosity manifested itself between the years of 1908 and 1920. Thereafter interest declined, probably because more convenient and practical methods (e.g., measurement of the sedimentation rate) had been developed. Nevertheless, for special cases, interest in the viscosimetry of blood and other body fluids has remained until the present time.

During my first year of internship I was naturally concerned about my future, so I set a firm goal for myself. I wanted to work in some branch of medicine which would give me an adequate income while at the same time allowing me sufficient time to devote myself to problems of basic research. A practice in ophthalmology seemed ideal to meet these two requirements. I therefore seized the first opportunity to enter the department of ophthalmology at the University of Zürich as a resident early in 1906. My new chief, Professor O. Haab, was an outstanding clinician and skilled surgeon. The somewhat one-sided morphological orientation prevalent in the clinic did not quite suit my views; however, I had ample opportunities to make diagnostic observations of a more dynamic character—for example, in analyzing oculomotor disturbances.

According to the technique employed at that time, the examiner relied on the patient's report as to the site of the double image when a moving light with changing directions was flashed before his eyes. With such a method the examiner was, of course, too dependent on the patient's intelligence, and quite often an exact diagnosis had to be foregone. I decided, therefore, to develop a method which would give more objective results concerning the co-ordination of eye muscles. I shall not describe the procedure in detail. Suffice it to recall that by employing an apparatus called "co-ordimeter," it was possible to determine the motor defect quantitatively. Furthermore, it was possible to evaluate with satisfactory accuracy the effects of treatment through repeated controls. The apparatus has undergone improvements and modifications since its inception, but the novel principle has held its own till now. More important to me personally was the clear insight I gained into the problem of motor co-ordination which—many years later—added greatly to my understanding of the analysis of motor responses during stimulation in the region of the thalamus and subthalamus.

The same was true of a thorough investigation of stereoscopic vision, which presents an instructive example of the integrative function of the central nervous system. In conjunction with the above interests, I tried to develop a procedure for making stereoscopic photographs, with the hope that I might capitalize on it and obtain thereby a certain degree of financial freedom. In fact, I succeeded in making three-dimensional transparencies which gave a real view into the depths of the object. The pictures, however, lacked certain desirable qualities which I was trying to incorporate when World War I halted my attempts. At the end of the war my position was more secure and other problems were occupying my attention.

Before the war I had completed my residency in ophthalmology and had furthered my education through a brief period of study in Paris. Soon thereafter I took over the practice of an ophthalmologist in an attractive city and important railroad intersection in the vicinity of Zürich. By the spring of 1908 I was living rather comfortably as a practicing eye specialist and was, therefore, in a position to marry my fiancée, Louise Sandmeier, who had worked in the outpatient department of the Zürich Eye Clinic. As a former doctor's aide, she was well prepared to offer efficient help in her husband's office, and thus we were fortunate enough to overcome our financial difficulties for the time being.

Leap into the Unknown—New Years of Training

The security and compensation derived from an extensive practice had negative aspects. I had set up a laboratory in which I spent my free time working on problems of hemodynamics, particularly in relation to blood viscosimetry, and on problems of motor co-ordination. The ever increasing demands of the practice, and especially the many professional consultations and opinions, left me with less and less time to pursue my scientific interests. I would come home from stimulating scientific meetings in Zürich and feel downright unhappy and dissatisfied because my hands were tied. A deep conflict resulted then between my sense of duty to provide for my family and my longings for pure science. Finally, a critical decision had to be made, as a position became available for me at the Institute of Physiology in Zürich. I can remember so well the exact spot in my garden where I decided in favor of science, despite the fact that I now also had a child to support, and that the decision entailed a considerable reduction in income. Of course I discussed the problem beforehand with my wife, who agreed to the step which was so significant for my later life.

The move was made in 1912. It wrought mental tensions which were not always easy to bear. My new teaching assignment made it necessary for me to review scientific material—old and new—and much was actually learned while teaching. Because of the poor health of my chief, Professor Gaule, a pupil of Carl Ludwig, personal contact with him for purposes of scientific discussion was rather limited, and I was more or less on my own.

I found no lack of pressing problems to tackle. Predominant among these was the economy of energy in the mechanics of circulation, which presents a dynamic parallel, for example, to the architectural patterns of spongeous bone, known to be built so as to insure optimal bearing strength. Take the head of the femur as an example. While the conditions obtaining in hemodynamics are not so obvious as in static systems, they are, nevertheless, of fundamental significance. In order to understand properly the hemodynamic situation, we must realize that the energy output of the heart is greatly dependent upon the configuration of the vascular system, especially of the arteries. Significant criteria are (*a*) the relation between the cross-sectional area of a vessel and the sum of the areas of its branches; (*b*) the angle between the branching vessel and the axis of its trunk; and (*c*) the distance to be covered between the heart and the capillary bed of an organ.

Given the above parameters, it was possible to set up an idealized model for an optimal vascular energy system for purposes of comparison with the performance of conditions prevailing in a living circulatory system. The formulation of such an ideal model may be regarded as an example of theoretical biology. The second procedure, testing the theory in vivo, represents, on the other hand, unequivocal experimental biology. I presented the above work for my *Habilitationsschrift*, which was accepted by the medical faculty in 1913. My presentation was not as convincing as the evidence found in osteology in regard to the adaptive structuralization of spongeous bone, partly because the former requires mathematical treatment before it becomes obvious and the latter presents itself directly to the eyes of a scientifically naïve observer. As I glance back after fifty years of experience, I would now tackle the problem somewhat differently; nevertheless, my basic attitude of laying a theoretical foundation before setting up an experimental procedure would remain unaltered.

In my position as *Privatdozent* I was authorized to give laboratory courses, which I organized according to my own inclinations—i.e., biophysically, but not without clinical perspectives. This ideal situation was, unfortunately, terminated by the outbreak of World War I. In the general mobilization of the Swiss army which followed, I, along with everyone else fit for military service, was called to active duty. My work at the physiology institute was completely interrupted. As the war went on, and the increasing superiority of the Allies became apparent, it was sometimes possible to return to work for a few months. I even contemplated continuing my scientific training abroad. Above all, I wanted contact with general physiology.

I found it in the laboratory of Max Verworn, Pflüger's successor in

Bonn. Verworn had extensive experience with animal physiology, acquired as a pupil of Haeckel. He was especially familiar with so-called elementary organisms and the basic requirements for life. A widely read book by Verworn entitled *Allgemeine Physiologie* (1922) contains more information concerning his work. Along with the formal lectures and laboratory work, the almost daily private contact at tea time with Verworn, when we discussed teaching methods in general, the work of our colleagues, and even topics in art, literature, and philosophy, did much to broaden me and prepare me for the future. I will be forever thankful for the kindness shown to me by this man. He never let me be aware of the vast distance which separated him—a famous, experienced, and wise man—from myself, a young and inquisitive scientist. I was allowed complete freedom in experimental work and was able, therefore, to concentrate further on problems of hemodynamics.

As a ready supply of dogs was available for experimental purposes, I was able to investigate in living animals the regulation of regional blood flow, i.e., its adaptation to the changing needs of specific organs. At that time the concept of the "peripheral heart" was a topic of much discussion, especially among clinicians who understood thereby the total muscular component of the arterial system. The pulse was ascribed partially to an active force, i.e., the centrifugal wave of arterial contraction released by the contraction of the heart and resulting in the forward propulsion of the blood.

The nonbranching sector of the common carotid artery seemed to me to be well suited for experimentally testing the above concept. The technique used was as follows. Through a small longitudinal incision in the proximal part of the common carotid artery a glass stopper was so inserted as to stop the flow of blood. To prevent any backflow into the area under investigation, the system was also closed off cranially with a stopper provided with a system for optically registering pressure changes in the thus isolated arterial section. The systemic blood pressure was occasionally monitored in the femoral artery, particularly in connection with artificial pressure increases in the carotid artery. All attempts to alter the blood pressure, either in the isolated section of the carotid or in the peripheral arterial system, ended in failure. At the end of my year's leave of absence I could only report negative results.

Soon thereafter I learned by reading the papers of Hering, Jr., and Heymans that I had just missed an opportunity to make an important discovery. My own procedure involved the common carotid up to the point where it bifurcates, thus excluding the carotid sinus. Had I included the sinus, I could not have failed to observe a massive fall in pressure due to the now well-known reflex control of blood pressure. This oversight really irked me, but I consoled myself with the thought that similar failures had certainly happened to many other investigators. In any case, I didn't allow myself to be detracted from the study of hemodynamics.

Upon returning to Zürich, it was not possible for me to continue the experimental work aimed at clarifying the adaptation of blood supply to the changing requirements of individual organs. I was called upon for further military service in addition to my teaching schedule, which took up all my time. Further research, then, had to wait until the end of World War I.

An Unexpected Turn of Events

As mentioned previously, my chief, Professor Justus Gaule, head of the department of physiology in Zürich, had suffered from poor health for many years, which hindered him from being very active in teaching and prevented him completely from doing research. Conditions finally became so critical that Gaule announced his resignation just before the winter semester of 1916. I was asked to take charge of the lectures and laboratories temporarily until the appointment of the permanent holder of the chair. I would have personally preferred to spend several more years as a *Privatdozent*, with adequate time for research, rather than to be acting chairman with all the administrative and teaching duties. Nevertheless, with healthy optimism and steadfast determination I began the work ahead of me. In relying on the experience gained during my years with the handling of mechanical and optical equipment, I planned to use such extensively in the laboratory experiments. I was also counting on drawing from my internship experience, and particularly on the operative skills I had acquired as an assistant surgeon and as an ophthalmologist. Finally, conceptual references between normal and pathological physiology as well as the insights gained into general physiology under Verworn turned out to be most helpful in the new situation.

Zürich Faculty

It should be noted that in the German-speaking region of Switzerland appointments to professorial chairs were at that time rather complicated and entailed far greater attention to the so-called "school" of the prospective candidate than, for example, in the United States, where much more liberal principles for selection operate. Additional difficulties arose in general from the fact that the relatively young University of Zürich lacked a corps of graduates trained in science. Therefore, German candidates usually had an advantage from the beginning, and many positions were occupied by Germans, some of whom were really outstanding. This method for gathering academic personnel was in vogue during the time of the expansive tendencies of the Wilhelmian epoch. In any event, the German professors took it for granted that a Swiss person could not be considered seriously for an academic position in a theoretical medical discipline; a Swiss scientist was more likely to be intrusted with a practical assignment.

Under these circumstances, then, a proposal was prepared at the end of the winter semester which foresaw calling a German professor to the chair in physiology. With due consideration of "his seniority and much larger training," he had produced far more scientific papers than I and had undeniably good qualities, especially in the field of physiological chemistry. In spite of this, he had not yet been called to a leading position in Germany and was still in line for one.

Since, however, the administration and management of the institute during the winter semester had gone along smoothly under my acting chairmanship, and because the lectures and laboratories had been well attended, the university authorities decided to re-examine the entire situation more thoroughly. An invited opinion written by Verworn which had been withheld by the faculty till then was also brought to my support. Finally, the summer semester turned out to be another success, to which two very capable assistants generously contributed, E. Rothlin and A. Fleisch—subsequently professors, respectively, of pharmacology at Basle and of physiology at Lausanne. The decision of the nominating committee came out in my favor, and in the fall of 1917 the chair for physiology was officially intrusted to me.

Development of a Program for Instruction and Research

Now that I was responsible for the development of physiology, it was mandatory for me to become familiar with the management and setup in other universities. I had the great fortune of being able to get to know and to observe the English physiologists of the classical period, as they were still working in their laboratories. Starling gave me complete freedom to gain an insight into his programing and methodology for lecture sessions and lab work. Through Langley I came to understand how the institute in Cambridge was run. I saw Sherrington at work only briefly, as he was very busy and implied that he did not want to be bothered. With the help and kindness of one of his assistants, however, I was allowed to find out about everything of interest to me. Many years later I met this assistant—who now holds a leading position in the United States—at an international congress (I believe in Montreal). Naturally the topic of conversation turned to Professor Sherrington. Because of my own later experience, I had long since come to understand Sherrington's reserve and aloofness.

In addition to this visit to England and later travels, I also participated in various congresses to which I owe a great deal for the broadening of my knowledge. I can still vividly remember the demonstration of dogs suffering from rickets presented by E. Mellanby, later Lord Mellanby, with the help of his wife, later Lady Mellanby, at the International Physiological Congress in Paris in 1920. At that time Mellanby demonstrated the effects of malnutrition—the concept of vitamins was still controversial. One could hear the differences of opinion being argued more critically in the corridors than in the demonstration hall in the presence of the speakers themselves. A great scientific event also occurred at the congress in Edinburgh in 1923, where, under the leadership of J. J. R. MacLeod, a series of lectures included those by Banting and Best in which the chain of events which led to the discovery of insulin was unfolded. I returned from still other scientific meetings enriched in experiences and knowledge which could be incorporated into my lectures by way of illustrating them with experimental material. The meetings of the *Deutsche Gesellschaft für Naturforscher und Ärzte* were particularly stimulating and important for me. At these sessions I attended primarily the general lectures. Otherwise, I sat in on those given by the internists. As a teacher, I was much concerned with the advances in internal medicine, as my students, upon entering the clinical semesters, should be able to correlate clinical material with their knowledge of physiology.

A special feature of these meetings was the chance to become personally acquainted with other scientists in the more relaxed atmosphere outside the lecture halls. Apart from shop talk, these personal contacts provided important insights for evaluating, to some extent, the publications of the various institutions. Such first-hand impressions saved me a lot of time in selecting literature for study.

Research Projects

For the time being hemodynamics remained the chief subject of research in my institute. It included research work concerning the autonomic properties and the reactivity of isolated arteries. It was clear to me that information obtained on an isolated arterial section could not by itself be decisive for the intact living arterial apparatus. On the other hand, I was convinced that the inherent functional properties of the arterial tube, even though normally subject to nervous influences, would be of great significance in themselves. In line with these thoughts, arterial rings were removed from various parts of the arterial system and tested for their spontaneous behavior while submersed in physiological salt solution. In addition, the rings were stimulated mechanically and electrically with varying parameters as well as chemically with biologically active substances—among others, adrenalin and acetylcholine. These experiments were extended over a period of years and yielded the material which, with inclusion of the reflex mechanisms, provided a general insight subsequently elaborated in 1930 in the monograph *Regulation of the Circulatory System.* From the close relationship and synergic functioning of the circulatory and respiratory apparatus, it followed automatically that *The Regulation of Respiration* be handled in an analogous manner (1931).

From discussions with a few colleagues, I occasionally heard that reference to the concept of a meaningful organization of physiological systems was here and there regarded as an expression of teleological tendencies. In replying to such comments, I have always maintained that living matter can only exist in the form of organization oriented toward success; indeed, that the investigation of such organization poses the central problem of biology. The knowledge and insight gained by experimental methods and the collected pool of facts allowing a synthesis between organization and performance truly constitute the grand aim of an *integral physiology*, which can never be fulfilled with the mere collecting of facts. The deleterious effects of disturbances, as in sickness, confirm the above viewpoint. The development of this theme was worked out and later formally expressed in the monograph (1948) *Die funktionelle Organisation des vegetativen Nervensystems* (*Functional Organization of the Vegetative Nervous System*).

The shift to a seemingly new topic—namely, examination of active regulatory dispositives at the higher level of the diencephalon—will readily be understood as a logical consequence of a long-range project. From an earlier programmatic work entitled "Correlations between Psychic and Vegetative Functions" (1924), in conjunction with and from knowledge of certain clinical experiences and from exploratory experimental investigations of Karplus and Kreidl, certain conclusions could be drawn. It became apparent that before further progress could be expected, a new experimental technique which could adequately fulfil the more differentiated demands of the modern investigation would first have to be developed. For it was my goal to test the behavior of experimental animals (cats) subjected to electrical stimulation and diathermic lesions without impairing the freedom of movement of the animal by immobilization or narcosis.

For this purpose, the very finest electrodes were needed which could be inserted into the hypothalamus without flexing and bending. In addition, to use the induction coil as a stimulating device was out of the question, for the relatively slowly arising autonomic effects in the face of the rapidly occurring potential deflections produced by induction could be all too easily overshadowed by reactions from somatic sensorimotor systems and could, under certain conditions, not even have time to be formed. I was more hopeful for a form of stimulation with pulsating direct current, provided that the cathodic electrode points could be depolarized between the single impulses, thus maintaining a consistent stimulus intensity also during prolonged series of stimulation. The decisive advantage therein proved to lie in the possibility of adapting duration and shape of the stimulating pulses to the time properties of the nervous elements under examination.

Apart from these precautionary measures concerning stimulation technique, the problem of anatomical identification of the stimulated structure had to be solved so as to allow the closest possible correlation between symptom and reacting substrate. Since required accuracy can never be achieved on the basis of electrode placements alone, microscopic control of serial histological sections of each experimental brain is necessary. Three atlases composed of photomicrographic reproduction of serial sections cut perpendicularly to each other gave invaluable assistance in the topographical analysis of stimulation sites. In addition, these atlases served to register in each individual case the histological finding as well as to prepare cumulative map files of all points stimulated during the many years of investigative work. Cross-references among these three standard atlases allowed localization of each site of stimulation in all three planes, thereby providing three-dimensional registration, which in many cases was indispensable to demonstrate the relation between topographical and functional organization. Cinematography was used extensively from 1927 on as a further aid in recording observations. It enabled us to make detailed comparisons between symptoms of experiments separated from one another by years. This would have been impossible by reliance on verbal notes alone. Finally, a filing system was developed which contained references to the symptoms produced by stimulation; this enabled one in the train of data integration to obtain full particulars of a desired case together with the verbal protocol, photomicrographic localization, and cinematographic documents.

The technical aspects of this entire program to investigate the functional organization of the diencephalon were reported in detail in a monograph (1932) entitled *Die Methode der lokalisierten Reizung und Ausschaltung subkortikaler Hinabschnitte* ("The Methodology of Localized Stimulation and Destruction of Subcortical Brain Areas"). This as well as the second part, published 1938, concerning blood pressure and respiratory effects elicited by localized diencephalic stimulation did not become too well known because of World War II. The group of competent workers in this field was small at that time, and all the type of this edition was destroyed in Leipzig during World War II.

At the very beginning of the exploratory experiments (1925) I had reckoned with from two to three years for gathering data sufficient to obtain a certain insight. But the mere manual work involved in the technique described above used up this much and even more of my time. Also, a heavy teaching schedule did not make things go any faster. Nevertheless, in 1927, the first results were made known at a meeting of the Deutsche Physiologische Gesellschaft in Frankfurt. Of course, following the conclusion of the first series of about fifty cases, no insight into general laws governing the functional organization was obtained; the symptoms were too inconsistent. Therefore, a second experimental series was carried out—which did not, however, do much to clarify the situation.

Only little by little and ever so slowly did the veil lift a bit here and there so that twenty-five years had passed before I could finally think of putting together all the many single research publications that had appeared over the years which had been concerned with individual symptoms. The vast number of experiments turned out to be decisive; for generalization concerning symptoms, syndromes, and localizations could be supported only by such a large body of data. An integrative review of all these efforts was published in two monographs (1947, 1948). They were well received, and in 1949, "for your discovery of the functional organization of the diencephalon and its role in the coordination of the functions of the inner organs," the Nobel Prize was bestowed upon me. The reward was shared with Egaz Moniz, who had developed the prefrontal lobotomy as a therapeutic method in the management of certain psychoses.

The long way which culminated in this high distinction has been presented here in a rather detailed manner because during the war Switzerland was totally closed off and precious little information concerning my investigative methods and results had reached readers abroad. Even with the war's end the fact that all my publications were written in German, the accepted written language of central and eastern Switzerland, proved to be for many years an almost insurmountable barrier in re-establishing a close scientific contact with the Anglo-Saxon countries.

Apart from behavioral and autonomic symptoms, interesting somatic motor effects came to light during the course of the experiments. Through these the relationships of certain formations of the thalamus as well as of the mesencephalon with the so-called extrapyramidal motor system were established. Last but not least, our attention was drawn to psychomotor phenomena on which I reported in a most recently published treatise (1962) entitled *Psychologie in biologischer Sicht* ("Psychology from the Standpoint of a Biologist").

Incidents, Personalities, and Anecdotes

During my active years as professor of physiology on the medical faculty at Zürich, the above described work was often interspersed with noteworthy incidents and problems which have remained vividly in my memory. One of these could be cited as an example of "fortune in misfortune." When I first came to the physiological institute of our university, there was a noticeable shortage of both equipment and space, without which a successful work program was rather difficult—or, more plainly, impossible. Significant improvement was out of the question for the time being. The basement and first floor of the four-storied building which had been constructed during the time of the famous physiologist Hermann, the predecessor of Gaule, were occupied by the physics department, which was also cramped for space. As a result of these unsatisfactory conditions, the department of theoretical physics and a succession of its famous staff members, such as Einstein, von Laue, and Schrödinger, had to work in the smallest space of all. A "higher power" intervened in this precarious situation. On the evening before New Year's Eve in 1923, just before retiring, I received a telephone call informing me that our institute was going up in flames. As I arrived on the spot, the entire top floor was already burning. The fire department went to work immediately. The captain of the fire squad was assured that it would not be necessary to evacuate material from the lower floors. As though to spite this comforting prognosis, however, the fire suddenly broke through the ceiling and threatened to destroy the main portions of our institute. It was high time, then, to get books—and anything else of value—out of the building as quickly as possible and to take them through the deep snow to neighboring institutes. During this "operation evacuation" our basic sense of democracy, valid for all social levels, was dramatically illustrated. For, in addition to the staff members of the physics department and other institutes, members of the executive branch of our state government were also on hand doing their very best to help out. Since only my chief assistant and myself were informed about the value of the inventory, we became responsible for giving directions as to the priority for objects to be saved. Thus it arose that the shoe came to be on the other foot, in that our employers, the political authorities, had to take orders from their employees, i.e., from the professor and his assistants. On the following day, after the fire was finally extinguished, we had to collect our possessions from the neighboring buildings. Of course, everything stored in the top floor was lost. In addition, the building itself had been seriously damaged. This state of affairs gave the cue to the second, happy, part of my story; for, during the repair work, an additional floor was added and thus our need for space alleviated. We moved into the newly repaired and expanded institute with the sincere hope of being able to devote ourselves to our work without disturbance.

This expectation, however, all too soon proved to be illusory. In our direct democracy a constitutional law exists whereby action can be initiated by the people provided that a sufficient number of signatures are submitted. A movement of the community touching at the very heart of medicine and biochemistry arose banning all animal experiments in the canton of Zürich. Members of the physiology institute in Zürich were called upon by the medical faculty to combat this attack, which was aimed at destroying a technique indispensible to scientific progress. We had to prepare ourselves for the battle, which, unfortunately, would take up a lot of time. In place of scientific work, it now became necessary to write popular newspaper articles and to speak at public gatherings in order to present the true interest of the people. The problem of financing the campaign, in the face of the opposite community drive on behalf of the protection of animals, was not a simple matter. When the polls opened, our side was understandably on pins and needles. Members of our campaign headquarters and many interested colleagues had assembled in a hotel room to keep informed on the incoming results from the city and the rural areas. Happily, our efforts had not been in vain. The popular vote resulted in a two-thirds majority in favor of freedom of research with reasonable restrictions. It is impossible to imagine what the fate of our faculty might have been had animal experimentation been declared a criminal offense.

Another equally laborious but more constructive undertaking into which I was drawn by chance turned out to be more than I had bargained for. The Naturforschende Gesellschaft (Swiss Society for Scientific Research) had taken upon itself, due to the promptings of one of its members, a competent meteorologist, to set up a committee for the purpose of constructing a research station at the highest point in Switzerland accessible by railroad—namely, on the Jungfraujoch, over 11,000 feet above sea level. The scientific promoter of the plan died before he could carry it out. Therefore, a new presidium had to be selected for the commission, and it came about that the job fell to me. I had suspected that acceptance would entail no small sacrifice, but in various respects this was a great underestimate.

Originally a Swiss undertaking was envisioned. I myself tried to have the project internationalized. One of the main reasons was the thought that thereby new contacts between representatives of countries which had been enemies during World War I could arise, which could help promote understanding among peoples of different nations. A second point in my program was to include all natural sciences, and particularly biology. One source of resistance was laid down in the initial formulation of objectives of the research station, according to which it was to be used primarily for meteorological studies and for work on geophysical problems. Fortunately the branch of the federal government charged with the main authority was farsighted enough to interpret the formulation of the objectives of the plan so that all disciplines of scientific research having an established interest in work in the high Alpine region should receive equal consideration.

With agreements on internationalization and nonrestriction as to field of research secured, it was time to look around for partners who were prepared to make a financial contribution for the project. We had the satisfaction of receiving positive responses from many countries, among which may be mentioned the then Kaiser Wilhelm Society in Berlin (presently Max-Planck-Gesellschaft), University of Paris, Royal Society of London, Academy of Sciences in Vienna, National Foundation for Scientific Research in Brussels, and, finally, the Rockefeller Foundation in New York, which, however, declined to participate on the international committee. Naturally, it was of prime importance that the Jungfrau Railway Company reaffirmed its active and financial co-operation, which it had promised before the grant for construction of the railway had been made, as well as its readiness to help out in any other problems concerning construction and operation.

No effort could be spared in overcoming the conditions which were to be expected in working on the rugged, fissured precipices. One had to reckon with unexpected stone slides and water breakthroughs as well as unseasonal heavy snowfall. Another problem was the extreme diurnal variation in temperature. The stone material to be used for the building was carefully selected to withstand the intensive heating by high-altitude solar radiation during the day and exposure to freezing temperatures during the night. A completely unexpected event made a joke of all our careful calculations—for in an area which had been stable and inactive for seventy years, an avalanche suddenly broke lose, interrupting the flow of supplies for valuable weeks.

But at long last, in the summer of 1931, the research station was dedicated in the presence of prominent representatives of the participating countries and institutions as well as Swiss government authorities of the highest rank. A special volume prepared for the memorable occasion included contributions from W. Nernst and v. Ficker (Berlin), Ch. Fabry and L. Lapicque (Paris), Sir F. G. Hopkins and G. M. B. Dobson (Oxford), A. Durig and W. Schmidt (Vienna), E. de Wildeman, Gand and J. Jaumotte (Liège),as well as from many others. Every donor country was represented by two delegates. With the reading of the declaration statement "For the Scientific Brotherhood" which had been prepared by the physiologist Lapicque, we fraternally joined hands.

After being responsible for directing the commission through five years of development and construction in addition to a further five years of service as director of the newborn institute, I felt relieved of a great burden when I finally stepped down. A. v. Muralt, from Bern, proved himself more than adequate and an excellent choice for the succession.

I should mention another event which brought additional honors and duties to our institute—the Sixteenth International Congress of Physiology in Zürich (1938). It should not be forgotten that we stood at that time at the brink of World War II. The annexation of Austria by Hitler was then an accomplished fact. At the last minute, partly out of political, partly out of racist motives, we were exposed to a considerable change in attitude from foreign colleagues and officials. Also, personal tensions between participants of the congress could not be ignored. It was not even certain whether the congress would be held at all. Nevertheless, it must be credited to those attending this memorable meeting that proper discipline was maintained and unpleasant incidents were avoided by suppressing any allusions of a political nature in the lectures and in the other events of the congress.

In connection with the deterioration of the warlike situation, the Swiss physiologists were put into an unusual position. Till then they had been associated partly with the German Physiological Society and partly with its French-speaking counterpart. A new way had to be found in loosening our ties from both of the warring factions. With the support of K. Spiro, the biochemist on the Basle medical faculty, I made a motion for the founding of a Swiss Physiological Society.

Inevitably, the next step was the founding in 1943 of a periodical, *Helvetica Physiologica et Pharmacologica Acta*. It is understandable that at first the circulation of the new periodical was rather limited. Everyone's interest was completely directed toward the war. In addition, the passage of printed matter out of Switzerland into, for instance, the United States was barred. Even after the war, the demand for the new journal was small. Yet we had to be satisfied with what had been achieved. Today we note that the journal is enjoying an increase in circulation.

To end this sketch, I have the satisfaction of announcing a gratifying undertaking which is intimately connected to my life's work. As early as 1940 I had assumed the initiative for founding a study group devoted to brain research. Periodically, physiologists, psychiatrists, brain surgeons, internists, pharmacologists, neuro-anatomists, psychoanalysts, and psychotherapists would come together at the physiological institute. At first, we wanted to get to know one another's points of view and to find a common language for the various terms and concepts.

Thanks to the financial support of the Rockefeller Foundation and later to that of the Swiss Academy of Medical Sciences, through its Commission for Brain Research, this study group achieved its goal with ever expanding participation until 1950. Today the original plan has culminated in an institute for brain research, to be opened in 1963.

If one considers my own interest in the functional organization of the brain along with its psychic manifestation—an interest which was expressed as far back as 1924 and which was never lost sight of—one will well understand that the decision of the faculty and the responsible authorities to create a chair for brain research has filled my young old heart with the very deepest satisfaction. Equally gratifying is the fact that I can regard the future of the institute with confidence, as one of my earlier co-workers, K. Akert, presently on the medical faculty, has been named its director.

A last point remains to be mentioned—research costs money and I am glad to acknowledge the help I received. While the small communities which support our Swiss universities were not able to provide adequate means, financial assistance by the Rockefeller Foundation and by a personal benefactor, Benjamin Stern, was of decisive value. In the last few years the Swiss National Foundation for Scientific Research furthered our endeavors.

In anticipation of a possible question from my readers, especially those in America, I must answer whether or not during my active period I found time for a hobby. Through fortunate circumstances, in view of my inclination to financially unpromising basic research, I was awarded a cash prize from the Swiss Marcel Benoist Foundation during the relatively early years of my work. This money was invested in a simple summer house south of the Alps in the region of the so-called "sun terrace of Switzerland." There I tended my vines and cared for my garden whenever I found it necessary or possible to relax a bit. My reward was not only a harvest of grapes and the pleasure given by the southern plants, but also acquisition of a variety of bits of information as well as the manual skills practiced by the farmers there since, presumably, as far back as Roman times. And the Italian attitude and language contributed much to my relaxation and enjoyment. I would quickly recover from overwork and in the presence of lizards, scorpions, Aesculapius snakes, and other crawling beasts so alien to eastern Switzerland, feel myself a new man. In this rustic setting, my mind would often turn to contemplating questions of prehistory, and I would become mentally refreshed and rested.

And now, after sixty years of service on behalf of science, I contentedly put down my pen with the hope that perhaps my work has contributed to scientific progress in my own field, especially toward the understanding of regulatory functions at the integrative level of the organism.

GEORGE HEVESY, Ph.D. (hon.), D.Sc. (hon.), M.D. (hon.)

A Scientific Career

I was born in Budapest the 1st of August, 1885. After terminating my studies at the Gymnasium of the Piarist Order in that city, I studied a short time in Berlin and later in Freiburg, mainly chemistry and physics, where I took my degree in 1908 and received an honorary degree forty years later. The subject of my doctoral thesis was the interaction between metallic sodium and molten sodium hydroxide, an interaction responsible for a poor yield often obtained when producing sodium by electrolysis of molten sodium hydroxide.

Being interested in high-temperature chemistry, after obtaining my degree, I proceeded to Zurich to work under Richard Lorenz, the then most eminent representative of that branch of science. The Technical Highschool of Zurich was in those days, as it is today, a great place of learning and teaching. The Swiss chemical and pharmaceutical industry could not have reached that very high standard it represents today without the aid of a great number of able chemists, most of them trained at the Technical Highschool of Zurich. When I joined that institution, the permanent head of the chemistry department was Willstätter.

Einstein's First Lecture

Shortly after my arrival at Zurich, Einstein was appointed associate professor of theoretical physics in the university of that city. I was one of the audience of about twenty who attended his inaugural lecture on the determination of the ratio of charge and mass of the electron. (Einstein left after a few years for Prague and returned later to Zurich to fill the chair of theoretical physics in the Technical Highschool.) When Einstein visited our laboratory, I had the privilege to show him round. I remember vividly

When George von Hevesy, physicist, was the first to separate "isotopes," the word had not yet been coined. He is the father of the radioactive-tracer technique, now so widely used in medical practice and research. He resides in Stockholm, Sweden.

his astonishment upon being shown a hydrogen electrode. He thought such an electrode to be a fiction only.

Twenty-three years later, after terminating my Baker lectureship in the Cornell University at Ithaca, I met Einstein at Pasadena. I visited a barber shop whose owner, a son of the City of Constance, praised the beauties of life in California, mentioning that his only wish in life was to be permitted once to cut Einstein's hair. I told him that this wish would not be easy to fulfill as, according to rumors, it was Mrs. Einstein who performed this work. When I told Einstein about the barber's wish, he remarked: "Da er sich auf Ihrem Kopfe nicht austoben konnte, wollte er meinen Kopf haben" ("As he could not sufficiently exercise himself on your head [I had poor hair] he wants to have mine").

Einstein talked repeatedly to me on the problem of causality. He disagreed with Bohr's views on this topic. He asked me to take over a message to Bohr. He wished an explanation on a classical basis.

When Lorenz left Zurich for the University of Frankfurt (incidentally, I was asked after his death to fill his chair, which I could not accept), Willstätter called on me to make the short statement: "In Germany the assistant belongs to the professor, in Switzerland to the laboratory—you stay here." I did not, as I got much interested in the catalytic synthesis of ammonia by Haber, a discovery which at that date rightly impressed deeply all those interested in chemistry.

My monthly salary in Zurich of the equal of $36 was entirely adequate, as I was charged for a very nice room and two good meals $15 a month. When I was promoted to a "first assistant," I was told that my salary would be raised to $60 a month, the highest sum ever allotted an assistant.

When I was leaving the laboratory one evening together with Willstätter, he told me that he was moving to Berlin to take over one of the Kaiser Wilhelm Institutes. I asked him, much astonished, why he was leaving. He was the permanent chief of the chemistry faculty and had a very fine laboratory and postgraduate students from all over the world were anxious to work under his guidance. His answer was: "If the fatherland calls, my duty is to go." Thirty-two years later I was present at the meeting of the Danish Academy of Sciences when the president, S. P. L. Sörensen, death written on his face, read a letter from Willstätter requesting that the *Proceedings* of the Academy should no more be sent to him. He went on, saying: "I have no home any more. I have lost all my belongings, which I do not much mind. What chagrins me is that I lost my fatherland."

Haber wished me to work on another field than that of catalytic synthesis. I was to investigate whether or not oxidation of molten zinc is followed by emission of electrons. No one in Haber's institute had experience in the field of the conductivity of electricity in gases. I proposed therefore to Haber that I proceed to England to acquire some knowledge in this new field of physics and return later to his laboratory. Haber entirely shared my view, and I left in the first days of January, 1911, for Manchester to work under Rutherford.

Years with Rutherford

The physics laboratory of the University of Manchester was housed in a spacious building. The chief equipment of the institute was electroscopes built from cocoa boxes, sealing wax, sulphur rods, gold leaves, and reading microscopes. Once adjusted, the electroscopes were not permitted to be cleaned, and the smoky atmosphere of Manchester left its visible marks all over the laboratory. The years I had the privilege to spend in Rutherford's laboratory in Manchester, between 1911 and 1914, witnessed some of the greatest discoveries in the history of physics. I could follow from close quarters the discovery of the atomic nucleus and how Rutherford devised, carried out, and interpreted the results of experiments. All this was done with the greatest ease, without visible effort.

Niels Bohr came to Manchester in 1912. He remarked quite recently in an after-dinner speech that I was the first one he met when he entered Rutherford's institute. Rutherford—and not he alone—soon realized Bohr's genius. When I was enjoying Rutherford's hospitality one Sunday afternoon soon after the discovery of the atomic nucleus, I happened to ask him about the origin of β-rays. The α-rays clearly originated from the nucleus, but what about the origin of β-rays? Rutherford answered promptly, "Ask Bohr," and the answer was at once given by the latter, emphasizing the difference between nuclear and secondary β-particles. Bohr was not always easy to understand. When he briefly stated, "Argon is not the right argon," he made a statement that was at that date not easy to interpret. It was then, in 1912, already clear to him that it is not the mass number but the atomic number that is decisive for the place of an element in the periodic system. Soon after, this fact was decisively brought out by Moseley's work. I consider myself lucky to have had the opportunity to help Moseley set up the first X-ray spectrograph. We turned to the steward of the chemistry department, Mr. Edwards, who handed us a beautiful, very large potassium ferricyanide crystal which found application in Moseley's spectrograph. A magnetic device served to bring small metal disks covered with the element to be investigated into the electron beam, which had to excite the X-rays. Moseley's fundamental work brought out, among other things, that, while the atomic weight of argon is higher than that of potassium, its atomic number is not—that "argon is not the right argon," as stated by Bohr previously. Moseley has also shown that the anomaly of the positions of tellurium and iodine in the periodic system disappears if we consider the atomic number instead of the atomic weight.

When I arrived at Manchester, Rutherford wished me to study the solubility of actinium emanation in various liquids. It was not an easy task in view of the short life of that emanation, now called actinon, the half-life of which is 4 seconds only. It was, however, a very good school to learn to handle short-lived substances. I was then engaged with the study of the electrochemical properties of radioelements of unknown chemical character and the measurement of their valency from diffusion data.

The early origin of the famous Geiger counter goes back to those Manchester days as well. Rutherford and Geiger counted α-particles by making use of a galvanometer which registered the arrival of each α-particle. The ionization produced was magnified by using the principle of the production of ions by collision. The very much more difficult task of counting β-particles was solved later, after the first World War, by Geiger, then at Kiel.

When I was in Manchester, Rutherford was much interested to come into the possession of a strong radium D sample. Large amounts of radium D were stored in the laboratory, but imbedded in huge amounts of lead. The great German chemist Haber intended to pay Germany's war debts after the first World War by extracting gold from the ocean. First he undertook to check the correctness of the available gold analyses of sea water. He found the gold content of the ocean to be very much lower than previously found. He summarized the depressing results of his expedition by stating: "Dilution is the death of all value." Rutherford could have made the same remark when glancing at the hundreds of kilograms of lead chloride extracted from pitchblende and presented to him by the owner of the Joachimsthal mines, the Austrian government.

Radioactive Tracers

One day I met Rutherford in the basement of the laboratory where the lead chloride was stored. He addressed me by saying: "If you are worth your salt, you separate radium D from all that nuisance of lead." Being a young man, I was an optimist and felt sure that I should succeed in my task. Trying during a year all sorts of separation methods and making the greatest efforts, it looked sometimes as if I succeeded, but I soon found out that it was radium E, the disintegration product of radium D, a bismuth isotope, which I separated. The result of my efforts was entire failure. To make the best of this depressing situation, I thought to avail myself of the fact that radium D is inseparable from lead, and to label small amounts of lead by addition of radium D of known activity obtained from tubes in which radium emanation decayed. From such tubes pure radium D can be obtained.

It was the Vienna Institute for Radium Research which owned in those days by far the greatest amount of radium and, correspondingly, of radium emanation. This fact induced me to interrupt my stay in Manchester and to proceed to Vienna. In the Vienna institute there were very large amounts of lead chloride, obtained from pitchblende as well, and Paneth, assistant at the institute, not cognizant of my efforts at Manchester, made very extensive studies to achieve separation. His great efforts were as abortive as mine. We associated in the application of labeled lead. The first use of this method, early in 1913, was the determination of the solubility in water of sparingly soluble salts such as lead sulphide and lead chromate. We then proceeded to study the electrochemistry of bismuth and lead by making use of the method of radioactive indicators. We could show, among other things, that Nernst's law of the dependence of the electrode potential on the ionic concentration is valid even at exceedingly low concentrations. Paneth then directed his interest toward the interaction of the lead ions present in the surface layer of lead sulphate and the labeled lead ions of the surrounding solution. I studied the interaction of the lead atoms of a lead foil and also of lead peroxide with the lead ions of a solution, employing labeled lead foils and non-radioactive lead salt solution, or vice versa. In the last of the numerous joint investigations with Paneth, we succeeded in preparing visible amounts of radium D from radium emanation. By comparing the electrode potential of radium D peroxide and of lead peroxide, we were able to show that these cannot be distinguished.

During my stay in Vienna I undertook balloon ascents in the company of Hess and Paneth. On one of his trips Hess took an electrometer with him to follow the change in the ionization of the air with height. He assumed it to be due to terrestrial radiation and correspondingly expected it to decrease with height. The opposite, however, was found by him to be the case. This observation led to the discovery of cosmic radiation. With such simple means and without much effort this great discovery was made.

Madame Marie Curie

When passing through Paris on the way to Manchester, I never failed to call on Marie Curie. I was sure to find her amidst experimental work. She was usually surrounded by several girl assistants precipitating or crystallizing preparations. The only protection that she made use of were finger caps of rubber. When engaged with the concentration of actinium in rare-earth samples, she generously presented me with an actinium preparation. I consider this specimen one of my most precious belongings. As the years pass by, the bottle containing the radioactive sample is getting more and more colored, indicating the many years which have elapsed since I met that most remarkable personality and great pioneer.

At a later visit to the Institut de Radium, I met Joliot, who was then a young assistant engaged in the study of the electrochemistry of polonium, which many years earlier was in the center of interest of Paneth and myself. Also, Irène Curie worked in the laboratory of her mother. When I saw her in 1938, she mentioned that by neutron bombardment of thorium she had obtained a lanthanum-like radioactive body. I asked her if she was sure that this substance was not actinium. She answered that she was pretty sure she was dealing with an element much lighter than the member of the radioactive disintegration series.

A few months later Otto Hahn and Strassman made their fundamental discovery of nuclear fission. I first met Hahn in Vienna in 1913. Already at that date he had made such fundamental discoveries as that of radiothorium and mesothorium and of the separation of radioelements by making use of the recoil phenomenon. The years to come brought new discoveries of great importance, many of them in collaboration with Lise Meitner. When I asked Rutherford in 1912 whom of his students he considered to be the most merited one, he answered without hesitation "Otto Hahn."

On my way to Manchester I usually stopped in London. On such an occasion I had the opportunity of being present in the House of Commons at the introduction of the much discussed budget by Lloyd George, then Chancellor of the Exchequer, who characterized his introduction of heavy death duties and other taxes as "bringing rare and refreshing fruit"!

I was also present when J. J. Thomson in April, 1913, delivered his Bakerian Lecture in the Royal Society on the two neon parabolas obtained in his positive ray studies. He did not make any allusion to the analogy between the two neons and the isotopes in the field of radioactivity. This omission induced me to write to him drawing his attention to the analogy between the two kinds of neon, on one hand, and radium D and lead, on the other. He stated in his answer that he did not share my view. While not adopting the view that the heavier constituent of neon was a compound NeH_2, which could have given the observed atomic weight within the limits of experimental error, Thomson was not convinced that this explanation was absolutely excluded. As Lord Rayleigh remarks in *The Life of Sir J. J. Thomson*, he had always been haunted by this suspicion about hydrogen compounds and, for that reason, hesitated for a time to accept Aston's later results about isotopes of other elements. When we were on a ski trip in Finse in Norway, Aston related that when he first succeeded in getting two lines on a mass spectrum photograph— one indicating Cl^{35} the other Cl^{37}—Thomson refused to look at the photograph, which, Aston added, was the most beautiful one he ever obtained. Aston was an ingenious and most merited experimenter, who was the first one to prove the complexity of the common elements.

In 1914 Moseley moved to Oxford and, being much interested in roentgen spectroscopy, I intended to work with him. We wanted to study the roentgen spectrum of the elements 68 through 72. I was already in Holland en route to Oxford when the first World War broke out, soon followed by the tragic death of Moseley. While talking on a field telephone at Gallipoli, a bullet struck the head of that ingenious and most remarkable man. By a curious coincidence, eight years later I had to occupy myself very extensively with the roentgen spectrum of the element 72.

Measurement of Self-diffusion

During the first World War, being a Hungarian subject (I am now a Swedish subject), I did military service in the Austrian-Hungarian army. I spent much of that time as technical supervisor of electrolytic copper works. While located in Carpathian plants, I fitted up a laboratory on a very modest scale and studied the difference in the chemical behavior of the active deposit of thorium when present in ionic and colloidal state. For several months after the end of the war it was not possible to leave Hungary. During these months I started with my friend Groh to study self-diffusion in molten and in solid lead, using radium D as an indicator. We melted a radiolead rod on the top of an inactive lead rod, heated this solid system to 200°–300°, and determined the dislocation of the radium D atoms. From the extent of dislocation, the rate of self-diffusion of lead was calculated. This early, rough method was improved later during my stay in Copenhagen. Together with the Russian scientist Mrs. Obrutsheva, we condensed the lead isotope thorium B on top of a lead foil and counted the number of scintillations produced by the α-rays emitted by the disintegration products of thorium B. Upon heating of the sample, thorium B diffused into the lead foil, resulting in a reduction of the number of scintillations observed. From this reduction, the diffusion rate of lead in lead could be calculated. Heisenberg, then lecturer in Copenhagen, very kindly helped us with these calculations. Later on in Freiburg, Seith and I availed ourselves of the recoil phenomenon to measure self-diffusion in lead. This is an exceedingly sensitive method, which permitted measurement of diffusion rates as slow as 10^{-14} cm^2/day.

The Rockefeller Foundation started to support my investigations in 1930 and continued most generously to do so for the following twenty-five years.

Niels Bohr's Institute

In the first days of May, 1919, I left for Copenhagen to spend some time with Niels Bohr at the charming summer house in Tibirke. At that time his premises were at the Technological Institute of Copenhagen, from which he directed the construction of his new institute. When he had to decide on a name for the new institute, he hesitated between "Theoretical Physics" and "Atomic Physics." His choice fell on the first one; he felt that the latter might be too exacting and possibly too special as well. In front of the Technological Institute there is a statue of Oluf Römer, the first physicist to measure the velocity of light. I once pointed out when passing this monument that space is available for a future monument of Niels Bohr. My companion smiled at this remark. Today he would not smile any more.

It was settled with Bohr that I should be back in Copenhagen in spring, 1920, to start my activities at the new institute which was to be opened by that date. I spent the following six months with my friend Zechmeister in Budapest carrying out exchange studies by the application of radioactive indicators. When dissolving in water both 1 mol of labeled lead nitrate and 1 mol of non-radioactive lead chloride, or labeled lead chloride and non-radioactive lead nitrate, after separation of the two compounds we found the radioactivity equally distributed between $PbCl_2$ and $PbNO_3$. When dissolving non-radioactive tetraphenyl lead and radioactive lead nitrate, after separation all radioactivity was conserved in the nitrate sample, as the lead atoms of tetraphenyl lead are not exchangeable. When I met Svante Arrhenius in 1922 he told me about his interest in the above-mentioned work. The experiments with labeled lead chloride and non-labeled lead nitrate, or vice versa, are the most direct proof of the correctness of the theory of electrolytic dissociation.

After the war I was anxious to go to England as soon as possible. The atmosphere at that time, however, radically differed from the one that prevailed after the second World War. When in 1921 I wrote from Copenhagen to Rutherford, a very liberal man, that I wished to visit England, he answered that it was still too early for a former enemy to come to England. In 1923, when he was elected president of the British Association meeting which was to take place in Liverpool, he invited me to address that meeting on the discovery of hafnium. I recall a lunch party at Liverpool in which Lord and Lady Rutherford, Niels Bohr, Millikan, Aston, Coster, and myself took part. Lady Rutherford remarked that this party included four Nobel Laureates. Rutherford added, "And some embryos."

Rudolf Schoenheimer

During my stay in Liverpool I was told about the work of Blair-Bell who claimed a successful cancer therapy through administration of lead compounds. These results induced me, when at the University of Freiburg some time later, to study the distribution of labeled lead compounds between cancerous and normal tissue. A study of the distribution of labeled lead and bismuth in healthy rabbits was carried out earlier, in 1924, in Copenhagen. I approached the great pathologist Aschoff to delegate one of his collaborators to help us in our work. He first delegated the director of a hospital on the island of Formosa and later, to help him, his chief chemist, Rudolf Schoenheimer. This was Schoenheimer's first experience with tracer work, a field to which he later, jointly with his eminent colleague Rittenberg, made unsurpassed contributions. Schoenheimer was already at that date a very nervous man. He moved his limbs incessantly, smoked cigarettes, and consumed coffee on a much too liberal scale. When our collaboration terminated, he left Freiburg and I was not permitted to see that most merited man again.

Separation of Isotopes

When I went to Copenhagen in the spring of 1920, Bohr's institute was not yet ready. I associated with the eminent physicochemist Brønsted to investigate a problem of great interest to both of us, namely, the partial separation of isotopes on a preparative scale. We based our procedure on the more rapid rate of evaporation of the lighter isotope from a liquid. We distilled mercury in high vacuum at 40° and prevented the more rapidly evaporating lighter isotopes from being reflected back into the liquid mercury by freezing them on a glass surface cooled with liquid air. By repeating this process some hundred times, we obtained a light and a heavy mercury fraction. The results were controlled by both density measurements and atomic weight determinations, the latter being carried out by Hönigschmid in Munich.

When partially separating the isotopes of chlorine, we made use of the above-mentioned method again. We distilled very concentrated solutions of hydrochloric acid in water and obtained several liters of water containing hydrochloric acid with different isotopic chloride composition. I suggested to Brønsted that he have a look at the density of the water obtained. He objected to my suggestion, as shortly before two eminent German chemists, Vollmer and Stern, had searched without success for other isotopes of hydrogen and oxygen than H^1 and O^{16}. These workers carried out diffusion experiments through porous membranes. When I, after Urey's discovery of deuterium, reminded Brønsted of my suggestion, he answered: "A discovery like this should not be made fortuitously; it should be based on careful considerations like Urey's."

Bohr was highly interested in our separation experiments and keenly followed our progress. Bohr's greatness is due not only to his ingenuity but to the unique catholicity of his interests, his sagacity, and his immense conscientiousness. When as a young man he intended to publish his first "letter" to the editor of *Nature*, he wrote that note over and over again. Finally his brother, who later achieved the fame of a great mathematician, suggested he should now mail the "letter." Niels Bohr was shocked by this suggestion, since, he said, this was the first trial of the first concept of the "letter." In this spirit all his papers were written.

Most scientists write for their contemporaries. Niels Bohr wrote not only for these but for many generations to come. Every word written down by him was weighed and reweighed repeatedly. He delivered the Rutherford Memorial Lecture in 1958, but it took him three years to write it down in a final form. In this lecture he gives a full survey of the development of every aspect of the quantum theory. I had the unique privilege to observe from close quarters the immense work he put in this survey. He scrutinized every statement most carefully and by doing so created an unparalleled masterwork.

Simultaneously with the isotope separation studies, I carried out among other things some tracer work on the interchange between the atoms of lead compounds and lead, all in molten state.

In 1921 Bohr's institute was opened. Those working at the institute at its start were, beside its director, H. Kramers, H. M. Hansen, I. C. Jacobsen, James Franck, who was invited for a short visit, and myself. In my first study at the institute I measured the conductivity first of a single crystal of sodium nitrate and then after it was molten and resolidified into a polycrystalline mass. This crystalline conglomerate was found to have a specific conductivity fifty times higher than the single crystal. From this result it was concluded that deviations from the ideal crystalline state promote electrolytic conductivity. While increase of temperature produces a reversible loosening of the lattice, we are here faced with an "irreversible loosening" of the crystal structure. This was a most modest beginning in a field that later proved to be of great importance.

Hafnium

Bohr's first fundamental papers, published in 1913, in which the quantum theory of the atomic structure was introduced, dealt only with the structure of the atoms of hydrogen, helium, and lithium. In January, 1922, I learned during a walk together with him that he now had extended his theory to the entire periodic system, giving among other things an explanation of the appearance of the rare-earth elements in that system. Their number according to his theory was restricted to fourteen, from which it followed that the unknown element 72 cannot be a rare earth, it has to be a homologue of the titanium group.

In the summer of that year I became interested in geochemical problems. Returning to Denmark, I proposed to Coster, who previously had studied roentgen spectroscopy with Siegbahn in Lund, that he should teach me the roentgen spectroscopic technique and that we ought at the same time to have a look at zirconium minerals for the missing element 72. The first spectrum obtained by him demonstrated the presence of the element in zirconium minerals, and further studies revealed its presence in all commercial zirconium samples, which indicated a very close kinship between zirconium and the new element hafnium. By a very protracted fractional crystallization of ammonium zirconium hexafluorides, hafnium could be prepared in a pure state.

The discovery of hafnium was not accepted without opposition. Urbain, in Paris, a few years earlier crystallizing crude ytterbium salts, observed twenty-six optical spectral lines not shown by the initial sample. He ascribed these lines to the presence of the previously unknown element 72 in his sample. After the discovery of hafnium, it was, however, demonstrated that none of these lines is to be found in the spectrum of hafnium. In spite of this fact, Urbain upheld his claim to have discovered element 72. Rutherford took great interest in our work—all our extensive correspondence with *Nature* passed through his hands—and suggested that I should send a paper on the chemistry of hafnium to the editor of *Chemical News*. He remarked in his letter that the editors of this periodical were strongly pro-French and I should not mind if they refused to publish my paper. In Sheffield, my friend the physicist Lawson ("interned" as a prisoner of war in the Institute of Radium Research of Vienna) handed my contribution over to the editor of *Chemical News*, Professor Wynne. He remarked that he was pleased with the paper but they might have something to say about the word "hafnium," adding: "We adhere to the original word Celtium given to it by Urbain as a representative of the great French nation which was loyal to us throughout the war. We do not accept the name which was given it by the Danes who only pocketed the spoil after the war." The paper was, however, published by *Chemical News* without remark.

Another opposition to the discovery of hafnium came from London. Alexander Scott, the chief chemist of the British Museum, could not identify a fraction of a sample of an Australian titaniferous sand. After our discovery was announced, he thought this fraction to be hafnium. Scott's paper induced the *Times* to publish in its February 2, 1923, issue an editorial under the title "Hafnium," stating: "Science is, and doubtless should be, international, but it is gratifying that this chemical achievement, the most important since the late Sir William Ramsay isolated helium in 1895, should have been the work of a British chemist in a London laboratory." Scott's sample, sent us for investigation, did not contain a trace of hafnium or zirconium.

The determination of the hafnium content of a great number of zirconium minerals and historical zirconium samples was a fascinating task. Berzelius determined the atomic weight of zirconium by analyzing its sulphate. This method supplies too low values for the atomic weight. This error was, however, compensated by the presence of hafnium, almost twice as heavy as zirconium, in his sample. Venable in South Carolina, who spent many years with the determination of the atomic weight of zirconium, applied a modern method devised by Richards at Harvard. He could not find the reason why his determination led to a clearly too high value. After the discovery of hafnium, he sent us a sample of his zirconium, and, after taking into account its quite appreciable hafnium content—which we determined—he could correct for the presence of hafnium in his sample and arrive at a correct value for the atomic weight of zirconium.

Through my work with hafnium I came into contact with the great Austrian chemist Auer von Welsbach. He invested a part of his very substantial royalties obtained for his patent of cerium-iron alloys (applied in cigar-lighters among other things) in a beautiful estate in Carinthia on which he built a castle. The rough crystallization of rare earth was carried out in one of his nearby situated works, and the final crystallization was done by himself in his castle. He was at that date and for many years to come the only man who possessed highly purified samples of all elements of the rare-earth group. When staying with him, he expressed his astonishment that when separating hafnium from zirconium I had chosen to handle large amounts of fluorides, which are highly unpleasant compounds to work with. He achieved all his great success in the field of rare-earth chemistry by crystallizing double sulfates. We found out later that there is no significant difference between the solubility of zirconium and hafnium double sulfates, and if we had chosen to crystallize these compounds, we would not have been able to separate hafnium from zirconium. All hafnium commercially available for the next twenty-five years was prepared by crystallizing the double fluorides.

V. M. Goldschmidt

Auer von Welsbach presented me with small samples of octohydrosulphates of all elements of the rare-earth group. This gift enabled me to measure the density of these compounds and to observe a systematic decrease of the size of the ions of rare-earth elements when proceeding from cerium to lutetium, a contraction which explained the extreme kinship of zirconium and hafnium, which are more closely related chemically than any other elements of the periodic system. (When testing the rare earth for radioactivity, making use of Auer von Welsbach's samples, we discovered that samarium emitted α-rays.) In Oslo, V. M. Goldschmidt simultaneously observed the contraction of ionic size proceeding from one rare earth to the next one and denoted this rare-earth contraction as the "lanthanide contraction." Goldschmidt described his and my work in his posthumously published book *Geochemistry*, a most fascinating reading, like everything that he wrote. V. M. Goldschmidt was one of the most able men I ever met. Endowed with an immense knowledge and a fabulous memory, he was full of fertile ideas.

A few weeks prior to the occupation of Norway, I spent a few days with him at his home on Holmenkollen near Oslo. He predicted the tragic happenings of the coming years, which very few foresaw. He mentioned that his pupil and former assistant Lunde soon would become a "Gauleiter" of Norway. Lunde was later the minister of propaganda in the Quisling government. Goldschmidt predicted that the Norwegian coast batteries would fail to fire at the invading enemy, which they in fact did with very few exceptions. He was also endowed with much humor. When Quisling came into power, Goldschmidt was imprisoned and all his property seized. Being short of phosphorus fertilizers, the government released him and instructed him to prepare phosphorus from Norwegian minerals. All his property, however, remained confiscated. When German colleagues passed en route to Rjukan, where they had to inspect the heavy-water works, they called on Goldschmidt. He invited them for dinner, encouraging them to eat with the remark: "Please go on eating, gentlemen, all you consume is state property."

Tracers in Biology

During the work with hafnium, I continued the tracer work and in 1923 applied radium D and thorium B as tracers in the study of the uptake of lead by bean seedlings and also in the removal of labeled lead by non-labeled lead from such seedlings. This was the first application of radioactive tracers in biological studies. The following year we extended these studies to the distribution of lead and bismuth in the animal organism.

Potassium is one of the few radioactive elements found in nature outside the members of the disintegration series. We were interested to find out which of the potassium isotopes is radioactive. For this purpose we carried out a partial separation of the potassium isotopes, applying the same method used when separating the isotopes of mercury. A few kilograms of metallic potassium were distilled and a heavy and a light potassium fraction obtained. From the difference in the activity of these samples and the difference in their atomic weight, the mass number of the active isotope could be calculated. Among other instruments that were used to measure the activities of our samples was the first counter built by Geiger in his institute at Kiel. The atomic weight of our sample was determined by Hönigschmid in Munich. From these data it was concluded that the mass number of radioactive potassium is 41. The first one to draw my attention to the fact that this result was probably wrong was Baxter, when I visited him at Harvard. He had found that, in contrast to all other atomic weight figures determined by Hönigschmid, that of potassium was wrong. Baxter proposed to determine the atomic weight of our potassium samples. From his results it followed that the mass number of radioactive potassium is 40. The two greatest authorities in the field of atomic weight determination thus arrived at different results as to the atomic weight of our potassium samples. To reach a decision, we extracted the small calcium content of an old potassium-rich mica. If K^{41} were the active isotope, then the calcium isolated should contain Ca^{41}. Aston could not, however, find any Ca^{41} in our sample. Thus K^{41} does not disintegrate and is not radioactive. Baxter was right. A few years later Fermi and collaborators observed the production of an artificial potassium isotope when bombarding potassium with neutrons. We obtained Fermi's product by bombarding scandium and also calcium with neutrons. As scandium has only one stable isotope, we could conclude from our investigations that Fermi's radiopotassium has the mass number of 42.

Activation Analysis

Auer von Welsbach was very cautious in giving away his very valuable rare-earth samples, but one day when I was staying with him he was in a generous mood and told me to choose one of his samples, of which he said he was willing to give me a larger amount. I chose dysprosium without having any special reason to do so. Ten years later, after the discovery of artificial radioactivity, we exposed Auer's dysprosium to slow neutrons and succeeded in producing an exceedingly strongly active radiodysprosium. No element is known that can be activated more intensively than dysprosium and europium. Exposure of Auer's europium to a neutron beam also led to the formation of a very strongly active radioeuropium, while no active gadolinium could be prepared by using radium-beryllium as the source of neutrons. At that time my friend Professor Rolla, of the University of Florence, who prepared a few kilograms of gadolinium oxide, sent me samples of this material which he wished us to analyze for europium by roentgen spectroscopy. We had earlier analyzed several of his samples making use of the quantitative method, applying secondary X-rays, which was worked out in the Freiburg laboratory. Having no access to a roentgen spectroscope in Copenhagen at that time, we tried together with Miss Hilde Levi to analyze the samples by exposing them to a flux of slow neutrons. All the samples contained some europium. By preparing standards containing a known amount of pure gadolinium and pure europium, we could arrive at quantitative figures for the europium content of Rolla's samples. This was the start of activation analysis, which has since become an important tool in analytical chemistry. It was possible by this method to determine, for example, the minute amounts of sodium and potassium in a nerve fiber.

Deuterium as a Tracer

Urey's epochal discovery of deuterium took place while I worked in Freiburg. Most kindly he promptly supplied us with some liters of water containing 0.6 per cent of deuterium oxide. This low heavy-water concentration sufficed to study the interchange of the water molecules of the goldfish and the surrounding water and also to determine the water content of the human body, making use of the principle of isotope dilution already introduced a few years earlier (1931) when we determined the lead content of rocks. The mean lifetime of the water molecules in the human body was determined as well. When I returned to Copenhagen in the fall of 1934, August Krogh called on me immediately upon my arrival. He wished to apply labeled water in his permeability studies.

I initially intended, upon returned to Copenhagen, to do work with deuterium on similar lines as later published by Schoenheimer and Rittenberg. The possibility of obtaining artificial radioactive isotopes, however, induced me to abandon this plan and to concentrate on the application of radiophosphorus in biological studies.

Radioactive Phosphorus

As a neutron source we had only radon-beryllium, later radium-beryllium mixtures, at our disposal. When Niels Bohr celebrated his fiftieth birthday, his friends presented him with 600 milligrams of radium, which he most kindly put at our disposal. With such modest neutron sources, the only tracer of an element of physiological importance which could be produced having sufficient activity was radiophosphorus. We irradiated 10 liters of carbon disulphide from which carrier-free P^{32} could be easily separated. All our preparations, however, had an activity below 1 μC. The first problem attacked was whether the mineral constituents of the skeleton are renewed or not during life. Labeled phosphate was administered to rats, and the specific activity of their plasma inorganic phosphorus and skeleton apatite phosphorus compared. The comparison indicated a 30 per cent renewal in the course of the first 24 hours. The amount of phosphate involved in this process exceeded twenty times the phosphorus content of the blood (including that of the red corpuscles). Thus a large part of the phosphorus present in the soft tissues must have been released and applied in the replacement of skeleton phosphorus. This result demonstrated the dynamicity of phosphorus metabolism. These conclusions were published about the same time, in 1935, that the first paper by Schoenheimer and Rittenberg appeared in which they demonstrated the dynamic nature of fat depots. It was followed by a great number of other most illuminating papers in which deuterium, and later heavy nitrogen, was applied as a tracer. Since P^{32} has a half-life of fourteen days only, happenings through life cannot be followed using this tracer. However, applying C^{45}, we succeeded a few years ago in showing that only one-third of the calcium atoms of the skeleton of the mouse are replaced during life.

The above-mentioned first application of an artificial radioactive isotope as a tracer was followed by our investigation of whether and to what extent the phosphatide molecules of the brain are renewed. These investigations were extended to other organs and to the formation of labeled phosphatides in the chick embryo following the injection of P^{32} into the fertilized egg. We transfused in vivo labeled plasma of a rabbit to a sister rabbit and followed the rate of disappearance of the labeled phosphatide molecules from the circulation of the second rabbit and their accumulation in various organs. The next step was the study of the rate of renewal of the ATP, creatine, and similar molecules, partly in collaboration with Professor Parnas in Lwow, Poland. With Armstrong and also with Krogh and Holst, we studied P^{32} incorporation in dentine and enamel. In one of the early applications (1937), the penetration of P^{32} into yeast cells was traced and shown to be an almost one-way process. This investigation was made possible by co-operation with Linderström-Lang and Olsen at the Carlsberg Laboratory. The first investigations of the uptake of P^{32} by plants (1936–37) was also carried out in co-operation with them.

In 1940 Professor Hastings, who had formerly visited Copenhagen, invited me to deliver the Dunham Lecture at Harvard University. Denmark was occupied, and messages to the United States could be sent only by the United States Legation in Copenhagen. When I called on the minister asking him to forward a cable to Professor Hastings stating, "I shall be in New York the 21st of June," the minister remarked, "You better write 'I intend to.' " It was a wise remark, as I did not succeed in getting to the United States and the Dunham Lecture was ultimately delivered by Schoenheimer.

We observed, with Aten, that while phosphate penetrates comparatively slowly into erythrocytes, it is incorporated very rapidly into labile organic acid-soluble molecules. Thus the red corpuscles are a kind of trap, though imperfect, for P^{32}, a fact which makes it possible to tag red corpuscles with P^{32} in vitro, reinject these into the circulation, and from the dilution figure calculate the red corpuscle volume of the subject in the course of a day. This method of red corpuscle volume determination found an extended application. The first clinical determinations could be carried out with the minute P^{32} activities prepared by us by irradiation of carbon disulfide with neutrons emitted by a radium-beryllium source. To investigate the formation of phosphatide or of casein in the milk of the goat, which was the subject of the dissertation of A. H. W. Aten, larger activities were needed. These were put at our disposal by the extremely great kindness of Ernest Lawrence. He supplied us later also with Na^{24} and K^{42}. We used these isotopes, among other purposes, to study the rate of interchange of vascular with extravascular ions. We were much impressed by the observation that within the first minute a very large fraction of the sodium ions of the circulation, for example, was replaced by extravascular sodium. Today we know that the exchange rate values obtained by the tracer method supply minimum figures only.

Max von Laue's and James Franck's Nobel Medals

My work was interrupted for only one day during the enemy occupation of Denmark. When, on the morning of Denmark's occupation, I arrived in the laboratory, I found Bohr worrying about Max von Laue's Nobel medal, which Laue had sent to Copenhagen for safekeeping. In Hitler's empire it was almost a capital offense to send gold out of the country, and, Laue's name being engraved into the medal, the discovery of this by the invading forces would have had very serious consequences for him. (Three years later the invading army occupied Bohr's institute.) I suggested we should bury the medal, but Bohr did not like this idea as the medal might be unearthed. I decided to dissolve it. While the invading forces marched in the streets of Copenhagen, I was busy dissolving Laue's and also James Franck's medals. After the war, the gold was recovered and the Nobel Foundation generously presented Laue and Franck with new Nobel medals.

The Nobel Prize

In December, 1935, on their journey home from Stockholm, where they were presented by King Gustaf V with the Nobel prize, for their fundamental discovery of artificial radioactivity, Frédéric Joliot-Curie and his wife stayed for a while in Copenhagen. It was then that Joliot mentioned that he, his wife, and the third French Nobel laureate, Jean Perrin, proposed me for the Nobel prize. During the war Niels Bohr with his extreme kindness remarked to one of his friends that one of the numerous disturbances created by the war was that I could not receive the Nobel prize. The shocking refusal of the acceptance of the prize by Domagk, Butenandt, and Kuhn at the order of their ruler made the Swedish Academy of Sciences reluctant to distribute further prizes during the war. In 1944 the Academy decided, however, to allot me the prize for 1943. With the war going on, no festivities were held, and the prize, contrary to the usual custom, was handed over to me in a meeting of the Academy of Sciences by the president.

Radioactive Tracers in Radiobiology

In 1940 we got interested, with L. v. Hahn, in the formation rate of desoxyribonucleic acid, DNA. While the incorporation of P^{32}, for example, into adenosinetriphosphate of the growing liver indicates mainly renewal of these molecules and not an additional formation, the incorporation into desoxyribonucleic acid indicates the latter to a very large extent.

By investigation of the effect of ionizing radiation on the incorporation of P^{32} into DNA, it should thus be possible to find out if irradiation blocks DNA formation. Together with Professor Hans von Euler, we studied in Stockholm the incorporation of P^{32} into the DNA of the Jensen sarcoma of rats and found in each of the investigated 100 rats exposed to roentgen rays a marked depression of P^{32} incorporation, and thus a marked depression in the rate of formation of DNA. Similar results were obtained when investigating P^{32} incorporation into the DNA in the various organs of growing rats. Indirect radiation effects were observed by us as well. These were among the first applications of radioactive tracers in radiobiological studies. Our joint investigations, among others, were extended to the determination of the number of fertilizing asp pollen, the atoms of which can be located in a seed. The incorporation of P^{32} into DNA of the nucleated erythrocytes of the hen was found, in collaboration with Ottesen about the same time, to be quantitatively conserved during the lifetime of the erythrocytes, which enabled us to measure the life-cycle of the red corpuscles of the hen.

Prior to and during the war I saw a lot of Professor Krogh, famous physiologist and a man of great kindness, to whom I was much indebted. While staying in Stockholm, he wrote down a detailed program of further permeability studies in which radioactive tracers would have to be applied. It is much to be deplored that he could not witness the great further success of his eminent pupil Ussing in this field.

Radioactive Carbon

My chief activities since 1943 have been in Stockholm and, for some years after the war, in Copenhagen too. During the last years I have been attending solely to my laboratory in Stockholm. I extended the radiation studies to the measurement of C^{14} incorporation into DNA in the organs of growing mice, which was found to be depressed in contrast to incorporation into proteins. My colleague Forssberg and I studied the effect of irradiation on bicarbonate, glucose, and fatty acid metabolism and other problems, applying C^{14} as a tracer. These studies, among others, led to the discovery of a fatty acid fraction of the liver having a very rapid turnover rate. For the last years we have been interested in physiological and clinical problems of iron metabolism.

In 1953 I had the privilege to deliver the Aschoff Memorial Lecture, which is given each year in the University of Freiburg to commemorate the great pathologist. Aschoff was not only one of the great pathologists of this century but a man of great wisdom and vision. The British pathologist Robert Muir wrote in his obituary note on Aschoff, published during the war, "I think one may say that in the period since Virchow's time, he has been the outstanding figure." He showed some interest in our early work with lead and was quite enthusiastic about the determination of the volume of the body water by applying heavy water as an indicator, which was the first clinical application of isotopic tracers. In my Aschoff Lecture I mentioned that our investigations had led us to the conclusion, not unanimously accepted by the audience, that the formation of hemoglobin is not radiosensitive, that so long as erythropoetic cells with an incomplete hemoglobin content are present in the bone marrow, even if the organism is exposed to roentgen radiation, additional hemoglobin is laid down in these cells. Since then this conclusion has been fully corroborated by work carried out in our laboratory, and especially by the beautiful work carried out in Oxford by Lajtha and his associates.

When we started with Paneth in the first days of 1913 to apply radium D as a tracer of lead, the word "isotope" was not yet coined. Groups of radioactive substances such as mesothorium and radium, or ionium and thorium, were denoted by Soddy as "chemically inseparable elements." Much has happened since those days!

LEO LOEB, M.D.

Some Personal and Professional History and Philosophy

Personal and Professional History

I was born on September 21, 1869, in Mayen, a town in Germany situated near the place where the River Mosel enters the Rhine in a hilly, volcanic region. During World War II a great part of this town was destroyed by bombs. Here I lived the first six years of my life. My mother, who was a delicate, sensitive woman, with a fine singing voice, died when she was thirty-two or thirty-three years of age and I was three. My father died at the age of forty-nine from tuberculosis, in the Italian Riviera, where he had gone with the hope of regaining his health. I was, thus, at the age of six without parents. At the end of this period I myself had what appeared to be an attack of tuberculosis that caused swelling of lymph glands and an affection of the skin. I was considered a delicate child; however, in the course of time I recovered from this attack.

My only brother, Jacques, ten and a half years older than I, then took me to the home of my maternal grandfather, who lived in Trier, a city situated on the Mosel, possessing interesting ruins of Roman buildings. We went by train, by way of Cologne, and I still remember this journey. At the home of my grandfather there lived also an uncle and an aunt, a younger sister of my mother. While I was in Trier, I went to the gymnasium, and I learned to swim in the Mosel River.

When I reached the age of ten, I left Trier and went to Berlin to live in

Young Dr. Loeb was the first official physician for Philosophy Professor John Dewey's new experimental primary and secondary school connected with the University of Chicago. The full significance of some of his basic discoveries about the individuality of tissues and the relationship of sex hormones to cancer did not become apparent until late in his life. Dr. Loeb died December 28, 1959, Professor Emeritus of Pathology, Washington University School of Medicine, St. Louis, Missouri.

the family of my uncle Harry Breslau and his wife, who was another sister of my mother. My uncle was a professor of medieval German history at the University of Berlin. He and my aunt had two young children. The older one was Ernst, who later became a professor of zoölogy at the University of Frankfurt and subsequently at the University of Cologne. When the Nazis began to dominate Germany, he and his family moved to Brazil, where he became professor of zoölogy at the University of São Paulo. Helene, the younger child of my uncle, who was very young when I was with the family, later married Albert Schweitzer and worked with him in his hospital at Lambaréné in French Africa.

In Berlin I went to the Askanische Gymnasium, where my brother had studied previously. During my stay in Berlin I suffered from hypertrophic adenoids, and a prominent ear and throat specialist, who had taken a leading part in the development of the operation for this condition, removed these glands. I still remember the occasion. He applied neither general nor local anesthesia in this operation but merely scraped the roof of my pharynx a number of times with a sharp spoon. The operation was, in a certain sense, a successful one so far as its objective was concerned, but subsequently I suffered for several years from severe headaches. This operation had still another effect which I had not expected. I had been an average student in school, but from then on, I became one of the best students in the class.

While I was in Berlin, my health gradually deteriorated, and after I had been there for about six months, it was thought advisable for me to interrupt my school work and attend to my physical needs. I was then taken to Wiesbaden, a health resort in western Germany, where I lived an outdoor life and did not study. After about six months, I went to Dürkheim, a town in the Palatinate, also a health resort. Dürkheim is situated in hilly, wooded country and is surrounded by vineyards. Here I stayed for several years and studied in the school which corresponded to the gymnasium. A great part of my time was devoted to daily walks in the woods and on the hills and to playing with other boys. After several years, when I had finished school in Dürkheim, I moved to the university town of Heidelberg, situated along the river Neckar and, likewise, surrounded by wooded, hilly country. I enrolled in the gymnasium and did good work in my classes. I walked in the woods and rowed on the Neckar River. During the last few years of my stay in Heidelberg, I lived with the family of Professor Hilgard, a teacher in the gymnasium, who later became director of the gymnasium in Bruchsal. After his death, I corresponded with Mrs. Hilgard for many years and kept in touch with her as long as she lived. A branch of the family Hilgard emigrated to the United States, where they assumed the name of Villard, and one of the Villards became very prominent as a builder of transcontinental railroads. During the years when I was at the gymnasium, I usually spent the long summer vacations with my brother Jacques in various towns situated on the coast of Belgium and Holland, but we also visited such resorts as Berchtesgaden and Reichenhall, at the border between Austria and Bavaria. Subsequently, I also went in the summertime to Switzerland, where I did some glacier climbing. While I was still in Heidelberg, I took lessons in horseback riding from a former German cavalry officer, and for many years I continued to ride, even after my arrival in St. Louis. Thus I continually kept in mind my physical requirements, in order to improve my bodily strength.

I shall now interrupt this narrative for a brief discussion of the German gymnasium as it was when I attended school. The gymnasium consisted of nine grades, each requiring one year of attendance, to complete the course. A boy would start at the gymnasium usually at the age of about nine and at the age of eighteen should have completed the course. The last year was spent in the Oberprima and the year preceding it in the Unterprima. The curriculum gave a prominent place to the study of Latin, which extended over nine years. Ancient Greek was studied during the last six years. The work in both these languages was very intensive and very thorough so far as grammar and syntax were concerned. There was also provision for the study of French and German, but the study of the English language was left to the choice of the individual student. In these languages also, emphasis was laid on grammar and syntax. While in Latin and Greek and also in French and German we read the work of authors prominent in their time, it was mainly the linguistic problems which were considered. Physics and mathematics and, secondarily perhaps, some biology were taught. But these subjects received only minor attention. This emphasis on formal linguistic study with neglect of literary aspects and the relegation of physics and biology to subordinate positions I found not satisfactory; therefore, when I was promoted to the highest class, the Oberprima, I decided to leave the gymnasium and to continue, if possible, my work at the University of Heidelberg, in order to take up studies of my own choice. It was possible for me, at the end of one year, to take a state examination which entitled me to become a regular student at the university. I passed this examination successfully in the year 1888 or 1889, so far as I can remember. Then I left Heidelberg to continue my studies at the universities of Berlin, Freiburg, and Basel. In each of these universities I stayed only one semester, in accordance with the custom of not confining one's studies to a single school but of studying at various universities in order to be able to work under prominent men. In Freiburg, Professor Weismann lectured on the factors determining the evolution of animal life, and in Basel, Professor Bunge, a well-known biochemist, and Professor Miescher, a physiologist, were members of the faculty. Professor Bunge was also a leader in the movement to abolish the use of alcoholic drinks.

During this early period of my university life, I felt very keenly the dominance of a pronounced and exclusive nationalism and militarism in Germany—a spirit which had been much strengthened as a result of the Franco-Prussian War in 1870; a spirit which was incompatible with the devotion to the ideals of liberalism and of universal brotherhood which had been so pronounced in some former times, for instance, in 1848, in Germany. I did not approve the prevailing nationalism and decided to leave Germany and continue my studies in the University of Zürich. Here, from 1890 to 1892, I took the fundamental scientific courses which constituted the first part of the study of medicine. There lived in Zürich then a number of well-known German poets and writers representative of European liberalism whom I often met—Henkell, Wedekind, Mackay, and others. I was also on friendly terms with Hinrichsen, who later became director of state institutions for the treatment of mental diseases, and with Tomarkin, who subsequently had a position in the Department of Bacteriology in the University of Bern. On various occasions I visited the family of Professor Gaule, who was a former assistant of the well-known physiologist Ludwig in the University of Leipzig. Professor Gaule had married an American, a Miss Leonard, a graduate of an American women's college. Her sister, Anne, a graduate of Smith College, lived in the Gaule family and studied modern languages and literature at the University of Zürich and subsequently at the University of Berlin. During this period Anne met my brother, and they were married in 1890 in Easthampton, Massachusetts, where her parents lived. After the wedding I met them in Le Havre when they were en route to Zürich.

Having passed the first part of my state examination, I decided to begin my clinical studies at the University of Edinburgh for one year, and then I continued my clinical studies at the medical school of the London Hospital, where I obtained my first practical experience in clinical medicine when I visited the homes of outpatients in Whitechapel on the east side of London. I also went occasionally to other medical schools in London, and thus I had the opportunity to hear well-known lecturers. My experiences in these two medical schools were very interesting, but in 1895 I returned to Zürich to complete my medical studies. In the following two years, from 1895 to 1897, I finished the various clinical branches. At the end of this period I passed the Swiss state examination in medicine and thus obtained the right to practice medicine in that country. This took place in Bern, the seat of the federal government. The right to practice was separate from the degree of M.D., which required the completion of a medical thesis.

For this purpose I undertook experimental investigations in the pathological institute of Professor Hugo Ribbert in the University of Zürich. I carried out transplantations of white skin of the guinea pig into defects in black skin of the same animal and of black pigmented skin into defects in white skin. The results were interesting. They showed that in transplanting pigmented skin into defects in white skin, the chromatophores of the pigmented skin invaded the neighboring white skin, but possibly also the ordinary pigmented epithelial cells took part in this movement. These movements continued for a certain length of time. The completion of these investigations required about a year, and at the end of this time, in 1897, I received the M.D. degree.

I have already mentioned that my brother first went to Zürich after his return from the United States following his marriage to Anne Leonard. He then spent some time with his wife in Naples in the Marine Zoölogical Station, continuing his research on problems of the general physiology of invertebrates. When he later accepted a position first at Bryn Mawr College and soon afterward in the Department of Physiology at the newly founded University of Chicago, I made my first visit to the United States to see them again. This was in the summer of 1892, when they had a cottage at Woods Hole, Massachusetts. In 1894 I visited them again at Woods Hole, and again returned to Europe to complete my studies. In 1897 I left for the United States for good and settled in Chicago, where at this time my brother was professor of physiology at the University of Chicago. In this city I lived for about five years, from 1897 to 1902, at first preparing myself for the practice of medicine. I then passed the state examination of Illinois, which gave me the right to practice in that state as well as in certain others. My office was near the University of Chicago, and some of the teachers at the university were my patients. One day Professor John Dewey, who taught philosophy at the university, came to see me and asked me to be the physician of his experimental school connected with the university. I accepted this invitation and at the same time taught in the Department of Pathology of the medical school which later became the Medical School of the University of Illinois. However, my experimental research continued, and for this purpose I rented a room behind a drugstore to keep my animals. After about ten months of practice of medicine, I gave it up and devoted my entire time to research. Many years later, when I was giving a lecture at the University of Chicago, the druggist from whom I had rented the room was in the audience. He came to greet me and said he had in the meantime studied medicine and had become a specialist. I was glad to meet him again on this occasion.

I was carrying out experiments concerning the process of wound healing in the skin of the guinea pig and was especially interested in the mode of ingrowth of the regenerating epithelium into the blood clot covering the wound. I observed that the strands of epidermal cells could separate from one another and penetrate independently of other strands into the clots and again could separate into new strands. These observations suggested to me that it might be possible to cultivate epithelium and also other tissues in clots in test tubes, separated from the organs and organisms in which they had originated. I continued these experiments for a considerable time, first in Chicago and then in the Department of Pathology in the Johns Hopkins School of Medicine, where I spent several months.

Johns Hopkins was at that time the leading medical school in this country. Here were Osler, Thayer, and Barker in internal medicine, Halstead in surgery, Welch and Flexner in pathology, Mall and Ross Harrison in anatomy. It was very interesting for me to meet all these men. As to my experiments in tissue culture, I felt certain that this research would succeed. As to the actual ingrowth of epithelium into blood clots, this should depend, among other factors, on the degree of density of the clots. The presence of erythrocytes would presumably render the texture of the clots more dense and, therefore, more resistant to the ingrowth of the epithelial cells. However, it seemed probable that tissue transferred to test tubes under otherwise adequate conditions might at least partly survive, even if no visible ingrowth into the clot took place.

Subsequently, during summers spent at the Marine Biological Laboratory in Woods Hole, I studied the movements and migration of amoebocytes, especially of *Limulus*, but also of other organisms, and I compared these reactions with those observed in the epidermal cells of mammals.

I returned from Johns Hopkins to Chicago, where, in association with other experiments on normal tissues, I undertook transplantations of a sarcoma of the thyroid gland of a rat. This sarcoma had developed spontaneously in a rat, and all these transplantations led to the conclusion, among other findings, that not only cancer cells and embryonal cells but also normal adult tissue cells may be potentially immortal.

In 1902 I received an offer from Professor Adami, who taught pathology at McGill University, of a research fellowship in his department. This offer I accepted, and I stayed a year in Montreal. I continued my research mainly on comparative transplantations of tissues and tumors. The spirit in the laboratory was friendly, but it was difficult for me to stand the cold winters in Montreal, and in 1903 I therefore accepted an offer of Professor Allen J. Smith of a position in the Department of Pathology of the University of Pennsylvania. From 1904 to 1910 I was assistant professor of experimental pathology in the department and continued my work on the transplantation of tissues. These experiments concerned mainly the relationship between the genetic constitution of host and transplant and the effect of their relationship on the fate of the transplants, especially on the duration of their life. I also studied the mode of defense of the host against the graft. The defense was associated largely with the activity of the lymphocytes of the host.

I also carried out a series of comparative studies on the coagulation of the blood in invertebrates in association with investigations on amoebocytes to which I have already referred. These experiments on invertebrate blood were performed in the Marine Biological Laboratory in Woods Hole. In this connection, I also studied coagulation of vertebrate blood. This research showed that specific adaptations exist between the genetic constitution of tissue coagulins and the type of blood, the clotting of which these coagulins induced. These studies on the coagulation of blood were extended to an investigation of thrombosis, with particular regard to the effect of inhibiting substances such as those present in *Anchylostoma*. The latter experiments were made in co-operation with Professor Allen J. Smith.

Dr. Weir Mitchell, a well-known neurologist and neurophysiologist connected with the University of Pennsylvania who was especially interested in the research of *Heloderma*, suggested further investigations in this field. We undertook such a study in co-operation with other investigators. The results of these experiments were published as a separate volume by the Carnegie Institution of Washington in 1913, I believe after the death of Dr. Weir Mitchell.

I also studied the production of deciduomata in the uterus of the rabbit, guinea pig, and some other vertebrates. We established that these transitory tumors were due mainly to two factors: first, a sensitization of the uterine mucosa by the hormone of the corpus luteum, followed, secondarily, by the application of mechanical stimuli such as wounding of the uterine mucosa or introduction of a foreign body into the lumen of the uterus. The work on the formation of deciduomata and placentomata was a phase in a wider investigation of problems concerning the sexual cycle which I undertook at that time. In this connection I studied, for example, the significance of the corpus luteum for the duration of the sexual cycle and also analyzed otherwise the effects which the corpus luteum exerts on the sexual cycle. At the same time I experimented on the effect of various environmental factors, including heat and chemical solutions, on the growth and on the immune reactions of tumors. During this period of my connection with the University of Pennsylvania, also initiated in our laboratory were studies on the genetic-hereditary factors determining the development of mammary gland carcinoma in various strains of mice. These investigations were undertaken in co-operation with Miss A. C. E.

Lathrop, who owned and managed a farm in Granby, Massachusetts, where she could inbreed various strains of mice by crossing near relatives. These studies were taken up on a larger scale subsequently and were continued until the death of Miss Lathrop in 1920. They were then extended for a certain length of time with the aid of her successor. Miss Lathrop was a good helpmate in this work, and I hold her memory in high esteem.

In 1910 I left the University of Pennsylvania to accept the invitation from the Barnard Skin and Cancer Hospital in St. Louis, which was especially devoted to the care of cancer patients. A laboratory in association with the hospital for experiments and other research in cancer was planned, and I was asked to direct this research. In accepting the position I made it clear that I planned to devote my investigations mainly to fundamental problems of cancer. I have lived in St. Louis continuously ever since—for forty-eight years now.

During this period at the Barnard Hospital, from 1910 to 1915, I was concerned mainly with three sets of problems: first, heredity and genetic factors in general with respect to various aspects of tumor growth; second, the effect of factors such as colloidal copper and hirudin and some other substances on growth-inhibition of transplanted mammary tumors in mice and primary tumors in the human species and, as well, the resistance which developed in tumors of animals against these growth-inhibiting agents; third, the influence of hormones, especially ovarian hormones on the development of tumors, particularly of the mammary gland in mice. These last studies were an extension of some of our earlier investigations on the sexual cycle and on growth processes and tumor development in the sex organs especially of mice and rats. We recognized at that time the interaction of hormones and genetic factors in these processes.

In 1915 I left the Barnard Hospital and became professor of comparative pathology in the School of Medicine of Washington University. In 1924, when Dr. Opie left Washington University to return to New York to accept the position of head of the Department of Pathology at Cornell University, I succeeded him at Washington University as professor of pathology. I was at that time about fifty-five years old, and I remained active in this position until 1937, when I became emeritus professor of pathology. At the same time I was made research professor and thus had an opportunity to continue my experimental investigations for four years longer. In 1941 I retired from this position also, at the age of about seventy-two years.

I should mention here that in 1922 I married Georgiana Sands, a daughter of Dr. and Mrs. Norton J. Sands of Port Chester, New York. Georgiana Sands was a graduate of Vassar College and subsequently studied medicine at Johns Hopkins and then served as an intern at Johns Hopkins Hospital under Dr. Osler, who was professor of internal medicine. After conclusion of this internship, she returned to Port Chester and practiced medicine for several years. My wife has been a good companion and much interested in my scientific activities. I owe her much. We now have lived together for more than thirty-six years, twenty-nine of them spent in our home in Clayton, a suburb of St. Louis, where we lead a happy life together.

Over the course of many years, from about 1895 to 1942, I carried out an extensive series of transplantations of various types of normal tissues and also of tumors. In these investigations, I paid special attention to the influence of the genetic relationship between donor and host on the results of these transplantations. I also considered the relative significance of the primary or preformed constitution of tissues and body fluids as well as of the secondary or immune substances on these processes. I concluded that in each organism of the higher types of animals we can distinguish organismal and organ differentials. Organismal differentials represent the genetic relationship of an organism and its constituent parts to their own organism as well as to strange organisms. These organismal differentials are characterized by specific physical-chemical factors which are the same or almost the same in every organ or tissue in the same individual and which differ in a graded manner from the organismal differentials in every other individual. The organ differentials and tissue differentials, on the other hand, differ from each other in every individual and may be very similar to those in other individuals, except that they differ in respect to the organismal differentials, which may have a modifying effect on the organ differentials with which they are associated.

As in the former periods, so also in this period preceding and following my retirement, I spent the summer months usually at the Marine Biological Laboratory in Woods Hole, where I studied the factors that determine the characteristics of amoeboid movement and of agglutination of cells as well as the production of experimental amoebocyte tissue. As in former periods, I used as material for these investigations mainly the amoebocytes of *Limulus*, but also those of other crustaceans.

After my retirement, I spent a considerable part of my free time in writing and in 1945 published a book entitled *The Biological Basis of Individuality*. I discussed the physical and chemical factors underlying individuality and also considered the psychical characteristics of man and animals. I am now occupied with writing two additional books, one concerned with the causes and nature of cancer and the other with the psychical factors of human life.

While spending the summer of 1950 in Woods Hole, I suffered another attack of tuberculosis. I returned to St. Louis in the fall and was treated with streptomycin during the ensuing months and recovered, but after this experience I never returned again to Woods Hole. Instead, I have spent my summers in St. Louis, where I have continued my writing.

We may now briefly recapitulate some of the scientific problems in which I was principally interested during the years of my scientifically active life. They were, in the first place, the growth processes of tissues in general and of tumors in particular. In both cases I considered the two factors involved in growth, namely, cell multiplication and cell movements. The cell movements I studied mainly in amoebocytes, with particular reference to the dependence of these movements on the physical and chemical conditions of the cells. We then studied, in association with our collaborators, the characteristics of cancerous growths of epithelial origin as well as of connective tissue origin and, furthermore, the effect of growth-inhibiting as well as growth-stimulating factors. We were especially interested in the increase in growth energy which our observations indicated could be induced by means of transplantation of cancerous tissue. Such an experimental increase in growth energy apparently cannot be produced in normal adult tissues, but there are some indications that it may be possible to induce it in transplanted embryonal tissues. This increase in growth energy in transplanted tumor tissue is probably related to the increase in growth energy which may be observed in tissues in the course of their progressive transformation into cancer. We were also interested in the question whether it was possible to induce a cancerous tissue to resume the growth characteristics of the normal tissue from which it originated. These experiments, however, gave negative results.

We could follow the development of cancer step by step, and we noticed a graded increase in growth energy of tissue taking place during this transformation. The factors involved in the cancerous transformations of normal tissues and their relationship could be expressed by the equation $S \times H = C$, where S represents the growth-stimulating factors, H the degree of genetic-hereditary responsiveness of the tissue to these stimulations, and C the resulting cancer tissue.

Among the stimulating factors, we found of special interest the proof that those hormones which are normally growth-stimulating may, because of this characteristic, become a very important cause of cancer. This is very significant, because the hormone action represents, in this case, a normal growth stimulus, in contrast to carcinogenic hydrocarbons, which exert an abnormal growth stimulation of tissue. This observation indicates that it is the growth stimulation as such which causes the transformation of normal tissue into cancer. We arrived at this conclusion because of our previous findings regarding the action of certain hormones on growth and related processes. Thus not only had we observed the inhibiting action of corpus luteum on ovulation, but we recognized also the secondary action of the luteinizing hormone, progesterone, on the uterine mucous membrane, which led, after the subsequent application of mechanical stimuli, to the production of tumor-like formations in the uterus which we called deciduomata or placentomata and which represent transitory tumors, because after cessation of the stimulation they regress to the normal condition of the mucous membrane. Growth processes are, therefore, presumably not only a characteristic of tumors and of cancer in particular but the essential cause of cancer; they are, however, accompanied by secondary tissue changes, especially chemical changes.

In this connection we may refer also to various other kinds of growth processes which may lead to the development of cancer. These are essentially the processes of wound healing and perhaps of compensatory hypertrophy. Both these conditions represent adaptive mechanisms which follow destructive processes either by mechanical injury or by the injurious actions of various micro-organisms. When these growth processes exceed certain limits of duration or intensity, they may end in the development of cancer, which again represents an irreversible state of growth. How far the action of certain viruses in the origin of cancer—the knowledge of which we owe mainly to the investigations of Peyton Rous—are related to the causative growth processes which we have discussed remains to be determined.

Besides these investigations, we analyzed experimentally factors which act on the circulation as well as factors which produce edema in various tissues and organs; however, we do not need to enter into a discussion of the conclusions arrived at in the study of these problems.

On the other hand, we considered of general significance the analysis of organismal and organ differentials which resulted from our transplantation experiments. In this connection, we might mention that, partly in association with our investigations of amoebocytes which are constituents of the blood of arthropods, we also studied factors which influence coagulation of the blood in these animals as well as in higher vertebrates. We found that a factor is present in the tissue of these animals which accelerates the coagulation processes in the blood plasma. We could conclude from this work that coagulins exist in the tissues whose accelerating action on the coagulation depends on the genetic relationship between the organism possessing the blood plasma and the organism which provides the tissue coagulins. It follows from these observations that the organismal differentials, in association with the tissue coagulins, somehow help to determine the degree of effectiveness of the latter, provided that we consider the action of the tissue coagulins to be an expression of the activity of organ differentials—and such an identification seems justified. The structure and function of organ differentials in general in these various species of animals seem to vary in accordance with the organismal differentials characteristic of these various species. However, a problem that remains to be determined is to what extent we have to deal, in such cases, with direct or indirect effects of the organismal differentials which help to determine the nature of the organ differentials.

Some General Problems of Human Life

From an early period of my life, since I was seventeen or eighteen years old, I have been interested mainly in two sets of problems. First, problems of growth and related problems in living organisms, particularly in the genetic and constitutional factors as represented by organismal and organ differentials and their action on these growth processes. These I have been discussing. I shall now briefly consider the second set of problems, which relate to the psychical factors in human life.

It should be noted, first, that it is possible to distinguish various spheres or levels of human activities. While these spheres seem to be distinct, actually several of them usually are combined or interact with one another to different degrees and intensities in individual cases. Also, human aims and actions in general usually represent a combination of a number of factors, but in this discussion I shall simplify the analysis by considering in each instance only one especially prominent factor.

There is, first, the sphere or level of the fundamental processes, such as respiration, alimentation, metabolism, sexual activity, motor activity, and so on. The higher levels which follow all belong to the psychical sphere. In the more primitive of these, hypnosuggestion is a prominent constituent.

Hypnosuggestion is a psychical factor in some ways intermediate between a suggestion as ordinarily understood and a state of hypnosis. It is stronger and more intense in its effects than mere suggestion, and less intense and restricted then the state of hypnosis. We therefore apply to this condition a term combining both these states and call it "hypnosuggestion." Hypnosuggestions dominate a great part of our usual psychical activities of learning, tradition, conversation, and fashion. Indeed, they occupy much more of our mental life, of our opinions and attitudes, than we are aware, and they tend to transform human beings, more or less, into automata. We are inclined to regard many hypnosuggestions as expressions of our free creative will. However, any word, sentence, or expression of attitude on the part of another person or of one's self is liable to induce within one's self hypnosuggestions which may either co-operate with already existing hypnosuggestions or thoughts or interfere with or antagonize them. In the latter case, a struggle within the psychical sphere of the individual may develop. A state of antagonism between the products of thinking and of hypnosuggestion may exist within us. Thought tends to make us free in a restricted sense, while hypnosuggestion, as stated, quite commonly serves to make us into automata. It does not tend to convert us into understanding beings; rather it may make us conventional and even cruel, although it does not have such an effect in all instances.

The next higher sphere is that of reasoning thought, and here we may recognize certain subdivisions. There is a type of thought that aims at one's own narrow, direct advantage—to gain superiority in the social struggle and obtain material and psychical goods.

In contrast, the next higher category is concerned with wider, deeper thoughts and interests and wider, deeper aspects of reality, such as are represented by certain problems of philosophy and science and the study of human relations. In this realm we tend to identify our own interests with those of our fellow human beings and with those of humanity as a whole.

A brief statement as to the origin of the psychical sphere of human activity may be interjected here. Two types of reality which affect human life in general can be distinguished. (1) There is the reality of the constitution of our body sphere and, in particular, of the central nervous system. Function in this sphere depends on the physical-chemical nature of the material of which these organs and tissues consist. (2) These organs and tissues interact with a reality represented by our environment, which includes the external as well as the internal environment. The interaction of these two types of reality creates the psychical sphere of thoughts, emotions, and hypnosuggestions. The existence of the psychical sphere depends, therefore, partly on the chemical-physical activities of the material constituents of our body and partly on the environment. Alterations in the mechanisms of material constituents may therefore affect our psychical functions.

We may now consider some specific psychical activities which have a great influence in determining our life.

The Role of Reproduction and Imitation of Environment

Human beings tend to imitate the non-living as well as the living environment, and this tendency extends to processes which go on within ourselves in the different levels of the mind. This activity may be exemplified in the characteristics of the conditioned reflex. The conditioned reflex may essentially represent an imitation of certain sensations. We imitate our fellow human beings in dress and way of life, and our opinions largely imitate those of others. We hear thoughts expressed and we reproduce them in our own speech or actions. The thoughts may be the more potent if they are given to us in the form of commands. In several fields of single thoughts as well as systems of thoughts, conditioned reflexes are active. A picture or the sound of a word may evoke a new picture, a new thought, which in certain respects reproduces the original thought; but this does not apply to all spheres of thinking.

The games we play reproduce the competitive and aggressive spirit characteristic of hunting, boxing, and fighting in general, which are activities of real life. Playing cards and playing golf are examples of competitive or aggressive activities. Literature, painting, and sculpture are imitations of reality and reproduce in various modified forms emotions we feel. Music reproduces emotions, or in certain cases it may represent a playing with sounds. Science is a generalized, economizing reproduction of reality and within itself must be consistent. In science we make use of various modes of symbolization. The term "reality" used here is meant to be devoid of any metaphysical connotation; it merely represents a system of experiences. Because we tend to reproduce reality by means of symbols such as words and sentences, the symbols may become detached from and mistaken for reality and then function as independent hypnosuggestions.

By reproducing our living or non-living environment, a strange, a mysterious, constituent of our world becomes familiar to us, and we no longer fear it as we might fear the unknown. In a sense, we subdue our environment by imitating it. This is one of the functions of art, literature, science—to enable us to overcome our deficiencies and to help make us victorious in life.

The Process of "Psychization" as a Human Activity

Human beings and the more highly developed animal species share the essential features of the primary mechanisms of respiration and digestion, although certain finer differences of some of these mechanisms may exist in these various species. In addition, rudimentary elements of psychical functions may have developed in some of the lower species. The more primitive the species, the more rudimentary are the psychical factors. In the most primitive invertebrates, there is no longer any indication of the existence of psychical factors. Certain functions which in the higher species are, to a limited extent, directed by various impulses—in which some rudiments of thought or hypnosuggestion may be involved—are replaced in some of the lower forms by various tropisms, which have been especially studied by Jacques Loeb. But only in the human species has a complex structure of higher psychical factors been erected on this basis.

In this way, a process which is designated as "psychization" has been developed. Thus eating and drinking have become subjects of poetry and of scientific research. The ordinary events in the social life of the human being, such as seeing, hearing, resting, and primitive social interactions, have been transformed into complex concepts of home, nation, and humanity and into the specific features of individuality. And out of these have been developed the concepts of law and ideals as well as the concepts of virtue and vice. Within family life, devotion, reverence, and obedience have arisen, but antagonism and hatred have also. The sentiments of national pride and sacrifice for the good of the nation and for humanity as well as deeply felt enmity have been created. To the primary sex functions, love and devotion have been added as psychical correlates. Constituents of non-living nature as well as of the more primitive living world have in a certain sense been humanized; trees, mountains, the moon, the stars, the heavens have been made the dwelling place of angels, evil spirits, and gods, all representing magnified humans. Poetry and art in general tend to convert non-living things into living beings, and we are making similar conversions in our poetry of daily life. These are examples of various types of "psychization" which tend to make human life richer but also more dangerous and often more painful.

The Struggle for Material and Psychical Goods

To satisfy the primary needs of organisms and also needs derived from their psychical structure, the desire develops—for material goods and for simple, basic kinds of psychical goods, such as the expression of kindness, friendliness, understanding, and affection. Secondarily, there is added the desire for distinctive psychical goods, such as honors, praise, and the submission of others to one's self. And to satisfy these needs for material goods and for simple and distinctive psychical goods, a competitive struggle develops. In more primitive times, the institutions of royalty, nobility, and social caste were created; but various new types of distinctive psychical goods have gradually been added, represented, for instance, by titles and positions in the community structure. These struggles are frequently intense and cruel, in the attempt to acquire or to maintain these material and psychical goods. The social elevation of one person or one group often meant the lowering or degradation of another. However, these distinctive psychical goods quite commonly have enriched the life of the person or the group possessing them. They have added self-confidence and self-respect, and they have increased the ability to fulfil various social functions. On the other hand, in the group not possessing these distinctions, there may be a depression of the personality, a loss of self-respect, a feeling of inferiority, and even a decrease in bodily strength and functions. The possession of distinctive psychical goods tends to increase the desire for additional psychical goods. These effects are in certain respects comparable to an increasing desire for toxic substances such as alcohol. All opportunities are used to justify a desire for an increase in these distinctions. Racial, family, national, and individual characteristics are employed to justify these claims, which are often based on assertions of a specially favorable genetic constitution; however, in reality, these apparently well-founded claims are actually what might be called "pseudo-genetics." There is no definite evidence for real genetic superiority on the part of the victors in the social struggle. These victories may be the result of various types of environmental factors, and they may lead to rebellions and revolts on the part of the vanquished individuals and groups, which usually represent a majority in the community.

A struggle similar in certain aspects to the struggles which occur between different individuals and between different groups of individuals may also occur within the psychical system of a single person. Such an inner struggle can take place because there are different levels of activity and of conscious control in the psychical sphere of an individual. Various conditions may raise the degree of consciousness of a thought. A command which is obeyed may have such an effect of increasing the degree of consciousness. In general, thoughts or hypnosuggestions associated with strong emotions may achieve high degrees of consciousness. Thoughts concerning a wider and deeper reality may become more and more objectified and thus control processes possessing a lower degree of consciousness that may find expression in our wishes and aims. The objectivity of thoughts may reach such a high degree that it may create a level which appears to be a separate individual, a separate entity—still, however, subject to conditions in one's organ functions. On this highest level of consciousness, one may analyze his own personality, and it may appear to him as a strange individual. In this sphere we also imitate ourselves and may control our thoughts and attitudes.

In this brief discussion I use the terms "consciousness" and "conscious" as characteristics of thoughts which can be readily recognized to be a part of ourselves. The terms are not used to indicate the existence of psychical activities in general.

Deficiencies in Human Life and Attempts To Compensate for Them

A principal source of mental disharmony and suffering in human beings lies in the fact that one becomes aware of the various kinds of physical and psychical deficiencies which develop sooner or later in life. Essentially, the discordances in the human mind are caused by the fact that in the human species the functions of the elementary nervous system are combined with a pronounced development of certain parts of the central nervous system, which differentiates the human from other animal species and which enables man to recognize certain psychical factors in the process of living.

We may briefly indicate some of these deficiencies which cause discordances in human life:

1) To proceed from the vigor and health of youth to weakness and physical and mental deterioration ending in death is the characteristic life-cycle. We do not wish to accept this reality; we wish to live forever. We also observe the passing-away of persons we knew, friends and relatives who formed a part of our personality. This passing-away means a loss of part of ourselves, our own death. While the universe may continue to enlarge, our own individual universe is shrinking.

2) We are conscious of a great similarity between the human and other species of animals, especially in the primary sex sphere. This similarity is resented as a lowering of our dignity.

3) Much suffering is caused by the crude and often cruel struggle for material and psychical goods already mentioned—by the creation of social castes and by the insincerity which may develop in the sphere of social relationships when pseudo-psychical goods are used as exchange instead of real psychical goods, in order to obtain social advantages.

4) Another cause of human disharmony consists in the premature acceptance of thought systems, some of which originated in primitive times and even at present are sometimes recklessly imposed upon other individuals. Semantics may be used as an instrument in the social struggle. As an example, we may mention the application of the terms "materialism" and "materialistic." These terms may refer to physical particles which help

to determine biological and, in particular, psychical factors in human behavior, but they may also refer to an attitude which consists of the worship of material factors such as money as the essential aim in life.

5) The persistence of our civilization is uncertain because of the possibility of its destruction as the result of technological development. There is also a possibility of the destruction of our planet as the result of some cosmic event. These thoughts may make us uncertain of the permanence and absolute value of the principles which have guided us in our lives.

In order to counteract these depressive factors in our psychical sphere, humanity has conceived doctrines or has accepted thought systems transmitted to it which promise eternal life. Furthermore, science, poetry, literature, and art not only reproduce life and environment in general, but by means of such reproductions they also tend to make us victorious in our struggle to overcome the deficiencies of life. We can mitigate the severity of these struggles by eliminating as much as possible the injurious hypnosuggestions which are the expression of our deficiencies.

These thought systems which have been created by groups of human beings may have served the usually unconscious purpose for which they were produced—each relieved the fears of deficiency of human life in its own way—yet, while they were useful in this respect, on the whole, they actually seem to have increased the intensity and severity of the human struggle between individuals, between groups of individuals, and between nations. This undesirable effect was probably caused largely by the fact that the adherents of each of the various thought systems regarded their own as the only true and justified one and all the other thought systems as more or less untrue. They therefore felt that they should extend their own system and impose it on the others. The existence of these various thought systems had still another interesting consequence. Each thought system in its own way acted on associated systems of emotion. Each intensified or created some emotions and diminished or eliminated certain other emotions. Thus, secondarily, thought systems modify in various ways the emotional life of the human beings who adhere to them.

Science and Human Life

What is science?—During a life, one makes simple and free observations or, on the other hand, makes observations under experimental conditions. If these observations, so far as they are true and relevant, are joined together in a correct manner, they reproduce a part of reality in which these various observations and the conclusions based on them are consistent with one another. They make possible generalizations which gain in significance with the progress of science and which lead step by step to a wider and deeper understanding of life and the universe. Science thus creates a constant picture of reality; this is its function and significance.

We may distinguish between pure science, which is an attempt to reproduce a part of reality, and applied science, which serves as an instrument for the attainment of a practical purpose.

Science and ethics.—Science discovers the means that make possible a relatively healthy development of body and mind. Health of mind rests on harmony in the function of the constituent parts of an individual, as well as on harmony with social groups, narrow or wide, which may extend to all humanity. Science always enables an individual to recognize himself in others and others in himself. Science may thus serve as a basis of ethics.

Science and education.—The ability to adjust one's attitudes and activities to the realities of life and also the ability to appreciate science and make it effective in the conduct of life depend on the ability to avoid errors in thinking. Some of the principle errors in thinking and in estimating reality occur under the following conditions:

a) We tend to attribute a single cause to a condition when actually a combination of causes is active. An example is the frequent occurrence of a combination of genetic and environmental factors.

b) We often fail to distinguish between certainties and probabilities, possibilities and impossibilities.

c) We often assume that a single environmental factor has a single effect, whereas in reality it frequently has several effects acting on several constituent parts of the organism. This is especially important in the sphere of the physician and causes the frequent appearance of unexpected, unfavorable side effects in the attempt to apply a remedy in the treatment of a disease.

d) We must distinguish between quantitative and qualitative conditions in comparing two factors. We need also to distinguish between causal and symptomatic effects in analyzing the relationship between two conditions. This is another factor of significance in the therapeutic efforts of the physician.

e) We are especially liable to be misled in our analysis of potent factors if our own advantages and wishes enter into a situation. This may lead us into false conclusions.

It is important to teach students to avoid such errors in judgment, and it might even be useful if children in their precollege training were instructed in avoiding such errors. Instead of teaching students merely by lectures, it might be advisable to have them discuss actual situations before the class and define the attitudes most appropriate to various conditions.

Science and the physician.—The physician is principally interested in the treatment of patients who need his advice. He must impart to the patient a belief that he, the physician, possesses the ability to treat him successfully. He may encourage in the patient the hypnosuggestion of his capability, his interest, and good will. But, in addition, the physician must be able to deal with the condition of the patient in a scientific spirit. He must make use of the various biological sciences of physiology, pathology, pharmacology, microbiology, and psychology for this purpose, and he must be able to analyze the condition of his patient in a scientific, objective spirit. The physician may also need the aid of these sciences to instruct and advise the community in matters that affect the physical and mental health of large groups. In this case also, he must be able to approach the problem in the spirit of both a scientist and a physician; therefore, the physician must combine in himself the ability of the healer and the scientist.

It may now be pointed out that there seem to be two contrasting aspects in human life. In the first place, life may be felt as a wonderful experience of a continuous advance in the understanding of life and living organisms and gaining vistas into the universe and also expanding the mind by feeling at one with fellow human beings. But here we must also recognize that associated with these experiences are elements of deep tragedy based on the difference between the limitations of human life and our wishes as to its permanence. There is added to this contrast our suffering in the social struggle.

In conclusion, we may ask whether it will be possible to diminish the difficulties and cruelties in human life. There are various ways in which we may attempt to obtain such an effect; and the history of man has shown that such a diminution of cruelties in the life of individuals, groups, and nations is possible.

a) We should attempt to diminish the influence and power of hypno-suggestions and substitute, for these, thinking that is at the same time creative and critical.

b) We should try to diminish the power and significance of distinctive psychical goods so far as they may lead to depression of the individuality of others.

c) We should give simple psychical goods—kindness, understanding, appreciation, and affection—as much as possible to others, and we should not restrict the applications of simple psychical goods to certain limited groups, such as family and nation, although we should not diminish greatly our gifts to those nearest to us but rather should grant them to wider circles.

d) We should remember that every thought we have, every action we perform, has an effect suggesting imitation and reproduction. In addition, the logic inherent in living may induce us to continue our thinking and acting in a direction which we have begun. We should, therefore, guard against thoughts and acts which may lead to unfavorable results. Thus, with patience and good will, we may hope that the values of life will increase and its acerbities will diminish.

I am now nearly completing the eighty-ninth year of my life, and, considering the physical deficiencies and, in particular, the deterioration of my eyesight caused by this advanced age, I recognize that I may not be able to conclude the work—the writing of two books—I have been engaged in for a number of years.

In this autobiographical account I have not been able to mention my friends and to refer to my research associates who have co-operated with me in the work which has been described in this account; but their memory is dear to me and represents a precious part of my life.

OTTO LOEWI, M.D.

The Excitement of a Life in Science

My Childhood and Education

The background of a man's achievements is usually the most interesting part of his life story. An advantage of autobiography may be that its author reports more competently than others on his inner experience and its effects; yet, even so, fiction may come into play because a retrospective report may not always truly reflect the past as it happened.

Because of their fundamental and lasting influence on my intellectual and spiritual development I have to go back to the years I spent in the humanistic Gymnasium in Frankfurt am Main, my native town. In my time, heavy emphasis was put on the study of Latin (nine years) and Greek (six years). We were made familiar with more than the grammatical subtleties of these languages. Through reading and commenting on original texts, we also became acquainted with the civilization of classical antiquity, which covered almost the whole sphere of human aspirations. This kind of study had unique and lasting value, not so much by increasing factual knowledge, but by widening the horizon and encouraging the habit of independent thinking. At least equally important, it always seemed to me, is that during the formative years a young person spends a good part of study time on classical languages *because* they are *not* of immediate practical value and because the past has shown that this type of education usually favorably shaped the student's personality and influenced his whole attitude toward life. I was graduated from the Gymnasium in 1891.

One of my dearest memories from those school years is of the place

Dr. Loewi discovered acetylcholine, the chemical that transmits nervous impulses. Like most European-born scientists, he worked or felt at home in many of the scientific centers on that side of the Atlantic Ocean. World War II forced him to leave the University of Graz, Austria, and find a new home in the United States, where he was a member of the Department of Pharmacology, New York University College of Medicine, until his death December 25, 1961.

where until 1890 we regularly spent our summer vacations. It was my father's estate, which consisted of an old manor, a large, enchanting garden, and some vineyards. It was situated on a slope of the Haardt Mountains in the Palatinate, a wine district whose vintages have deservedly been as famous as those from the vineyards on the Rhine. Each time I went there with my family my feelings for our country place were deepened. My memories of each detail are as vivid as if they were from yesterday and not seventy years ago. The Haardt was where I first picked a lily of the valley and plucked my first apricots from a tree.

During the obligatory nine years that I attended the Gymnasium, I received poor marks in physics and mathematics. They were compensated by fairly good marks in the humanities. It was always understood that after graduation from the gymnasium I should study at a university. I was not one of those fortunate few who early display a definite talent which indicates the choice of study.

As a teenager I was already familiar with masterworks of the early Flemish painters through trips to Belgium. They deeply impressed me and caused me to become acquainted with works of art, particularly paintings, whenever possible and to read relevant literature. In fact, my leaning to art became so strong that I wished to study the history of art. The family, however, for practical reasons, was against this project and wanted me to study medicine. I gave in, and in the fall of 1891 went to Strassburg University. It ranked among the most excellent in Germany because after the Franco-German war Alsace-Lorraine had become German, and Strassburg, its university, received all kinds of privileges to attract the very best scientists as professors.

After my matriculation as a medical student, I began to attend regularly all the required preclinical lectures and courses. Right then and there I found out that a great scientist is not inevitably a good teacher. Consequently, I soon limited my attendance almost exclusively to the anatomy courses of Gustav Schwalbe, who was both an excellent scientist and a stimulating teacher. A good part of the time gained by playing hooky from medical courses I spent attending lectures at the philosophical faculty —lectures covering the exact sciences as well as the humanities. I was particularly attracted by Georg Dehio, at that time the outstanding scholar of the history of German architecture. Another man who deeply impressed me was Wilhelm Windelband, a highly regarded philosopher; Kuno

Fischer in Heidelberg, the most popular lecturer in philosophy, had Windelband in mind when in one of his lectures he remarked, "There are only two philosophers in Germany. The other one teaches in Strassburg." Only in the summer of 1893, during the fourth term of my medical study, did I seriously prepare for the first medical examination, called *Physicum*, to which one had to submit toward the end of that term. I was quite satisfied that I narrowly escaped failing.

The following year I spent in Munich. In the 1890's the revolution in literature which had been manifested first in the social and naturalistic plays of Scandinavian and German authors reached its acme. Berlin and Munich competed for the best performances. Munich excelled also in its performances of the operas of Wagner, who was at the zenith of his glory, and it had become the center of an exciting new movement in fine arts. These were the main reasons why I went to Munich. In the beginning I attended medical courses fairly regularly. But again my eagerness soon diminished, and I spent more and more time visiting the museums and exhibitions of what then was regarded as "modern art" and on other non-medical activities. After a year, in the fall of 1894, I returned to Strassburg. Only then, in the beginning of my fourth academic year, my indifference to medicine suddenly gave way to almost enthusiastic interest.

After signing up for the lectures, a student had to collect the signatures of the individual lecturers for his attendance record. One signature I needed was Professor Bernhard Naunyn's, the head of the clinic of internal medicine, an outstanding clinician and experimental pathologist as well as a stimulating teacher. His lecture was already in full swing when I arrived in the clinic. Even the corridor leading to the open door of the auditorium was filled to capacity. It was so quiet that, standing at the end of the corridor, I could catch every word of the speaker, whom, of course, I could not see. The sound and vigor of Naunyn's voice as well as his presentation of the subject so deeply impressed me that the next day I came half an hour early to be sure of a seat. From that day until the end of my studies I tried not to miss a single Naunyn lecture. I also volunteered for student practice because I wished to attend Naunyn's daily rounds in the wards and in the laboratory. In time I came into personal contact with this fascinating man and his excellent staff, among whom were Oscar Minkowski and Adolph Magnus-Levy.

Naunyn provoked my interest in several branches of medicine, but pharmacology was not one of them. And yet, strangely enough, I asked the famous "Father of Pharmacology," Professor Oswald Schmiedeberg, for a subject for my thesis. As a rule, people working in Schmiedeberg's laboratory were apprentices or competent scientists in the field from all over the world, rarely students who, like me, had no preliminary knowledge or training. What motive impelled me to this step? In the first part of *Faust* Goethe says, *Du glaubst zu schieben und du wirst geschoben*, or, as translated by Bayard Taylor, "Thou'rt shoved, thyself imagining to shove."

In the laboratory I again met Oscar Minkowski and also Arthur Cushny, Karl Spiro, and Walter Straub. Straub was still a student, but he had already been fairly well trained in experimental work in the laboratory of Carl von Voit, who was the teacher of Graham Lusk also. We became friends for life. It was Spiro who introduced me to the classic studies "On the Life of the Rhine Salmon in Fresh Water," of Friedrich Miescher, Swiss pioneer in biology. These studies were collected and republished in 1897 as *The Histochemical and Physiological Studies of Friedrich Miescher*. Time and again I have turned to this volume, which became to me a kind of scientific bible. While I owe my interest in medicine to Naunyn, Miescher's studies were chiefly responsible for my later choice of biology —strictly speaking, physiology—as a calling.

During the tenth term, I had to take my oral examinations (*Staatsexamen*). Everything went well until the last section of the last examination. The subject was surgery, and the last section included fractures and dislocations. I drew a question about interdental splints. I enumerated all of those referred to in the textbook, but the examiner inquired about yet another one. It was an obscure splint engineered by a dentist who had once worked with the professor. This splint had failed to make the textbooks, and it was only natural that I never had heard of it. For this failure I was not passed for six weeks. In my opinion, most examiners who are feared by candidates because of their strictness, pettiness, and insistence on unimportant details are narrow minded and frustrated because of a hidden, often justified, inferiority complex. They are not so much critical of but find fault with generally acknowledged achievements. Naunyn once wrote, "Criticism is indispensable, skepticism is the arrogant attitude of an ignoramus."

After my graduation from Strassburg in 1896, my parents fulfilled an old desire of mine by offering me a trip to Italy. I have returned to that country time and again. I would not like to have missed the enrichment of my life that I owe to Italy.

I Choose the Laboratory Rather than the Clinic

I was fully aware that I lacked sufficient knowledge and training in chemistry to meet the requirements of experimental work in any laboratory. After my return from Italy, I therefore took an excellent course in inorganic analytic chemistry in Frankfurt and then spent a few months in the biochemical institute of Franz Hofmeister in Strassburg. He was an ingenious biologist as well as an unforgettable personality. Meanwhile, Professor von Noorden, the internist of the city hospital in Frankfurt, offered me an assistant's position. Von Noorden was well known for his valuable studies on pathologic metabolism as well as on nutrition and dietetics. I had already decided to seek an academic career but did not know whether I should choose internal medicine or a basic medical science. Preparation for either branch of medicine by service in the ward combined with laboratory work appeared to me advantageous. I therefore accepted Noorden's offer and started in my post in 1897. The first ward I had to take care of was reserved for cases of far-advanced tuberculosis; in the second there were many patients suffering from a pneumonia which then was epidemic and proved to be particularly dangerous for vigorous young men. There was no therapy. The mortality was enormous. Because of these experiences, I decided not to become a clinician but to do research in basic medical science.

At that time, and ever since, I have looked at pharmacology as the science whose main goal is revealing physiological functions by the reactions of living matter to chemical agents. The very concept of using drugs in the study of functions oriented me to pharmacology.

On my request for advice about with whom I should work, Hofmeister strongly recommended Professor Hans H. Meyer, the pharmacologist at the University in Marburg an der Lahn. There was, fortunately, an opening in the department, and after an encouraging interview, I was accepted as assistant. Dr. Meyer was a great scientist and person. His scientific reputation reached its culmination after the publication of his pioneering studies leading to his "Theory of Narcosis" in 1899, and of his "Researches on Tetanus" with Fred Ransom in 1903. In 1904 he was invited to deliver the first Harvey Lecture in New York. I stayed with Dr. Meyer for ten happy years, from 1898 until 1905 in Marburg, then in Vienna.

The conditions in Germany at that time were most favorable for the development of scientists. In spite of the frequent rattling of sabers, under the reign of Wilhelm II almost everybody enjoyed both security and freedom. The universities were government owned, but the government hardly ever interfered with their far-reaching autonomy. As a rule, it contented itself with accepting the universities' proposals and paying the endowments and debts of the departments. If the debts were excessive, the department got a warning—and a little later the payment. Because of these enlightened policies, there was no need to rush work and publication. There was much leisure for keeping abreast of the literature—which, to be sure, was not so immense then as it is nowadays—for extensive discussions, and for concentrated thinking. I was not at all sure whether I had enough scientific imagination for a man who thought of spending his life in basic science. Therefore, at the interview with Dr. Meyer, I proposed and he agreed that my two first years with him should be on probation. Apparently, for this reason, Dr. Meyer encouraged me to make my own decisions about the subject matter of my investigations right from the first day. After I had made my decision, he discussed with me all of the details and then followed the progress of the work with great interest. His analytical talents and his imaginative mind were of inestimable value to me. So was his broad-mindedness and deeply rooted culture, which he expressed in digressions often lasting for hours into many aspects of human aspirations. In many respects I owe to Dr. Meyer a very large part of my education.

During the first years in Marburg, I chose my topics mainly from the field of metabolism, toward which I had been drawn by personal contact with such pioneers in the field as Naunyn, Minkowski, and Magnus-Levy and by intense study of the fundamental papers of Miescher. I started by investigating the action of phlorhizin, a glucoside that provokes glycosuria. This was my first approach to the problems of carbohydrate metabolism, to which I returned time and again. Another investigation concerned nuclein metabolism in man. After the publication of the results obtained in this study, Dr. Meyer recommended me, in 1900, to the faculty as *Privatdocent*, a title signifying the first step in an academic career. I delivered the obligatory probation lecture on "The Migration of Material in the Organism" because this subject gave me an opportunity to emphasize Miescher's pioneering work. In 1902 I published my paper on "Protein Synthesis in the Animal Body."

Up to 1901 no one had succeeded in maintaining animals in nitrogen equilibrium by feeding them with the degradation products of casein or fibrin in place of native protein, even if the degradation had not gone very far. It was therefore assumed that animals were not able to synthesize their proteins from degradation products. I knew about this state of affairs but was not especially interested in the question. My attitude changed remarkably overnight. One evening in 1899 I read a paper just published by the excellent biochemist Friedrich Kutscher, an associate of Albrecht Kossel in Marburg, "On the End Products of Trypsin Digestion." He showed that by prolonged digestion in an incubator, a pancreas can be decomposed so that any reaction characteristic of protein is no longer present. Right then I got the idea and the firm conviction that one would succeed in reaching protein synthesis in animals by feeding them the degradation products of a whole organ rather than of a single protein.

I started the experiments at once. For a long time I encountered great difficulties, particularly because most of the dogs did not relish the unusual fare. I persisted, however, because I had not the slightest doubt that I would succeed in the end. My perseverance was rewarded. In 1902 I was able to prove the correctness of my hunch that animals are able to rebuild their proteins from their final degradation products, the amino acids. This discovery has played an essential part in the science and practice of nutrition. It also was the first publication that made my name known as a researcher. I did not at all foresee such dividends. In 1902 I also published the first part of a series of papers called "Experimental Contributions to the Physiology and Pharmacology of Kidney Function."

To England To Learn

The relatively simple techniques I applied in the experiments I had published, and those I prepared for Dr. Meyer's lectures on pharmacology were almost the only ones at my command. Frequently, because of my poor training in the methods required, I dropped ideas that occurred to me. This meant, of course, a serious limitation of my scientific activity in the future, and I decided to remedy this shortcoming.

During the nineteenth century the humanities as well as the basic sciences were blooming, especially in Germany. World-renowned German medical scientists like Julius Cohnheim, the experimental pathologist in Leipzig, and physiologists like Rudolph Heidenhain in Breslau and Wilhelm Kuehne in Heidelberg attracted students from abroad. But it was the laboratory of Karl Ludwig in Leipzig that became a kind of Mecca for physiologists and other medical scientists from all over the world. He devised innumerable methods and apparatus for approaching problems until then inaccessible. After Ludwig's death in 1895, Germany little by little lost its leadership to England, where men such as Barcroft, Bayliss, Gaskell, Haldane, Langley, Sherrington, and Starling had become world-renowned physiologists. Being familiar with most of their papers, I decided to spend some time in England to learn methods and to meet at least some of its famous physiologists. I wished particularly to work with Ernest Starling because his papers covered so many sides of experimental physiology. I wrote to him in 1902, and he accepted me as a student in his laboratory. On the trip to London I did not neglect to stop for a week in Holland to enjoy the original paintings of the Dutch masters which I had known until then only from prints.

When I first saw Starling's laboratory, I was surprised by the striking contrast between its extremely limited space and primitive equipment and the very high level of the work that had come out of it. Like everybody else, I was charmed at first sight by Starling's appearance, his expressive features, his shining eyes. I soon recognized that he was the most dynamic and contagiously enthusiastic man I had ever met, full of ideas and optimism, as well as very critical of other people's and his own achievements. He possessed a serenity and simplicity, humility and a kind of naïveté that is characteristic of so many men of genius. He made the atmosphere of his laboratory warm, informal, and stimulating.

W. M. Bayliss, Starling's brother-in-law, was also working there—an inconspicuous man, always in high spirits and extremely modest. His interest, knowledge, and thought covered almost every branch of science important for progress in biology. Aside from his broad view, he possessed all the other qualifications needed for writing that unique book *Principles of General Physiology* (1917), which for many years had an enormous influence on everybody interested in the question "What is life?" Many facts offered in this book are now obviously out of date, but it still makes stimulating and exciting reading, and for fundamental principles and historical perspective, nothing has yet taken its place. Starling and Bayliss were very generous in offering me so much of their wealth of ideas, knowledge, and experimental experience.

It was in Starling's laboratory in 1902 that I first met Henry Dale. We at once found that our interests and aspirations had much in common, and we soon developed a close, lifelong friendship.

I greatly enjoyed the meetings of the Physiological Society, an organization that impressed me as being one big family. The atmosphere of the meetings was informal, and a fine kind of humor spiced the discussions. I had never experienced anything like this in continental meetings. At these meetings I had the good fortune to become acquainted with most of the British physiologists of that time.

A friend, Nathaniel Alcock, who worked with me in Marburg and later succeeded Brodie as Professor of Physiology at the University of Toronto, conveyed to me an invitation to spend the Christmas vacation in the rectory of his uncle, Dr. Kingsmill, in a community close to Norwich. The rector immediately excused me from attending the daily services in his home. On a Sunday morning, however, he said that his altar boy had fallen sick and asked me to substitute for him at the service in the local church. He carefully prepared and dressed me, and then—Otto Loewi, M.D., *Privatdocent* of Pharmacology in Marburg, functioned that day in a white vestment as acting altar boy.

During the stay in England, I came to admire the English people in every respect. This visit also left me with a warm feeling of friendship for individual Englishmen, beginning with the contemporary biologists and extending to the succeeding generations.

Vienna

After my return to Marburg, I continued to study the function of the kidney and the mechanism of action of diuretics with Walter M. Fletcher,

Velyan Henderson, and Nathaniel Alcock. In 1904, Dr. H. H. Meyer accepted an appointment as Professor of Pharmacology in Vienna. I substituted for him in Marburg and after a year followed him to Vienna.

The seven years spent in Marburg were very enjoyable. I valued a close association with Hermann Cohen, the famous neo-Kantian philosopher, although I did not understand his philosophy. I was also on good terms and in stimulating scientific contact with many colleagues of my age and with Professors Friedrich Mueller, Ludolph Krehl, and Ernst Romberg, the successive heads of the outpatient clinic in Marburg, which position proved to be for them a steppingstone to brilliant academic careers.

In Vienna I made up for what I naturally had to forego in Marburg, which had just one per cent of the population of Vienna. I frequently went to the *Hofoper*, then under Gustav Mahler, and to the *Burgtheater*, where Joseph Kainz stood out; he is considered to be the equal of the greatest actors of all time. I indulged in the pleasure of studying art treasures accumulated during centuries and of becoming familiar with the unique charm of that city and its gracious surroundings. The Easter vacation of 1905 I spent in Naples and worked in the famous zoölogical station. There I became well acquainted with Anton Dohrn, its founder, the highly cultured friend of Adolph Hildebrandt, the architect, Joseph Joachim, the violinist, and Hans von Marées, the painter who had adorned the station library with frescos of world fame. It was there that I met for the first time Ernst Theodor Bruecke, who later held the chair of physiology in Innsbruck. From our first meeting we developed a close friendship which lasted until his untimely death in Boston, where his old friend Alexander Forbes had offered him opportunity to continue his work at Harvard.

The Viennese medical school enjoyed a high reputation of long standing that attracted many students, from the United States especially. There existed an "American medical association in Vienna," and *Amerikanerkurse* (courses for Americans) were a standing institution. A growing number of young scientists and clinicians, at first mostly Viennese, applied for admission as co-workers in the pharmacological department. With those who were assigned to me by Dr. Meyer, I again studied mostly problems connected with carbohydrate metabolism. One of these studies proved that the preference of pancreatectomized dogs for fructose rather than glucose, as had been demonstrated by Minkowski, is not specific for this deficiency but is shared by dogs deprived of their glycogen by other means, e.g., by phosphorus poisoning. It was further shown that the heart, in contrast to the liver, cannot utilize fructose. It was finally discovered that epinephrine injections into rabbits completely depleted by starvation of their liver glycogen brought the glycogen back to almost normal values in spite of continued starvation.

Other investigations in Vienna were devoted to studies on the vegetative nervous system. I had imported the interest in that field from England, where Gaskell and Langley had discovered the existence of two divisions of the vegetative nervous system, and where T. R. Elliott during my short stay in Cambridge was just about to conduct the final experiments on the action of epinephrine. His classical paper on this subject was published in 1905. I did experiments in that field in Vienna jointly with Alfred Froehlich, well known for the syndrome named after him. A skilful experimenter and genuine musician, he was liked by everybody, particularly because of his serenity and equanimity. This gentle philosopher retained these qualities and developed them even more in 1938, when he was forced to leave his beloved Vienna. He went to the United States and adapted immediately to conditions of life very different from those he had been accustomed to in Vienna.

The best-known result of our studies on the vegetative nervous system was the observation that small doses of cocaine potentiate the responses of sympathetically innervated organs to epinephrine and sympathetic nerve stimulation. This reaction has proved to be so specific that it has been successfully used as a test for epinephrine or norepinephrine.

As I had done before, in 1907 I spent my summer vacation in the upper Engadin, in Switzerland. To me it has always been the most beautiful place in the world. During my stay in Pontresina, I was introduced to Dr. Guido Goldschmiedt, then Professor of Chemistry in Prague, later in Vienna, who vacationed in Pontresina with his wife and daughter, Guida. In 1908 I married Guida. She was my faithful companion, devoting her life to my well-being for over fifty years.

In 1909, I accepted the chair of pharmacology in Graz. It was with deep regret that I left Vienna after four stimulating and fruitful years.

Graz

Like Marburg, Graz is an old and picturesque town built around a hill known as the *Schlossberg*, which, incidentally, happens also to be the name of its counterpart in Marburg. Graz could count only one-tenth the population of Vienna, yet it was the second largest town in Austria and had fine concert halls, a playhouse, and an opera house. The performances well deserved their high reputation. As everywhere in Austria and Germany, the theaters in Graz were considered important educational institutions and therefore were maintained by the city rather than as private enterprises. We soon got on friendly terms with some of the many art and music lovers. During the winters of the twenties, we usually had monthly chamber-music concerts played in our home by friends who were professional musicians or excellent amateurs.

I remember well when and how I started to enjoy symphonic music. During my last year in the gymnasium, I was invited several times to the famous symphony concerts of my home town, but usually I could not help falling asleep. During my first year in Strassburg, a fellow student who was an outstanding cellist and music connoisseur encouraged me to accompany him to a few concerts. He also stimulated my interest in the structure of musical creations and helped me to understand something of their essence. Little by little and without a conscious effort I came to love music. We may possess hidden inclinations and qualifications which need only to be encouraged to be released and developed.

In Graz I had to deliver five lectures weekly during the whole long winter term. It took me more than two full years to prepare them. When a student became restless during a lecture, I always felt that it was not his fault but my own. Before and during the first minutes of a lecture or a talk, I suffered from a kind of stage fright. A similar kind of inhibition has apparently been the cause of my spending so much time and effort preparing every one of my publications and talks. It took me about six weeks to prepare my first independent paper for publication. When I apologized to Dr. Meyer for my long absence from the laboratory, it gave me some comfort when he answered, "Having worked on your subject for almost two years, you should respect your work enough to devote six weeks to its write up." Recently, New York's Park Commissioner Robert Moses published a short essay, "A Toast to O'Casey." Here one reads, "If as the result of enormous effort and diligence the words seem to come naturally and with effortless ease, is not this the height of art?" I really appreciated this thought, since it precisely described what I have always been striving for.

I remember quite well that this strong self-criticism began when, in my early twenties, I became acquainted with Guy de Maupassant's short stories. I was fascinated not so much by the content of the stories, which I often disliked, but by the perfect shading of expression, and still more by the justification of each word used. Even slight details that at first seemed irrelevant proved in the course of the story to be necessary or essential. The economy of wording has ever since been to me one of the most important measures of quality in writing.

In Graz, before 1914, my first associate from the North American continent was the late Velyan Henderson, at that time Professor of Pharmacology in Toronto, who had worked with me in Marburg also. Next came Franklin C. McLean, who was then a professor in Portland, Oregon. After World War I, before leaving for the United States, Carl F. Cori came, followed by Harold G. Wolff, Ralph G. Smith, now at George Washington University, and John L. R. Browne and Rhoda Grant from McGill University. We also enjoyed welcoming as visitors from the United States John T. Edsall, Wallace O. Fenn, Herbert S. Gasser, Ralph W. Gerard, Ross G. Harrison, and Jeffries Wyman.

To have regular though modest physical conditioning, I adopted the habit of climbing almost daily to the top of the *Schlossberg*, usually in company of one of my co-workers. I always liked discussions with younger people. Since most of them are not yet preoccupied with scientific problems of their own, they are susceptible to other people's ideas and willing to listen.

Many studies in Graz were again devoted to problems connected with carbohydrate metabolism. Adolph Jarisch, a highly gifted scientist, who for many years was my assistant and then became professor in Innsbruck, elucidated the mechanism of action of Claude Bernard's *piqûre*. Then, with isolated rabbit hearts perfused with Locke solution, we studied the conditions responsible for epinephrine hyperglycemia.

Our last contribution to the field of carbohydrate metabolism concerned a particular kind of regulation. We called it a proprioceptive metabolic reflex. It demonstrates a mechanism through which the central nervous system, which is informed of the general metabolism by humoral means, is informed of the state of the metabolism in individual organs.

A biography should not vie with a bibliography for completeness. I, therefore, mention only one out of many studies on the part played by cations in some physiological functions and in drug actions. From the results of these studies, the first of which was fully published in 1913 and the last in 1944, I concluded that the effects of digitalis glucosides on the frog's heart are due to those drugs' sensitization of the heart to calcium. This theory became the starting point for quite a number of studies in various laboratories. Its application enabled me to elucidate the particular reaction of the toad's heart to digitalis, until then unexplained.

I had the opportunity to give a short account of the first results obtained from these studies in Dundee when I was invited to attend the annual meeting of the British Association in 1912. Among the entertainments offered at the meeting was a trip to Glamis Castle, well known from *Macbeth*, owned since then by the Earl of Strathmore. When the visitors were gathered on the lawn surrounding the castle, one of the bagpipe players—to my greatest astonishment—shouted my name. He then led me to Lady Strathmore, the grandmother of Queen Elizabeth II. Lady Strathmore graciously guided me to many remarkable sites in the castle. After the tour I asked Starling how it happened that I alone was extended this privilege. He told me that Lady Strathmore had once mentioned to one of his friends how bored she used to be with such collective visits, because out of shyness the visitors never dared to talk to her. Starling immediately recommended me as one who would definitely not suffer from such shyness.

Following the meeting, Starling, to my great pleasure, joined me in a trip through the famous lochs in Scotland. Once before, in 1904, we had traveled together in the Austrian and Bavarian Alps. He then looked so keen and vigorous that the mountain guides asked me whether he was a guide I had brought along. Starling, who usually rounded Regent Park at a trot every day before dinner, climbed in one day what for others took two days. No guide was willing to go with him after the first excursion.

The Idea of Chemical Transmission of Nervous Impulse

Now I have to turn to the best known of my scientific achievements, the establishment in 1921 of the chemical theory of the transmission of the nervous impulse. Until 1921 it was generally assumed that transmission was due to the direct spreading of the electrical wave accompanying the propagated nervous impulse from the nerve terminal to the effector organ. Since the character of that potential is everywhere the same, such an assumption would not explain the well-known fact that the stimulation of certain nerves increases the function of one organ and decreases the function of another. A different mode of transmission had, therefore, to be considered.

As far back as 1903, I discussed with Walter M. Fletcher from Cambridge, England, then an associate in Marburg, the fact that certain drugs mimic the augmentary as well as the inhibitory effects of the stimulation of sympathetic and/or parasympathetic nerves on their effector organs. During this discussion, the idea occurred to me that the terminals of those nerves might contain chemicals, that stimulation might liberate them from the nerve terminals, and that these chemicals might in turn transmit the nervous impulse to their respective effector organs. At that time I did not see a way to prove the correctness of this hunch, and it entirely slipped my conscious memory until it emerged again in 1920.

The night before Easter Sunday of that year I awoke, turned on the light, and jotted down a few notes on a tiny slip of thin paper. Then I fell asleep again. It occurred to me at six o'clock in the morning that during the night I had written down something most important, but I was unable to decipher the scrawl. The next night, at three o'clock, the idea returned. It was the design of an experiment to determine whether or not the hypothesis of chemical transmission that I had uttered seventeen years ago was correct. I got up immediately, went to the laboratory, and performed a simple experiment on a frog heart according to the nocturnal design. I have to describe briefly this experiment since its results became the foundation of the theory of chemical transmission of the nervous impulse.

The hearts of two frogs were isolated, the first with its nerves, the second without. Both hearts were attached to Straub canulas filled with a little Ringer solution. The vagus nerve of the first heart was stimulated for a few minutes. Then the Ringer solution that had been in the first heart during the stimulation of the vagus was transferred to the second heart. It slowed and its beats diminished just as if its vagus had been stimulated. Similarly, when the accelerator nerve was stimulated and the Ringer from this period transferred, the second heart speeded up and its beats increased. These results unequivocally proved that the nerves do not influence the heart directly but liberate from their terminals specific chemical substances which, in their turn, cause the well-known modifications of the function of the heart characteristic of the stimulation of its nerves.

The story of this discovery shows that an idea may sleep for decades in the unconscious mind and then suddenly return. Further, it indicates that we should sometimes trust a sudden intuition without too much skepticism. If carefully considered in the daytime, I would undoubtedly have rejected the kind of experiment I performed. It would have seemed likely that any transmitting agent released by a nervous impulse would be in an amount just sufficient to influence the effector organ. It would seem improbable that an excess that could be detected would escape into the fluid which filled the heart. It was good fortune that at the moment of the hunch I did not think but acted immediately.

For many years this nocturnal emergence of the design of the crucial experiment to check the validity of a hypothesis uttered seventeen years before was a complete mystery. My interest in that problem was revived about five years ago by a discussion with the late Ernest Kris, a leading psychoanalyst. A short time later I had to write my bibliography, and glanced over all the papers published from my laboratory. I came across two studies made about two years before the arrival of the nocturnal design in which, also in search of a substance given off from the heart, I had applied the technique used in 1920. This experience, in my opinion, was an essential preparation for the idea of the finished design. In fact, the nocturnal concept represented a sudden association of the hypothesis of 1903 with the method tested not long before in other experiments. Most so-called "intuitive" discoveries are such associations suddenly made in the unconscious mind.

Many questions connected with and raised by the discovery of chemical transmission were studied in laboratories all over the world as well as in my laboratory. We found, for instance, that the effect of the *Vagusstoff* on the heart quickly fades because it is inactivated by an ester-splitting enzyme (cholinesterase). The *Vagusstoff* was soon identified as acetylcholine. Also, it was proved that the activity of cholinesterase is prevented by the alkaloid physostigmine. This was the first identification of the point of attack of an alkaloid and, to my knowledge, the first elucidation of the mechanism underlying all the effects of an alkaloid. Not until 1936 could I identify the transmitter liberated by stimulation of the accelerator nerve as epinephrine.

In 1926 the Committee of the International Congress of Physiology to be held that year in Stockholm requested me to demonstrate there the experiment on the frog heart. I did not feel too happy about this invitation. Like most experimenters, I had experienced time and again that experiments before a large audience often failed although they never did in the rehearsals. Fortunately, I was able to demonstrate in Stockholm the experiment not less than eighteen times on the same heart.

In 1928, I had the honor to be invited by the Royal College of Physicians in London to attend the tercentenary of the publication of William Harvey's book *De Motu Cordis*. The privilege of offering the first banquet at that ceremony was given to the "Worshipful Company of the Grocers." This ancient guild had once given Harvey a grant that enabled him to study at continental universities. As one of the ceremonies during the banquet, a silver horn filled with wine was passed around. Each time a guest drank from this horn his neighbor would rise and guard his back. This custom was instituted after a king of old was stabbed in the back while drinking.

Something else happened on that occasion that I never will forget. One of the foreign guest speakers thought this banquet a fitting opportunity to lodge the claim that one of his countrymen, and not Harvey, had been the first to discover the circulation of the blood. I became so angry about what seemed to me to be an unheard of absence of good taste that I shook my head and turned around expecting to see my English hosts react with similar indignation. How astonished I was to see all my English friends leaning back comfortably with broad smiles on their faces. With typical English equanimity, they considered the apparently insulting attitude of the speaker just a huge joke.

In 1933, I delivered the Dunham lectures at Harvard. During the time I stayed in Boston, my friendly relationship with Walter B. Cannon, which had begun at the International Congress of Physiology in Boston in 1929, developed into a warm personal friendship. My admiration for Cannon's human qualities matched my admiration for his scientific thought and achievement.

In 1935, I gave the Ferrier lecture to the Royal Society of London, with Frederic Gowland Hopkins in the chair. Guida and I greatly enjoyed Sir Henry and Lady Dale's hospitality. It was in their home on a rainy day that I came across Bayard Taylor's translation of the first part of Goethe's *Faust*. This translation follows the original almost to the letter and seems to have lost hardly any of the beauties of the original.

The Nobel Prize

In 1936, jointly with my dear old friend Dale, I was awarded the Nobel Prize in physiology and medicine. Twice during that unforgettable ceremony in Stockholm I was deeply moved. Heralded by trumpeters, the Laureates of that year made their entrance upon the stage, and at that moment, led by the almost eighty-year-old King Gustav, the whole audience rose to pay homage to science. Then after the prize was handed to Dale and me, the orchestra played the Egmont overture. The orchestra was located on the top gallery. To me the music seemed to come from heaven.

On the way back to Graz I stopped in Vienna to meet Sigmund Freud for the first time. I cannot better or more exactly describe my impression when alone with him in his studio than to say that he filled the whole room with his personality. I had a similar feeling with Joseph Kainz, the actor, and again when I met Einstein. These three figures were all men of genius, unassuming and even humble. People of this kind—of course, not all of them—take their achievements for granted.

1938

On March 11, 1938, I conducted with one of my associates an experiment that was supposed to be the last of a series which had all shown that afferent nerves, in contrast to efferent nerves, contain not even traces of acetylcholine. In the late afternoon my co-worker told me that the Nazis had just taken over the country. I was so strongly preoccupied with thoughts about our most recent finding that I did not catch the full import of that news! This almost incredible indifference still lasted while, before going to bed, we heard over the radio the deeply moving valedictory address of Schuschnigg as President of Austria.

I awoke from a deep sleep at three o'clock in the morning when a dozen young stormtroopers, armed with guns, broke into my bedroom, took me downstairs, and pushed me without any explanation into a waiting prison van that took me and others to the city jail. Later that night I was joined there by our two youngest sons, Victor and Guido. Our two elder children, Hans and Anna, were not in Austria at that time and, of course, did not return.

During the obligatory morning walks in the prison yard, I found that hundreds of other male Jewish citizens of Graz shared my fate. To increase the hardships of the jail, playing any game, reading, or writing were strictly prohibited.

When I was awakened that night and saw the pistols directed at me, I expected, of course, that I would be murdered. From then on during days and sleepless nights I was obsessed by the idea that this might happen to me before I could publish my last experiments. After repeated requests, a few days later I was permitted to have a postal card and a lead pencil to write, in the presence of a guard, a communication of my last experiment to be sent to *Die Naturwissenschaften*. Later in the day the guard came to tell me that he himself had mailed my card. I felt as relieved as if our whole future depended on that communication. After two months I was released from the jail, and in three weeks my boys were set free and could emigrate.

Forced by the Nazi authorities to leave Austria, I departed from Graz on September 28, 1938, for London. Before leaving, in the presence of Gestapo men, I had to order the Swedish bank in Stockholm to transfer the Nobel prize money, deposited with the bank in 1936, to a prescribed Nazi-controlled bank. Guida was forced to remain in Austria because the Nazis were dickering with the Italian government to dispossess her of some real estate in Italy which had been in her family for over one hundred years. Apart from this, the Nazis deprived us both of all our property and belongings down to the last penny. After a pauper's oath was presented, Guida was given a so-called "subsistence allowance." It was not until 1941 that she could leave Austria and join me in the United States.

A few weeks after my arrival in London I accepted an invitation of the Franqui Foundation to serve for eight months as a visiting professor at the *Université Libre* in Brussels. To my great pleasure, simultaneously Erwin Schroedinger and Albert Szent-Györgyi became Franqui professors, the former in Ghent, the latter in Liége. The late Leo Zunz, an especially kind-hearted man, head of the Department of Pharmacology at the *Université Libre*, gave me the opportunity to work, and Walter Dulière, a biochemist, immediately offered me his services as an associate. He proved to be a great help in my laboratory work as well as in the preparation of the lectures which I had to deliver in French. He had full command of the English and German languages and literature as well and a deep understanding of the respective cultures.

In contrast was another experience I had in Brussels, with a charming lady, an acknowledged poetess. I was struck that she did not know even by name Gottfried Keller and Conrad Ferdinand Meyer, Swiss writers whose poetry and prose, written in German, were considered classics in German-speaking countries. I was still more surprised that the lady did not know by name Timmermans, a Belgian author, born and living in Lier, a village quite close to Brussels. His excellent novels and short stories, written originally in Flemish, were translated into German though not into French. I became conscious for the first time of the barriers presented by language. This is most unfortunate, particularly when there is ever increasing striving after understanding of foreign nations. Are the great writers not so representative of the character and level of civilization of a nation as the great artists are, or even more so?

During my stay in Brussels, I enjoyed much pleasant hospitality. I remember with deep gratitude Mrs. Max Gottschalk, who, through enormous effort, succeeded in getting visas for my daughter and her family, thereby enabling them to leave Czechoslovakia in time.

A New Citizenship

In the summer of 1939, I spent some months at the country seat of friends in England. Then, because of the outbreak of the war, I had to abandon my plan to return to Belgium and went to Oxford on invitation of Professor Gunn, who held the chair of pharmacology at the Nuffield Institute. While there I received a call from New York University Medical School to join the faculty as a research professor of pharmacology and to work in the laboratory of George Wallace, unforgettable to everybody who was fortunate enough to meet this distinguished scientist, teacher, and friend.

When I appeared before the American Consul in London in order to get my non-quota visa, he said that everything was ready for me except for a little formality. He asked whether I could prove that I had been teaching during the last few years. I produced the decree by which I had been dismissed as professor from the University of Graz, but he shook his head and said that this would only prove that I had been dismissed, not that I had been in a teaching position. I suggested that he should ring up Sir Henry Dale, who would be able to give him any information about me. He rejected this proposal as he considered Sir Henry to be just a private person. He was quite at a loss what to do because he really wanted to help me. Finally, quite casually, I mentioned that, of course, he would find all my data in *Who's Who*. "You think you are in?" "I know I am." He sent for the book and felt quite relieved when he said that everything was O.K. Then I had to pass a physical examination and was eventually handed a sealed envelope by the doctor. After this procedure, I received my visa. I thanked the consul for the trouble he had taken on my behalf. When I reached the door, I turned again and said, "By the way, do you know who wrote this paragraph for *Who's Who*? I did. Good-bye, Mr. Consul." Upon my arrival in New York harbor, a clerk prepared my papers for the immigration officer. While he was busy doing this, I glanced over the doctor's certificate—and almost fainted. I read: "Senility, not able to earn his living." I saw myself sent to Ellis Island and shipped back to Mr. Hitler. The immigration officer fortunately disregarded the certificate and welcomed me to this country. I arrived here June 1, 1940. On April 1, 1946, I became an American citizen.

I am one of those lucky people from abroad who right from the outset could continue here the work they had to abandon in the country they had considered to be their homeland. I owe this privilege to the understanding of my situation, the broad-mindedness, and the generosity of New York University College of Medicine as represented by Deans Donal Sheehan and Currier McEwen as well as to the late George Wallace. The unique climate of the school and its high reputation are in great part the product of a strong feeling of responsibility and a disinterested striving of the individual faculty members to serve the school.

I have been an active member of the staff since 1940, when I was sixty-seven years old. Until 1955 I continued to work experimentally and to publish mostly on leftovers from earlier problems. In 1944 I received the Cameron prize from the University of Edinburgh and an honorary science degree from my new school; and in 1950 the same degree from Yale University. Also in the 1950's I received honorary degrees from the universities in Graz and Frankfurt.

In 1954 I became a foreign member of the Royal Society of London.

Frequent invitations to deliver lectures gave me the welcome opportunity of becoming acquainted with many excellent biologists and their activities as well as with a good part of the country. An ardent desire to see the West was met by an appointment in 1942 as Walker Ames Visiting Professor at the University of Washington. On the way back to the East via California, we stopped at some places because of the uniqueness of their beauty or because I had to lecture. At the California Institute of Technology I had the honor to be introduced to the audience by the late Thomas Hunt Morgan. In 1948, I spent three weeks as visiting scholar of the Richmond Area University Center. I had to lecture at sixteen universities and colleges, and thus we became acquainted with Virginia. The originality of Thomas Jefferson's architectural and layout plans made the University of Virginia, to me, the most outstanding of all the public buildings I have seen so far in this country.

In July, 1940, a month after my arrival in this country, I went to Woods Hole, Massachusetts, for a summer vacation. And since then until three years ago, Guida and I went there every summer, as do so many who once experience the unique atmosphere radiating from the Marine Biological Laboratory, which attracts renowned scientists from Europe as well. The atmosphere originates in the main from the opportunity for informal mutual interchange with broad-minded scientists and carefully selected, refreshingly curious students. Ever since my first day at Woods Hole, I have admired the high level of those students' discussion with their teachers. I myself felt as a student there. In fact, I owe to Woods Hole my introduction into quite a few areas of biology and the intensification of my interest in any aspect of cell structure, cell function, and their interrelations. Also in Woods Hole, I had the opportunity to keep abreast of the most recent progress in diverse branches of biology by attending many lectures given by competent scientists and by frequenting the library, considered to be the world's greatest of its kind. I met there old friends and made many new ones. As a matter of course, from the start I have felt at home in Woods Hole.

> *Caelum, non animum, mutant,*
> *Qui trans mare currunt.*—Horace, *Epistle I*
>
> Who rushes oversea will find
> The climate changed but not his mind.

Like the great majority of those who succeeded in leaving Hitler-dominated countries in time, during the first years we were not able to maintain the standard of life we were accustomed to. However, it took us almost no time to adjust to the different pattern of life. In fact, it appeared to us an almost negligible inconvenience, far outweighed by the luck we were blessed with—every single member of our family was able to leave

Hitler's part of Europe. Furthermore, my strong desire to continue my educational and scientific activities was fulfilled by my appointment to New York University and the opportunities given to me by the Marine Biological Laboratories at Woods Hole and the many other institutions where I gave lectures or addresses.

It was good luck indeed that I got an appointment in New York. At no other place in the world could I have met and become acquainted with so many outstanding biologists from all over the world and other renowned people. It is a truism to say how much more complete our picture of people we know only through their achievements becomes when we meet them, even if only once. New York, furthermore, excels by having a peculiarly stimulating climate—meant, of course, only figuratively—which appears to be the source of permanent, quick progress in every respect. During the relatively short time I have lived here, I have been privileged to experience a spiritual growth of this city which manifests itself in all spheres of cultural life. For instance, there has been a tremendous increase in musical activities and a remarkable deepening of understanding on the part of the people. And I have observed the overwhelming response of young and old to the admirable opportunities offered to them in the museums. These examples could, of course, be multiplied indefinitely.

Until the Hitler catastrophe, I felt perfectly happy during the almost thirty years I spent in Graz. In fact, everything I needed or desired for my scientific and educational activities, including enough excellent co-workers, as well as a fairly large, interested audience, was there. Because of the age limit, even under normal political conditions I would have been obliged to metamorphose from an active to a retired professor. As such, one frequently is invited or allowed to stay as a permanent guest in a corner of an institute. It is quite understandable that, as a rule, the retired professor becomes to his host just as welcome as the mother-in-law to a young married couple. Anyway, my curiosity and receptivity so far have not diminished. Therefore, I am happy and deeply grateful to the fate that transported me to this country, my new homeland, and to this unique city, where I continue to enjoy the stimulating, almost rejuvenating influence in new friendships and the wealth of new impressions and experiences.

ESMOND R. LONG, M.D.

A Pathologist's Recollections of the Control of Tuberculosis

The last fifty years have seen great changes in the prognosis and treatment of pulmonary tuberculosis, once the most widely fatal of all human ailments, a disease that has cost the world heavily in lives and health, expense of prolonged medical care, and personal and family sacrifice. The story of the decline in tuberculosis is colorful and dramatic and fortunately has been put on record in many accounts that are inspiring as well as informative.

My own interest in the disease has covered all of that half-century. I have spent a large part of my life on matters related to it in one way or another, not the least of which was some personal experience with it as a patient. In the light of all that has happened since, I can only count that experience as an event of great good fortune.

Initiation in Tuberculosis

My first knowledge that I had tuberculosis came on a summer afternoon when I suddenly coughed up several mouthfuls of blood while playing a desultory game of tennis on a University of Chicago tennis court. The shock settled a growing problem. I was a second-year medical student and candidate for the Ph.D. degree in pathology. I enjoyed my work and was ambitious to learn, with good example all around me, but for some hitherto unexplainable reason was profoundly and increasingly tired all the time. Never since have I been so weary. That I was playing tennis when the break came may seem absurd, but in 1913 exercise was a first line of ther-

Dr. Long conquered tuberculosis first in himself, as a patient. Then, as a physician, organizer, and administrator, he was one of the most important figures in the forces of medical science which only recently, within living memory, conquered the enigma of the disease and reduced it to the dimensions of a preventable problem. In retirement as Professor Emeritus of Pathology, University of Pennsylvania, Director of its Henry Phipps Institute, and Director of Medical Research of the National Tuberculosis Association, Dr. Long continues his scientific activities from Pedlar Mills, Virginia.

apy for many vague ailments, and I was too fond of sport not to give it all the trial I could. I did worse things before I was through.

Education in Chicago

How I came to be there at all can be told fairly simply in retrospect. I had majored in chemistry at the University of Chicago, with an indefinite expectation of becoming a chemist, relying on chance and developing interests to determine what kind. My selection of chemistry was natural. My father was professor of physiological chemistry at Northwestern University Medical School, and I had spent many hours taking the equivalent of freshman chemistry under his instruction. He was intimately acquainted with Julius Stieglitz, John Ulric Nef, and others under whom I studied later at Chicago. Stieglitz in turn was a close friend of H. Gideon Wells, of the department of pathology at the university's medical school, who happened to be in need of a chemical assistant about the time I graduated from the university. Stieglitz recommended me, Wells stirred my enthusiasm in explaining the work, and I accepted happily. The post was humble but of great potential opportunity.

Before recounting how I spent the first two years of an ultimately long and cherished association with Gideon Wells, I should say something about the background of the limited attainments I brought to the position. I was born in Chicago in 1890 and grew up in a suburb, Auburn Park, which my parents hoped would become a progressive one in the fast-growing city. It failed to do so at the time but had other advantages. My mother, with a deep interest in cultural resources, started me on literature and languages at an early date with home tutoring and my father kept the ideal of a life of science in front of me all the time. There was a fair grammar school nearby, with an excellent teacher in the formative eighth grade, to whom I am lastingly indebted. Best of all at the time, we were not far from the Morgan Park Academy, a secondary school of the University of Chicago, in which instruction was excellent. I was deeply influenced there by my teachers in English and Latin and, indeed, for a time I thought I would be a Latin teacher. I was thoroughly disabused of that notion, however, when I took an undistinguished part in a gathering of student representatives from regional schools in a large one-day competitive examination.

I entered the University of Chicago in 1907, developed an abiding interest in history, and ultimately majored in chemistry. I undertook some athletics while in college, specializing, of all things, in the mile run—about as unsuitable an event for a prospective tuberculosis patient as could be imagined. Indeed, better medical attention at the time would have disclosed that I was already tuberculous, for I had long periods of cough and a few small pulmonary hemorrhages over a period of two years while a member of the university's track team. On the day when the real break came, at the end of my first two years of exacting graduate work with Wells, I went back to the laboratory in the evening, stained my own sputum, and found it full of tubercle bacilli.

While the course with Gideon Wells was thus startlingly broken, it ultimately proved of lasting value. In those two years I had assisted him on his own problems in chemical pathology, the field in which he was the acknowledged American leader, had worked on several problems he assigned me in the field of purine metabolism, which were to serve as the basis for my Ph.D. thesis, and had taken a substantial portion of the first two of the prescribed years of the medical course—much of it, to be sure, backward, studying pathology before anatomy, and unfortunately omitting some useful disciplines entirely, which I miss to this day. But I was maturing under the sunny mentorship and genial approach to scientific problems characteristic of Wells and growing up in all ways except in health. We worked twelve hours a day in the laboratory and classroom—Wells himself more than the rest of his staff—in crowded quarters at which students in the modern medical school palaces would be shocked, and much of the time in a sultry atmosphere of Kjeldahl fumes.

Climatic Therapy in the Southwest

When the catastrophe came, I found nobody had more friends. Advice flowed in from all sides, with suggestions ranging from Wells's sensible one that I go to the tuberculosis center at Saranac Lake to that of F. Robert Zeit, professor of pathology at Northwestern University, who looked at my sputum and said if it were his he would be on the way to Arizona that afternoon. As a matter of fact, that is where I did go later, but only after several moves and missteps. The advice that prevailed was given by Walter S. ("Daddy") Haines, toxicologist, life-long invalid himself, friend of my father, and very close associate of Norman Bridge, Rush Medical College internist who had broken down with tuberculosis in Chicago, migrated to California, and gained health there and a substantial fortune besides.

This was in the most romantic period of tuberculosis history, when sufferers were sent to enchanting climates to rest and play outdoors without being required or expected to take any annoying specific treatment. I had a near-disastrous prolonged pulmonary hemorrhage on the way out—brought on by a lengthy horseback ride at a mountain resort where I broke the journey for several days—but arrived in Los Angeles in seemingly good condition. There Dr. Bridge put me in the hands of a capable ex-tuberculous physician, Frederick Speik, who started me on a rather elastic rest regimen and gave me my first lessons in tuberculosis as a medical science. Fortunately or unfortunately—it had both aspects—I grew exceedingly restless and after a few months persuaded him to let me go to work in a unique institution in Arizona, a state with a supposedly even more salubrious climate for sufferers from tuberculosis than California's. Through my father's interest I had received an invitation to act as assistant in Tucson to Daniel T. MacDougal, the director of the desert laboratory of the Carnegie Institution of Washington, with special responsibilities as chemical assistant to the laboratory's expert investigator of photosynthesis, Herman A. Spoehr.

Here began a period as influential as any I ever spent. Every emphasis was on science for its own sake, and the major effort was to understand environment rather than control it. The place, under MacDougal, a jovial director, was bursting with enthusiasm, and studies were in course all the way from the laboratory itself to deserts as distant as Australia. I had had no training whatever in plant physiology, but from many long hours of discussion in the laboratory I acquired some elements of knowledge of the subject. MacDougal and Spoehr gave me problems of my own, and before I left I published several papers on the water balance and metabolism of desert plants. I learned to love the desert and felt perfectly in tune with it, with my own tent on the desert floor. This, I should say, was *the* period of emphasis on outdoor dry air for victims of tuberculosis.

But from the standpoint of health, it proved to be one more mistake. The long summer heat was oppressive and my activity was far too great. In the later months I had repeated small pulmonary hemorrhages. This was a complication not considered of much moment by the hundreds of tuberculous residents in southern Arizona in 1914, but in the face of all too evident simultaneous failing strength, it was a clear indication that the time had come for me to give up.

The Rest Cure

During those months a cousin of my father, Dr. John Crooks, practicing physician in Seattle, had berated me for putting climate so high and rest so low in my therapeutic regimen, holding out the promise of getting me on my feet in time, with some assurance of future safety, if I would abandon the idea of work and resign myself to complete rest. I left Tucson at low ebb in health in March, 1915, and a few days later began a regimen of total rest in a little open-air cottage in Seattle under the medical care of Dr. Crooks and the nursing care of his sister, Mrs. Helen Wren. I spent more than a year in bed, gaining weight, which was considered good, but with little change in physical signs for several months. The big glass X-ray plates of the period showed bilateral pulmonary infiltration, poorly defined in detail, however. In those days the photographic emulsions did not bring out the contrasts as do modern films. Ultimately the physical signs, on which more reliance was placed, cleared up to some extent—they have never disappeared entirely—and I was permitted gradual exercise that restored my strength. My sputum, which had been positive for tubercle bacilli on my arrival, became negative. Looking back, I am convinced that the prolonged inaction arrested the disease. About the role of the heavy feeding schedule that was an integral part of the regimen, I am not so sure. Four quarts of milk a day and sometimes a dozen eggs, with three regular meals besides, was standard. I put on some forty pounds. In the light of the teachings of half a century later, I shudder to think of the cholesterol bath in which my arteries must have soaked then.

The time itself was not unproductive. I read as never before and kept up a continuous correspondence with Gideon Wells, who supplied me with scientific papers. He had not given up the idea of sending me to Saranac Lake. When on my feet again I set up a little laboratory on the grounds, made autogenous vaccines for local doctors—some of which worked astonishingly well—and with a few bacterial cultures kindly furnished by the bacteriologist of the University of Washington, John Weinzirl, began a type of experimentation that I followed for some years thereafter. I had been much impressed at Chicago by the remarkable nutritional and immunological relationships of proteins with and without certain amino acids in their makeup, as worked out by Wells and the Yale chemist Thomas B. Osborne. I set up a program of bacterial cultures on pure proteins deficient in certain amino acids which showed quite clearly that some of these acids were necessary for some bacteria while other germs were less selective. It was heartening to be at work again, even on the modest scale of a six- by four-foot workroom. After years of absence I returned to Chicago, where arrangements were made through Wells for me to work at Saranac Lake, then the fountainhead of tuberculosis research in the country.

Saranac Lake in 1918

My long-deferred residence there began on sub-zero New Year's Day of 1918. I had a subsistence allowance from a special fund in the Trudeau Foundation and was under the direct tutelage of the phthisiologist Edward R. Baldwin, America's leading investigator of tuberculosis immunology. Baldwin had been inspired and taught by Edward L. Trudeau and each had deeply influenced Allen K. Krause. In preparation for my work I read practically everything these three had written, but in the long run it was Krause who influenced me the most. A former patient at Saranac Lake, when his disease was arrested he had taken a full-time position as director of the Kenneth Dows Tuberculosis Research Fund at the Johns Hopkins Medical School. At the same time he was editor of the *American Review of Tuberculosis*, active in research plans in the National Tuberculosis Association, and a frequent visitor at Saranac Lake. He had an encyclopedic mind and rare talent as teacher, speaker, and writer. An accomplished essayist with a remarkable medical-historical background and a gift for both popular and technical presentation, he soon held a dominant and authoritative position in tuberculosis research. He was influenced by Paul Roemer of Marburg even more than by Trudeau and Baldwin. Krause was responsible to a greater extent than any other man in the United States for the concepts of allergy, tuberculin sensitiveness, and immunity that governed American thinking in the pre-chemotherapy days. Tragically, within a few years his brilliant mind burned itself up, but his influence has persisted even among those who scarcely know his name. Weaknesses in his chain of reasoning were shown by his colleague at the Johns Hopkins Medical School, the able pathologist Arnold R. Rich, and in time the sharp distinction on which Krause had built so much—between mere tuberculous infection, supposedly acquired by everyone, and tuberculous disease, rare but dangerous—fell to the ground. However, his papers will long repay careful reading.

My own work began on a much lower level with simple attempts to work out in practice, with the good facilities of the Saranac Laboratory, some of the ideas I had developed in my primitive laboratory in Seattle. The way in which the tubercle bacillus abstracted nourishment from the surrounding medium and grew and multiplied seemed a good place to begin. Only a few people in America had bothered at all with this field of research up to that time, and I was soon in possession of new facts on the manner in which the bacillus converted complex proteins into simple substances for its own use and chose or discarded other elements from the abundant surplus around it. More or less fumblingly I was opening up a new field in this country, the importance of which was recognized two years later in the form of a substantial grant for further studies from the Medical Research Committee of the National Tuberculosis Association, a small group composed of Krause, Paul A. Lewis, of the Henry Phipps Institute in Philadelphia, and William Charles White, of the Tuberculosis League of Pittsburgh.

While at Saranac Lake I acquired some clinical experience. Baldwin accorded me considerable responsibility as an untitled and quite untrained resident at the Reception Hospital, a twenty-bed institution for advanced cases. Here I gave pneumothorax refills, fluoroscoped patients periodically with a rickety, old-fashioned X-ray apparatus, did the laboratory work, and in general learned much about the ravages of tuberculosis in patients who had passed the point of likelihood of cure. From time to time I attended conferences at the nearby Trudeau Sanatorium, where I was privileged in making close acquaintance with its leaders, the dean of clinicians Lawrason Brown, his associate Fred Heise, the pathologist LeRoy U. Gardner, and the self-trained, accomplished bacteriologist S. A. Petroff.

During the Saranac Lake period I began a connection with the National Tuberculosis Association that was to prove life-long. With others of the laboratory and sanatorium staffs, I attended the Boston meeting of the association that spring of 1918 and listened with imperfect understanding to papers on tuberculosis by the country's leaders. It was war time, and there was much discussion of the military significance of the disease. The principal authority and ranking officer on all such matters was Colonel George E. Bushnell, chief of the tuberculosis program in the Office of the Surgeon General of the army. He was particularly noted for his views on the dangers of tuberculosis as a primary infection in adult life and recognized for his broad knowledge of the epidemiology of the disease. All present listened to him with deep respect, I among them. If anyone could have told me that twenty-five years later I would be in his place in a larger army in another world war, I would have thought it utterly fantastic.

Two great events passed over the tuberculous patients in Saranac Lake with a relatively light touch that year. One was the war. We read the news avidly and, if we arose early enough, as few did, saw the drafted recruits selected from the able-bodied residents of town march to the morning train. As physical rejectees, we were outside the main current. The other event was the devastating influenza epidemic of the fall of 1918. Many of us were sick, some severely so, but the established routine of the community sent us to bed early in our individual attacks. Few deaths occurred among tuberculosis patients, but many among those who took care of us, from our mailman to the working staffs of the nursing cottages. We realized that we were a highly favored group, sheltered at the expense of those whose responsibilities made it requisite to stay on the job. Elsewhere in the country, where the advantages of Saranac Lake were not at hand, the epidemic took heavy toll among tuberculosis patients, with a conspicuous reverse effect on a previously declining mortality curve.

My year at Saranac Lake gave me essential training and new incentive. I returned to my old place at Chicago in January, 1919, as assistant in the department of pathology, on a light schedule of laboratory instruction, with half the day for rest and study for my Ph.D. examination, which I took that spring under Ludvig Hektoen. Gideon Wells, my real chief, was abroad as Red Cross Commissioner to Romania. The hours allowed for rest during those months, with more the following summer, insured against relapse, which was all too frequent among tuberculosis patients returning to work in those days, long before the advent of chemotherapy. One can never tell what would have happened, but I have always counted it as singularly fortunate that I could return to full-time labor gradually. I had run the course of the treatments of the day for tuberculosis, with full measure of climate, dry air, exercise, prolonged rest, superalimentation, and light work under supervision. I had missed only the one most esteemed of all at the time, pneumothorax, but I had administered plenty of that and so had a good background on the nature and treatment of tuberculosis, which, with youthful optimism, I now proposed to study.

Training as a Pathologist; Early Research

The years with Wells were continuously happy. He seldom directed but rather was solicitous always to discover new interests and new opportunity for his assistants. The fact that I had not yet graduated in medicine bothered him little in assigning me responsibility. We had a heavy teaching schedule in pathology and a thorough grounding in post mortem study at the Cook County Hospital. Wells, best known through his writings as a chemical pathologist, was also highly proficient at the autopsy table. No stickler for anatomical technique and never lost in anatomical detail, he was skilled in noting relations and in quick deduction and explanation. He conducted a superb course in microscopic pathology that taught the rest of us a great deal.

All this time I made some progress with research on the chemistry and metabolism of the tubercle bacillus, specializing first on its general nutrition. Wells himself was much interested in the chemistry of the whole subject of tuberculosis and especially in its chemotherapy. The Otho S. A. Sprague Memorial Institute, of which he was director, was an associated research organization in his department which gave him resources for special studies. Lydia M. DeWitt, a member of the Sprague staff, was assigned to the full-time task of investigating the treatment of tuberculosis by synthetic dye-metal combinations, modeled after Paul Ehrlich's successful development of salvarsan for syphilis.

In 1922, under Wells's inspiration, the three of us collaborated in writing a book, *The Chemistry of Tuberculosis*, which included material on chemical changes in the disease itself, its experimental drug therapy, and the chemistry and metabolism of the tubercle bacillus. The book has now gone through three editions, the third stressing chemotherapy more than its predecessors. For many years research on the drug treatment of tuberculosis led only to discouragement. The two major centers of early work in America, Wells's department at Chicago and one under Paul Lewis at the Phipps Institute in Philadelphia, met nothing but failure. However, a significant prophecy was placed on the record by Wells in the second edition of our book in 1933: "Since 1922 we have come to recognize more and more that chemotherapy in the sense in which Ehrlich introduced the term is more of a dream than a reality. A specific chemotherapy of tuberculosis has not been found, and may be a long time in coming because of inherent difficulties in the problem, but it is not a closed chapter. Probably success with some other bacterial infection will stimulate a new attack on the more difficult problem offered by tuberculosis." Twenty-five years later, and fifteen years after Wells's death, I had the privilege of bringing out a third edition with an expanded section on chemotherapy and long and detailed chapters on the highly effective drugs discovered between 1943 and 1952, streptomycin and isoniazid.

While teaching second-year pathology and carrying out as much research as possible on the tubercle bacillus, I was struggling to finish medical school, utilizing the summer periods, which were normally vacation breaks in those days when academic schedules still allowed for long vacations. But the summers in Chicago were hot, humid, and, for me at least, with my long background of ill health, highly debilitating. To escape this unfavorable influence, I registered for my summer vacation period in 1921 at the Stanford University Medical School, which, like Chicago, used the quarter system. Here I began my clinical work with classes in the Lane Hospital. It was a propitious move. The San Francisco climate was highly agreeable. I had several good teachers, notably T. Addis in medicine. He was a dedicated investigator of renal disease and at the time engaged in a controversy with L. H. Newburgh of Michigan, who believed that high protein diets disposed to clinical nephritis. Addis had his students on low-water, high-protein diets most of the summer. We proved none the worse for the experience and learned much of the ideals of medical research as well as its trials.

That summer of 1921 was a memorable one. I took a refreshing holiday after the Stanford quarter and climbed in the High Sierras, discovering with great joy that my old strength and energy had returned. As I made my way down the rough slopes of Mt. Tallac one evening I realized that I was through with tuberculosis as a patient. After all my mistakes and setbacks I had finished the job.

My cup then filled and ran over. In Denver, on the way back, I renewed acquaintance with Marian Boak Adams, a distant relative—we shared great, great grandparents who had migrated from England to America—and my life gained complete new meaning. The succeeding months, with heightened efforts in study, teaching, and research, and above all new plans, were crowded ones. We were married the following June and sailed immediately for Europe. Our destination was Prague, where I had arranged to study in the German university of that city with the pathological anatomist Anton Ghon, whose name is still associated with a characteristic lesion of healed childhood tuberculosis, the "Ghon nodule." We saw much of Germany enroute in those days of low prices, but also the sadly straitened circumstances of the aftermath of World War I.

Prague in 1922

Under Ghon, I was introduced to precise methods of dissection such as I had never known before. I made a dismal first appearance but was fortunate to become acquainted soon with two experts who gave me personal instruction—Kornel Terplan, assistant in the Pathological Institute and now professor of pathology at the University of Buffalo, and Béla Halpert, a Hungarian anatomist then a voluntary assistant in Prague like myself and now chief pathologist of the Veterans Administration Hospital in Houston and professor of pathology at Baylor University. I soon acquired some of their skill. The opportunity for study was great. Ghon assigned all the tuberculosis autopsies that summer to me and kept me busy searching in each case for the primary tubercle amidst the massive lesions of terminal disease. It was excellent training in a positive sense because of the basic prevalent view—all too true in the crowded sections of the great cities—that adult tuberculosis was reinfection tuberculosis, with anatomical characters determined by immunological factors stemming from an original primary infection in childhood; in brief, by the allergy set up by the first infection, a concept in which I was well grounded already after my studies with Baldwin and Krause. In a negative way the training was equally valuable, creating a reservoir of recollections to be held in reserve for later years in America, years of rapidly declining tuberculosis rates, when the disease in young adults was no longer always a reinfection but more frequently a primary one. The time of first infection is one of the basic differences between progressive pulmonary tuberculosis as I knew it as a patient and student and as it is today. Actually, the difference in anatomical character of the disease in young adults in the two forms is not so great as would have been predicted on the basis of earlier views about the predetermining effect of allergy. It is still a matter for study, however.

Before I left Prague for return to the States, Halpert and I toured pathological institutes of central Europe, observing with critical eyes what seemed to us inferior work after our months with the master Ghon. I was privileged with Ghon's friendship from then on, visited him on later trips, translated some of his work for publication in America, and kept in touch with him until his death from tuberculosis in 1936.

Studies on Tuberculosis at the University of Chicago

Back in Chicago with the new year of 1923, after spending final weeks of our European trip in Italy and Paris, Marian and I settled near the University of Chicago. I had much time to make up, for the university had granted me salary and time off in advance. The schedule in the department of pathology was much as before, and now I entered solidly on a line of research that had long been shaping up: the nature of the active principle of tuberculin. It seemed inevitable to me that this remarkable product of growth of tubercle bacilli in the laboratory, which in minute amount elicits a sharp inflammatory reaction in those infected with tuberculosis, must play an important role as an allergen in the disease itself, since it is presumably discharged constantly into the tissues of the host as a product of metabolism of the bacillus in the body. I discovered that it caused its intense inflammatory response in other organs than the skin—e.g., the lungs and kidneys—and induced a reaction of exceptional severity in the testis of tuberculous animals. The response to tiny amounts of tuberculin was so devasting to the organ and so destructive primarily to a specific cell, the spermatocyte, that the reaction appeared to be of basic significance. I used it frequently from then on and even brought out a "spermatocyte test" for the standardization of tuberculin but, delicate as it was, the test proved too cumbersome for routine use. Unfortunately I was never able to go on to study more subtle effects of the damage to chromosomal structures, still worth investigating in these days of revealing genetics. I learned only that regeneration did occur.

At the same time I commenced studies on the chemical composition of the active principle. I was exceptionally fortunate, for Wells assigned to the work a young assistant, Florence Seibert, who had come to the Sprague Institute through the interest of Wells's own former teacher at the Sheffield Scientific School of Yale University, Lafayette B. Mendel. Together we worked out several advances showing that the active principle was of protein nature, as had long been suspected but never proved. Dr. Seibert soon took on the major chemical studies of our joint enterprise and in the succeeding years became the leading student in the United

States in this field. She crystallized the active protein principle and in later years, after training under Svedberg, Pedersen, and Tiselius in Uppsala, made exhaustive electrophoretic studies of the substance and the changes to which it is subject under laboratory conditions.

This was only one phase of our research at the time, however. I became deeply interested in other fields in the experimental pathology of tuberculosis, particularly in cellular reactions to tubercle bacilli in fresh infections of previously normal animals and in animals sensitized and partially immunized by previous infection. In these studies I had the assistance of some of my Ph.D. students, particularly Sion Holley, who later went into hospital pathology, and Arthur J. Vorwald, who is now professor of industrial medicine and hygiene at the College of Medicine of Wayne University in Detroit. We studied cellular reactions in the testis, the cornea of the eye, and other organs with great profit. In the immunized animals we were engaged essentially in investigating cellular reactions to tuberculin that was itself attached to the cell-stimulating lipids of the bacillus. The latter were the major elements in reactions well studied later by Florence Sabin, C. A. Doan, and their associates in correlated work at the Rockefeller Institute—tied up, like mine, with the National Tuberculosis Association research program. These pieces of research led to honor for both Dr. Sabin and me in the course of time in the award of the association's Trudeau Medal.

Interest in Medical History

During these years my close connection with the Tuberculosis Association had carried me into a quite different line of work—semipopular writing and speaking on the whole subject of tuberculosis research. The National Tuberculosis Association had 2,500 affiliates in the different states, counties, and cities. In the course of forty years I have spoken to a great many of these. The association had its own popular magazine in its earlier days, the *Journal of the Outdoor Life;* I became editor-in-chief and wrote several series of articles with enthusiasm and also a facility of expression that has not held up in later years.

Somewhat as an outgrowth of the research involved in these articles, and again under the heartening stimulation of Gideon Wells, I entered upon another line of effort, which has since become one of my principal activities and sources of satisfaction—studying and writing medical history, specifically, the history of pathology and tuberculosis.

This is perhaps the place to say that my contributions to advance in knowledge of pathology outside the field of tuberculosis have been few. Such as I have made were the products of chance encounters at the autopsy table, including reports on highly acute meningitis, a number of tumors of special interest, vascular lesions of the abdomen, and a fair number of congenital anomalies seen in a large service in obstetrical hospitals associated with the University of Chicago. In much of this work I was associated with Paul R. Cannon, a lifelong friend, who ultimately succeeded Wells as head of the department of pathology at Chicago. Outside the University of Chicago the man who stimulated me the most was Howard T. Karsner, professor of pathology at Western Reserve University and now advisor in medical research to the United States Navy. He guided much of the organization of pathology in this country and inspired many students.

I taught some of the background of pathology regularly in the course of classroom instruction and finally, at Wells's suggestion, wrote a *History of Pathology*, which has had some use in medical schools throughout the country. It was supplemented by a collection of extracts from classics in the field which I brought out as *Selected Readings in Pathology*. This has had a gratifying reception and is now in a new and enlarged edition. I have held the conviction over the years that medical students, not to mention their teachers, should be thoroughly informed on the achievements of the past if they are to have any perspective on accomplishments of the present. Indeed, the distinction between past and present is shadowy, and it seems inescapable that all investigators should hold a reserved view of current research and avoid the indulgent retrospect sometimes accorded the labors and concepts of what is often viewed as the benighted past.

A commercial activity with some academic aspects might be mentioned. For years I served as editor in medicine for *Webster's International Dictionary*, defining or approving definitions of about fifteen thousand words, an exercise that required some background in etymology, which fortunately I had, and which in turn promoted a precision of expression that I would have done well to retain. Also to be mentioned here is the fact that belatedly along the line, in the midst of all these activities, I completed the requirements for my long-deferred M.D. degree.

I have always been glad that I was graduated from the Rush Medical College rather than from the modern, far better equipped, well-designed medical school of the University of Chicago on the south side. Training at Rush, by that time a perfectly appointed academic institution with its university affiliation, still carried the flavor of the great days of proprietary schools, a phase in American medical education not to be disparaged in the pride of present-day medical education. Rush had been one of the best of the proprietary schools. Some of the amenities, and not a little of the old time harshness, were still there. As late as 1920 at least two of the professors donned frock coats for their lectures. In a course like materia medica everything depended on memory, and woe to him whose memory was faulty. Brilliant teachers, of course, bridged the gap. The greatest of these in my time was James B. Herrick, to whom I owe much for my concepts of internal medicine.

The Henry Phipps Institute

During these years of tuberculosis research I had come to know the Henry Phipps Institute of Philadelphia well. Eugene L. Opie, one of America's leading pathologists and most noted investigators of pathological, immunological, and epidemiological problems in tuberculosis, who had succeeded Paul Lewis as its director of laboratories and research, was resigning to become head of the department of pathology at the large and rapidly developing Cornell University Medical College. In 1932 the University of Pennsylvania invited me to become director of the laboratories of the Phipps Institute in his place, in association with the eminent chest clinician Henry Robert Murray Landis, director of the institute's clinic, and Charles James Hatfield, executive director of the institute. By this time it was clear that I was not going further with general pathology, although I maintained the closest relations with pathologists and the American Association of Pathologists and Bacteriologists. It was certain, too, that such research as I might be able to accomplish in the future would be in the field of tuberculosis. The close co-ordination of the work of the Phipps Institute with that of the National Tuberculosis Association, which supported my research in appreciable measure and with which I was at all times in close connection, made the venture seem a natural one. My chief and mentor in all professional problems, Gideon Wells, had long been a friend of the Phipps Institute and proved cordial to the move, feeling that it afforded opportunity for the promotion of research on tuberculosis on a larger scale. The position carried with it a professorship of pathology in the University of Pennsylvania with opportunity for as much teaching as I desired and a pathology service at the Philadelphia General Hospital.

Thus, in the summer of 1932 I began my longest academic tenure. The Phipps Institute, founded by the philanthropist Henry Phipps, a partner of Andrew Carnegie, and the Philadelphia physician and health crusader Lawrence Flick, had become in 1910 an integral part of the University of Pennsylvania. It made a distinguished record in the study of environmental factors and racial differences in tuberculosis, experimental pathology, and methods of prevention of the disease under Flick, Lewis, Landis, Opie, the public health nurse Fannie Eshleman, and their numerous associates. It had become a place of widely recognized value for the training of tuberculosis workers in diverse fields and for public health physicians and nurses. It was a center affording at the same time an academic environment and a prominent place in the day-to-day practical fight against tuberculosis. Its thousands of clinical case records were priceless for the study of tuberculosis as a medical and social problem.

Florence Seibert and our technical assistants made the move with me. We went ahead rapidly with our tuberculin studies, fortified now by a new alliance with a member of the Phipps staff and the country's leader in the use of tuberculin in field epidemiological studies, Joseph D. Aronson. Tuberculin had become so highly purified in Seibert's hands that it seemed logical to set it up as a national or even international standard. The idea was enthusiastically promoted by William Charles White, chairman of the Committee on Medical Research of the National Tuberculosis Association, which supported our research. To make a long story short, after further purification of the substance by Seibert, it did become, under the name Purified Protein Derivative (PPD), the standard for the Public Health Service in this country and ultimately, in 1952, the international standard of the World Health Organization. In the 1930's, with Aronson as a member of the team, many studies were made of its value in comparison with that of other preparations—in colleges, on Indian reservations, in clinics, and elsewhere—which led to the necessary refinements and a graded system of dosages for its practical employment. In the course of several trips abroad I used the substance in many places, one of them the General Hospital of Moscow.

The association with Aronson led to further new developments. He was one of the earliest investigators in the United States to test the French tuberculosis vaccine BCG developed by A. Calmette and C. Guerin of the Pasteur Institute. James G. Townsend, of the United States Public Health Service and director of health for the Bureau of Indian Affairs, thought that BCG might be of value in attacking the grave problem of tuberculosis among American Indians and approached the Phipps Institute with a view to establishing a vaccination program. After several preliminary surveys, Aronson was set up with facilities for a large project which ultimately included Indian reservations in Arizona, New Mexico, the Dakotas, Wyoming, and Alaska. These studies lasted for more than twenty years, demonstrating a significant value in the vaccine in the unusual situations studied, where medical attendance was inadequate, mortality rates were high, and thousands of children were infected early in life.

The biweekly chest conference of the Phipps Institute and the numerous ramifications of our work in the field were slowly turning me in a small way into a clinician and epidemiologist. I was forced by the nature of the expanding work to acquire some proficiency in chest X-ray interpretation, which stood me in good stead in later years. For my instruction in this branch I was deeply indebted to H. W. Hetherington, chief of the institute's chest clinic.

Pathological studies on tuberculosis in which I was engaged during this period included investigations of the body's response in primary and superinfection, sex differences in response, nutrition and tuberculosis, tuberculosis in adolescence, and particularly the routes of transport of infection within the body. The last was an illuminating study of spread by lymphatics, blood vessels, and the larger natural channels with an assistant, Robert Faust, on a large number of cases in the autopsy service of the Philadelphia General Hospital.

In subsequent years my published papers were concerned chiefly with the procedures of tuberculosis control. In my own mind, at least, I was achieving a synthesis of the pathology of the active disease with its epidemiology. A background of understanding of the metabolic and anatomic changes it wrought seemed to give me a better basis for its demographic study.

The Wistar Institute

One other activity of this period may be noted. Through association with Alfred Stengel, vice-president in charge of medical affairs at the University of Pennsylvania, I had become a member of the board of managers of the Wistar Institute of Anatomy and Biology, of which Stengel was President. The board, which profited by the advice of a distinguished advisory committee for professional purposes, included representatives of the Wistar family, the Academy of Natural Sciences of Philadelphia, and the University of Pennsylvania. The activities of the institute were of great interest. The traditions established by H. H. Donaldson and M. J. Greenman still ruled, but their departure was keenly felt. Important studies on growth, genetics, constitution, and nutrition were under way. Stengel was an able administrator and rapidly restored the purpose and drive that had declined after Donaldson's and Greenman's deaths. Tragically, in the midst of excessive labors, Stengel himself died suddenly. By vote of the board I became president, a job for which I was unfortunately neither prepared nor fitted. The experience of the next three years was stimulating but not altogether happy. Factional differences occurred within the board and staff which I was incompetent to resolve. The family and university representatives did not agree on the promotion of trends in the institute. Harmony has long since been restored with the passing of some of the personalities concerned, but it was a real relief when the national crisis in 1942, and consequent more appropriate responsibilities for me elsewhere, enabled me to turn my Wistar responsibilities over to more competent hands. My principal contribution to the success of the institute was inducing the noted tissue culture experts Warren H. and Margaret Reed Lewis to join the staff on their retirement from the laboratories of the department of embryology of the Carnegie Institution of Washington at Johns Hopkins University.

Administrative and Extracurricular Activity

By that time, in the late 1930's, I had run out of time for any more significant laboratory research. At the specified age for retirement of administrators, Dr. Hatfield had removed himself from the executive directorship of the Phipps Institute and I had become director in his place. The management of the institute and the ever-growing demands for money to support its work kept me on edge all the time. In addition, I had reached the culmination of a large number of extracurricular endeavors with which I had been associated for years. Almost simultaneously, after long novitiates on councils, committees, and boards, I was president of the American Association of Pathologists and Bacteriologists, the National Tuberculosis Association, and the American Association for the History of Medicine. Over and above all this I was also, for three years of that time, chairman of the Division of Medical Sciences of the National Research Council, nothing like so large a job then as it is now, but one that was expanding in the gathering shadows of World War II. The associations in the Research Council were invaluable—with the current and recent chairmen of the council, Ludvig Hektoen and W. H. Howell, and with the hard working committee chairmen in the Division of Medical Sciences, particularly Robert M. Yerkes of the committee for research on problems of sex, Walter B. Cannon, chairman of the committee on endocrinology, and Francis G. Blake, chairman of the division's fellowship board.

Tuberculosis in World War II

In late 1941 all was changed by the entrance of the United States into World War II. Even before that certain needs were evident. Special skills were in demand. The Division of Medical Sciences of the National Research Council was called upon to formulate physical standards for recruits. I became actively engaged in a committee which wrote the standards to exclude active or potential tuberculosis. It included J. B. Amberson, Bruce Douglas, H. R. Edwards, P. P. McCain, J. A. Myers, and J. J. Waring, almost all of them previous presidents of the National Tuberculosis Association. This disease had been a problem of great magnitude in World War I, and the Veterans Administration, set up after the war, had been left with a huge legacy of cases for treatment and compensation. In the early months of mobilization for World War II the same dangers were apparent. The Medical Corps of the army, faced with the induction of eight million men, soon felt the need of an officer for tuberculosis control. Colonel, later Brigadier General, C. C. Hillman, chief of the Professional Service Division of the Surgeon General's office, invited me to try to qualify under the fairly rigid standards we were ourselves setting up. With a certain amount of generous ignoring of my past history, the Officers' Examining Center at Walter Reed General Hospital passed me, and I entered Colonel Hillman's office as consultant on tuberculosis with the rank of lieutenant colonel. In the succeeding months of 1942 and 1943 I visited each of the 95 recruiting and induction stations in the United States that were operating in co-ordination with the selective service system, overseeing the examinations for tuberculosis and passing on problems that pushed my meager clinical experience to the limit. I was accorded an able assistant, William H. Stearns, to cover my protracted absences from Washington. In those days of an expanding medical corps, we were soon promoted, with corresponding increase in the prestige of our office. There is little doubt that our efforts did tighten the control exercised over induction of potential cases. Mistakes were made, but the rate of development of disease from overlooked lesions, though not negligible, was far below that prevailing in any previous period.

My duties soon extended beyond tuberculosis. Even in the induction station inspection, carried out under the aegis of the Service Commands, I was soon concerned with the entire examining process. This seemed to me of the utmost importance, but Medical Corps officers in general looked upon it as a thankless task, vastly less interesting than hospital appointment or field service with troops. I accumulated other responsibilities and in time was deputy chief of the Professional Service Division of the Office of the Surgeon General under Colonel Arden Freer, who succeeded General Hillman when the latter moved to the command of Letterman General Hospital.

In the final months of the war, when American soldier prisoners were being recovered in large numbers, many with tuberculosis, and large Nazi labor and concentration camps were being overrun by our troops, I served overseas in Italy, France, and Germany. The United States army hospitals of eastern France in the overrun areas met a tuberculosis problem unique in military medical history. I had an opportunity to back up the work of Colonel Theodore L. Badger, consultant on tuberculosis in the European Theater, who had introduced modern prophylaxis in the midst of an exposure to massive contagion that might have gotten out of hand. I spent some time with Military Government in Germany after the war, my responsibilities suddenly and strangely changing to maximum preoccupation with the care and prevention of tuberculosis in the population of disrupted Germany.

Finally, back in the United States, I held responsibilities in the separation centers comparable to those of the earlier years of the war in induction stations. The separation centers discovered a good many cases of early tuberculosis of doubtful clinical significance and good prognosis that required some care. We set up a third tuberculosis hospital unit in Swannanoa, North Carolina, which I visited from time to time. Prior to that I had had abundant experience in our two major tuberculosis hospital units, at Fitzsimons General Hospital in Denver and Bruns General Hospital in Sante Fe.

Tuberculosis Therapy with Artificial Pneumothorax

The principal treatment for tuberculosis up to the middle 1940's, in our armed forces as elsewhere, was artificial pneumothorax. It seems strange today, less than twenty years later, that so much value was attributed to the procedure. It appeared logical enough at the time, however, and was held in almost as much repute as chemotherapy today. Used at first only in "selected cases," as was chemotherapy in its initial period at a later date, it was soon employed in practically all cases, just as drug treatment is today. The justification was far less, however. The dangers of isoniazid therapy today are slight. The hazards of pneumothorax were constantly before us. Although the Phipps Institute administered the treatment routinely on an outpatient basis in its chest clinic, some of the best papers by the staff were on its complications and dangers. In spite of these, it remained the universal first line of attack. I remember vividly a huge campaign in the progressive health department of Detroit, designed to find all the unknown cases and get them under pneumothorax treatment promptly. The supposed success of the therapy interfered with my own efforts to stimulate research. Once, when I tried to induce a financially well fortified state affiliate of the National Tuberculosis Association to provide more funds for research, the executive director blandly countered, "Do you really need the money? Isn't it true that with mass X-ray surveys to find the cases and pneumothorax for their treatment we have all the weapons we need?"

Some years later Godias Drolet and associates in the New York Tuberculosis and Health Association showed by careful statistical methods that the noteworthy decline in tuberculosis mortality so impressive to us in the pneumothorax era was at a rate only approximately the same as that occurring without the treatment. The data were so startling that I have been inclined to withhold judgment on today's apparently extraordinary mass results with chemotherapy; twenty years from now a similar statistical analysis may show that other factors have been quite as important or more so. These remarks do not apply to individual cases under the best of individual medical treatment. No one would deny the superiority of modern drug treatment under such conditions, or the not infrequent good results with carefully administered pneumothorax.

Chemotherapy

After the war I had a chance to observe and take part in a development of signal importance for tuberculosis research in this country. On my return from military government duty in Germany an arrangement was effected by Major General Paul R. Hawley, formerly chief surgeon in the European Theater and subsequently chief medical director of the Veterans Administration, whereby I continued to give about half-time to the Surgeon General's office, chiefly as consultant on separation center examinations and hospital arrangements for tuberculous patients, and half-time as acting chief of the Tuberculosis Service of the Veterans Administration, with which the army tuberculosis problem was inevitably closely tied. This was a short-term arrangement. In January, 1946, we were able to secure as full-time, permanent chief of the V. A. Tuberculosis Service John B. Barnwell, tuberculosis specialist, investigator, and associate professor of internal medicine in the University of Michigan. Under Barnwell's direction began a period of medical care and research never before approached in the Veterans Administration.

The time was ripe for progress. A vital tool for therapy, streptomycin, had been discovered by the soil microbiologist S. A. Waksman and his associates at Rutgers University in 1943–44 and tested in the Mayo Clinic and Laboratories by H. Corwin Hinshaw and William H. Feldman. Early in 1947 Barnwell and his associates, with Arthur M. Walker, formerly associate professor of pharmacology at the University of Pennsylvania, in direct charge of operations, set a program in motion that soon developed into the national proving ground for streptomycin and a series of antituberculosis drugs that followed it. A group of Veterans Administration hospitals and one army and one navy hospital, with duplicate or individual projects within the total plan, participated in a closely controlled investigation of the efficacy, safety, and optimum dosage of these drugs. The annual chemotherapy conference of this group, necessarily restricted for efficiency largely to participants in the program, became one of the most important tuberculosis meetings in the country. The therapeutic value of streptomycin was rapidly demonstrated and the dangers in its indiscriminate use revealed. In 1952, with the discovery of isoniazid, a similar and much larger program for that drug was established. This co-ordinated effort led to understanding of these drugs with a speed that would have been impossible in unco-ordinated trials throughout the country. As it was, the facts uncovered in the controlled V. A. and armed forces investigations led rapidly to essentially uniform and optimum drug employment in sanatoria, hospitals, clinics, and other tuberculosis institutions everywhere.

At the same time an independent but correlated program of tuberculosis research, with special emphasis on chemotherapy, was started within the framework of the newly organized Research Grants Division of the National Institutes of Health of the United States Public Health Service. With the participation of unpaid consultants from civilian institutions, study sections for different medical disciplines were set up to pass on projects and recommend allocation of funds by the research grants organization. A tuberculosis program projected by this body made a rapid start by taking over, as its study section, the streptomycin committee of the medical division of the National Tuberculosis Association, i.e., the American Trudeau Society, following discussions with its chairmen, H. McLeod Riggins and H. C. Hinshaw. This section carried on for years with some organizational changes under the able chairmanship of Walsh McDermott, associate professor of medicine in the Cornell University Medical College, editor of the *American Review of Tuberculosis* and active participant in research projects of the National Tuberculosis Association. A series of generous grants for chemotherapeutic research were implemented, many of them for an experimental approach in contrast to the clinical studies sponsored by the Veterans Administration. There were in addition, however, well co-ordinated trials of the new drugs in hospitals, with Research Grants Division funds, under plans set up by Carroll Palmer and his associates in the tuberculosis program of the Public Health Service.

To reduce complexities in approval of projects, a small "steering committee," of which I was made chairman, struggled with some of the basic problems. The hardest of these by far was the question of ethics in "controls." Operating, as we knew we were, with potent and effective drugs but not sure how good they were and how safe, we recognized as mandatory the establishment of control measures in which results in a drug-tested group could be compared in a wholly unbiased way with results in a group without drug therapy. Denying to half our subjects what we knew to be of some value and establishing safety measures and other forms of therapy for them occupied the major part of our time. Ultimately we reached a measure of agreement in this knotty problem that left everybody at least partially satisfied, and I believe the programs of those early days are now looked upon with satisfaction and relief as well within ethical and humanitarian bounds and at the same time sound for statistical analysis.

Last Years at the Phipps Institute

My own closing years at the Henry Phipps Institute were inevitably occupied in no small way with the programs I have just described. By that time the work of the institute had wide ramifications. The closest ties outside of the University of Pennsylvania were with the National Tuberculosis Association under its successive managing directors Kendall Emerson and James E. Perkins. Much of our work at the institute had support from the national association, particularly that of Max B. Lurie on inherited constitutional factors in resistance to tuberculosis and of Florence B. Seibert on the chemistry of tuberculin and immunology of the disease. Each had support also from the Research Grants Division of the Public Health Service, as did Joseph D. Aronson, for a variety of studies on mycobacteria.

In 1947, under appropriate arrangements made by the association and the university's vice-president in charge of medical affairs, Alfred N. Richards, I went on half-time service with the National Tuberculosis Association as its director of medical research, succeeding to responsibilities well developed over twenty-five years by William Charles White and by H. S. Willis in an interim period after the war. This simply doubled my duties, since those at the Phipps Institute remained essentially as before. Fortunately the National Tuberculosis Association supplied me with a highly competent medical research secretary, Virginia Cameron, under whom the details of our organization, concerned largely with grants-in-aid of research and fellowships for tuberculosis training, progressed smoothly. Our efforts were greatly assisted by Floyd Feldmann, medical director, and Agnes Fahy, in charge of research aspects of public relations, in the N.T.A. office. In the management of the Phipps Institute itself I was saved from the harassments of executive detail by a capable administrative assistant, Jeanne B. Wagner, and the services of a personal assistant, H. J. Henderson, research associate in the institute. In research I was helped greatly by one of our clinicians, S. C. Stein.

As time went by, international relations became steadily more important in both the Phipps and N.T.A. programs. I made numerous trips to Europe and to Latin America as representative of the National Tuberculosis Association and occasionally as consultant for the army. The association took a large part in plans and projects of the International Union Against Tuberculosis. The latter organization, with the prominent Paris phthisiologist Etienne Bernard as secretary-general and W. Gellner, formerly of the World Health Organization, as executive director, developed lengthy programs for review of progress in chemotherapy. A special responsibility, and a fatiguing one, that fell upon me was an attempt to bring some sort of order in the assemblage of knowledge on progress in various fields by co-ordinating the union's several technical committees.

At the Phipps Institute my strength, no longer what it had been, was given largely to problems of organization and financing. Our endowment was far from sufficient for our needs. Most of what was outside the skeletal organization was financed through project assistance, as in medical schools throughout the country. Laboratory investigation was reasonably well supported. The clinic received generous support from the Community Chest of Philadelphia, but under a long-term arrangement of diminishing funds. The handwriting was on the wall for tuberculosis institutions. Tuberculosis was becoming a governmental problem, the prevalence of the disease was declining, and control bodies with state and national responsibility were according it less prominence in allocation of funds by setting up chronic disease programs in which tuberculosis was but a part. It was becoming apparent that organizations like the Phipps Institute would soon be anachronisms. Indeed, a few years after my retirement at the statutory age and my succession by our staff member Julius L. Wilson, the Henry Phipps Institute for the Study, Treatment and Prevention of Tuberculosis, under its present director, Dr. Theodore H. Ingalls, became the Henry Phipps Institute for Research in Community Disease—a quite typical sign of the times.

My retirement from academic tenure commenced in 1955. It has made little difference in my way of thought and less than might be expected in my activity and associations, even though most of my time is spent in a quiet mountain retreat out of traffic. During the years of administrative concern much study and writing had to be postponed. On this I am still engaged. I have little sympathy with the prevalent condemnation of academic retirement. Such a period is needed for unhurried thinking. All the old associations remain at hand. The opportunity for congenial contact in scientific societies in which I have formed attachments through the years has proved a lasting asset. Most prized are the semiannual meetings of the American Philosophical Society and the National Academy of Sciences. Closer companionship in a home of forty years of shared devotion has been a great reward, to which has been added the joy of children and grandchildren. Retirement has brought no envy or dissatisfaction, in fact quite the reverse.

The fifty years' observation of tuberculosis noted in this personal account have spanned great changes in the treatment and prevention of the disease and in its gravity as a world health problem. At the opening of the twentieth century in America, with an annual tuberculosis mortality rate of about 200 per hundred thousand population, and with some ten persons sick or endangered by an already acquired infection for every one who died, phthisis was far and away the leader among the causes of death. Treatment at the opening of the century was primitive by comparison with modern methods, and there were few places where even that could be given intelligently. With all due recognition of the fact that a vast number of patients survived, the truth remains that most of those who passed the relative security of the "minimal" stage died of the disease within a few years after its clinical outset.

Today all is changed. The annual mortality is about a fortieth of what it was then, treatment is considered one of the great achievements of modern medical science, and a hundred or more good hospitals and sanatoria, not to mention clinics and doctors' offices, administer properly controlled therapy. Standard public health procedures for prevention of the disease are in effect everywhere. The saving of life and conservation of productive capacity have been great. There is now good reason to believe that unless an international cataclysm occurs carrying modern cultivated society down with it, tuberculosis will become a rarity. There is cause for enormous gratification in what has come about, and naturally great credit is accorded to the measures that have been used in combatting the disease. These are by no means a minor item in the combined budgets of the country, costing, as they do, several hundred million dollars a year.

Unbiased analysis of the momentous decline in tuberculosis, however, yields some facts not known to everybody. From 1900 to the present day, and indeed for decades before that, tuberculosis has been steadily declining. Each of the overlapping epochs of the last sixty years has been characterized by a standard treatment, which in every instance has been viewed with satisfaction and assurance in the practice of medicine. I have personally observed the gratification of our profession in treatment successively by climate, dry air, and horseback riding; complete rest supplemented by a diet far beyond the usual caloric needs; artificial pneumothorax with a dozen accessory operations to collapse diseased lung or remove it entirely; and finally a brilliant chemotherapy that has progressed in a few strenuous years from a cautious use of streptomycin to an almost universal employment of isoniazid in cases of every kind and stage. We have reason to believe that the rate of decline in mortality has been much accelerated in the chemotherapy years, but it will take long-range perspective to analyze that part of the curve satisfactorily.

In the meantime fewer people each year will die of tuberculosis. It was once a fatal disease of youth; now it is a chronic and no longer terrifying ailment of late middle and old age. Relatively few people now are infected in the early years. The old people with tuberculosis hang on long enough to die of cardiovascular or renal disease, pulmonary emphysema, or some form of neoplasm. This is indeed a triumph for medicine, of course, and, in a less vitally important way, of great interest to pathologists.

But medicine has had much help along the way. The huge benefits that have accrued in the development of our society, imperfect as the latter still is, have played a great part. Among these are physical expansion of the environment with less crowding and contagion, better housing, and cleaner food supply adequate in essential accessory substances, improved sanitation almost everywhere, shorter hours of work, labor-saving devices, more time for recreation, and so on. It is impossible to assess the value of these larger measures, and there is no thought of playing down what has been accomplished in the specific care and prevention of tuberculosis. Every understanding worker in the field—practicing physician, tuberculosis specialist, scientific investigator, expert in public health, or voluntary contributor of his time—is aware that he has watched an irresistible decline in tuberculosis as much as he has taken part in it.

But the two are not distinct. Among the improved standards of living themselves that are making modern society incompatible with endemic tuberculosis are many that stem back directly to the conscious efforts of these dedicated workers. Indeed, the acquired means at hand for the future control of tuberculosis are powerful, and it is worth noting in closing this story that the two great official and voluntary agencies, respectively, that are concerned with attack upon the disease in this country, the Public Health Service and the National Tuberculosis Association, have joined hands in an all-out program for its elimination as a public health problem. The time is ripe for such an effort.

IRVINE McQUARRIE, M.D.

Autobiographic Sketch

One of my convictions is that every person should have a purpose—that one should make a constant effort to better human welfare. The conscious purpose of my life has been twofold: to prod the frontiers of medical science until they yield a little—my own work in this area has been largely centered on the riddles of metabolism—and to share with others such knowledge as I have, with the frequently voiced hope that they too will share their knowledge. In science, as in all life, hoarding is useless. Only by sharing what we learn is the body of knowledge increased. It is in this spirit of sharing that I agreed to write some autobiographical notes.

It is only fair to warn the reader that these reminiscences may disclose some proselytizing. Very little of my life has been devoted to private practice, almost all of it to teaching and research. For me, teaching is almost a religion, so it is with fervor that I bear witness to the rewards of the scholarly way of life. I hope that some of the young men wrestling with a decision whether to teach and do research or to take up the practice of medicine may sense some of the satisfactions of the former and will make this the principal purpose in their lives.

I do not in the least deprecate the practice of medicine. That is one of the prime reasons for studying medicine. It is the private physician who bears the responsibility for care of the patient, who is on call around the

Dr. McQuarrie, who was head of the Department of Pediatrics, University of Minnesota, worked intermittently between 1958 and 1960 on this brief personal account of his life although he was handicapped by cataracts and surgery to remove them. It was finished after he died September 9, 1961, by Mrs. McQuarrie, with the kind assistance of several of Dr. McQuarrie's students, now prominent teachers and leaders themselves in medical schools throughout this country. "Their Professor" was an outstanding researcher, physician, and administrator who achieved his greatest eminence as a teacher, dedicated to his school, his students, and his patients, "the kiddies."

clock, who gives comfort and hope at the bedside, and who is largely responsible for the public image of "the doctor." Behind him, however, molding his career, are the men who taught him to be a doctor. We need these men. We need teachers, first-rate ones, if we are to have first-rate practicing physicians.

Much of my pay over the years has been the thrill of working with young people—seeing them progress toward their degrees, helping them get their internships, seeing some of them succeed in private practice and seeing others turn to teaching and research, many of them reaching the very pinnacle of success. Relationships with these inspiring and inspirable personalities have brought deeply satisfying rewards.*

Unlike Dr. George H. Whipple, whose autobiography appeared in PERSPECTIVES in the Spring of 1959, I did not always want to be a doctor.

I was born in Silver Reef, Utah, April 20, 1891. My father was a metallurgist and supervised the town's silver mill. Silver had been booming for several years, but by 1893 the great financial panic was in full swing, the mine closed down, there was another ghost town in the U.S.A., and people and records were moved elsewhere.

Father moved his family to St. George, Utah, and became foreman of a copper mine in which he had some shares. His responsibility for developing mining property in the area necessitated frequent visits to the mines, and he often took me with him. I grew to love these jaunts. We talked about the trees and animals in the country, geology, and a great deal about philosophy. He made these discussions thoroughly interesting and applicable to life and perhaps initiated a sense of values which gave some direction to decisions which would have to be made later.

With this background, mining seemed to offer attractive prospects, and mining engineering beckoned as a career. The University of Utah had an

* The influence of Irvine McQuarrie was not limited to his students and colleagues in medicine. When I went to the University of Minnesota as a graduate student in psychology in 1931, Irvine and Vira McQuarrie were the first members of the faculty to welcome us and to let us know that we had friends in Minneapolis. This was during the depth of the depression. He said, "If you ever need food or shelter or money, come to me. Or whenever you would like to discuss science, my office door is always open." With never a thought that he had other things to do, I appeared unannounced at his office many times, seeking advice on occasion, but more frequently pouring out the story of my research on the adrenal cortices. I believe that I was welcome there and that he shared my enthusiasms, although I must have been a formidable test of his tolerance on some occasions.—DWIGHT J. INGLE.

excellent department of mines, so when the time came for college, I registered there to prepare for my life's work—or so it seemed.

Three things altered the situation. First, my uncle, Menzies Macfarlane, became a doctor. As Father had talked about mining and philosophy, so this uncle talked about medicine.

Second, my mother became ill with arthritis, and her chronic and painful condition brought the family doctor to our home often. His visits were brief but frequent, and through them some insight about the fascinating subject of medicine was imparted to me.

Third, and most important, I met a young lady who was attending the university. Her name was Vira Perkins. We were married June 1, 1912.

It is my deep conviction that this early marriage had much to do with whatever success I have had. The idea of becoming a mining engineer was abandoned and the decision to study medicine was substituted. This decision, and all important decisions since that time, Vira and I made together. There remained the unanswered question of how to finance a medical education. The answer—two years of college for me, with Vira teaching school. In June, 1914, our first daughter, Oane, was born. This complicated the financial picture, but we were confident that somehow the rest of the way could be managed.

And it was, via the now quite common scholarship route. The competitive Willard D. Thompson Scholarship for Utah students to attend the University of California was awarded to me, and so we folded our nonexistent tent and silently moved away.

In Berkeley, Dr. George Whipple was dean of the medical school, University of California. He, more than any other man in our field, influenced my thinking and my career with his brilliant, incisive mind and ability to inspire men and stimulate their continued efforts. He could also quite properly assess the economic needs of a family of four, for by this time, 1916, our second daughter, Maris, had arrived. He decided that in this "special case" it was justifiable to bestow a second scholarship to meet the requirements.

With such manna in our financial wilderness, it was possible to spend two years with him at the Hooper Foundation for Research after completing the first two years of medicine. Here, as assistant in pathology, I did my first teaching on the university level, in the department of chemistry, which was located in San Francisco.

Other celebrities at the California medical school were Drs. Herbert M. Evans, George W. Corner, Phillip E. Smith, F. P. Gay, T. Brailsford Robertson, and Walter R. Bloor—a stimulating group indeed.

After receiving a Ph.D. in experimental pathology and biochemistry and completing the first two years at the medical school, I moved on to Johns Hopkins, where Drs. Whipple and Evans had held associate professorships in their respective fields. With their sponsorship the transfer was easily made.

Drs. Osler, Howland, Halsted, Myers, Dandy, Kelly, Welch, and a host of other top-notch authorities created a heady environment at Hopkins. After weekly ward rounds with Drs. Edwards A. Park and Grover F. Powers, and listening to the lucid lectures of Dr. James Lawder Gamble on infant metabolism and nutrition, it was clear to me that pediatrics was my choice of the clinical fields. While an internship in that discipline would have been most welcome, it would have been impossible to accept at the time for financial reasons. But the dream of someday returning to pediatrics was often in my mind.

My M.D. from Hopkins was received in 1921. At that time an internship at the Henry Ford Hospital in Detroit was highly sought after. In addition to the regular salary, its appointments and equipment were extraordinary, so when the opportunity to become a house officer was presented, I accepted it with alacrity. Two years later I was made director of the section of endocrinology and metabolism. After almost another two years, a situation arose which made it possible for me to choose between returning to pediatrics or remaining in the field of internal medicine.

The governing board of the hospital had decided to develop a special division of pediatrics, and they offered me a full year's leave, on salary, to study pediatrics at any place of my choice in America to further prepare for full-time work in that field.

Dr. Park had been called from Hopkins to Yale in 1921 to develop a new department on a full-time plan. After observing and visiting several outstanding teachers elsewhere, I sought his advice. When he offered an instructorship in his department, I readily accepted. The environment was stimulating and enjoyable, but I was obligated to return to the Henry Ford Hospital to head the department there.

A young man deciding what to do with his life should consider all the rewards of his work, and finances is certainly one of them. He has to decide how important money becomes in his own scheme of things, so perhaps it will not be amiss to share with him my feelings on this subject.

It would have been quite easy for me to accumulate modest wealth at that time. All that was needed was to stay in Detroit, a thriving industrial city, enter private practice in pediatrics, which was then a comparatively new specialty, and, like others, watch my bank account grow. Or I could have remained at the Ford Hospital as chief of the department in a secure and lucrative position. These were not irresistible temptations personally, but there was the family to consider. Had my wife and daughters been filled with social ambitions or envious of the possessions of others, life might have been very different. On the other hand, we did know something about the "austerity" program and wanted to avoid that, too.

For many men there is no such decision to make. They are "called" to private practice. From their first exposure to medicine, they want to be on the front line of medicine, which is at the patient's bedside. The interpersonal contacts mean more to them than does money; it is a bonus that the work they love is also financially rewarding.

I wanted to teach. It was just as simple as that. Soon an opportunity came. Dr. Whipple, who had left the University of California to establish the school of medicine in Rochester, New York, invited me to join his staff. The salary offered was just half that paid by the Ford Hospital, and a much smaller fraction of the one offered if I would stay. But there were other compensations to offset this at the university, so we accepted the offer.

Have I ever regretted the decision? This is a question any young doctor would ask if he were considering spending his life in teaching. My answer is NO!

We spent four very happy years in Rochester. In the spring of 1930 the University of Minnesota invited me to become professor and head of the department of pediatrics at that medical school. This assignment lasted for twenty-five years.

Although Yale and Rochester had been exciting, the situation at Minnesota was even more so. Undoubtedly one of the rewards of teaching at a great university is the close association and constant stimulation of the outstanding men in the various fields of knowledge. Here, in addition to the excellent staff of the medical school, was a galaxy of renowned scholars.

At the top was the president, Lotus Delta Coffman. And there were

J. B. Johnston, dean of science, literature, and the arts; Everett Fraser, dean of law; Albert Ernst Jenks and Wilson Wallace, anthropology; Elmer E. Stoll, Oscar Firkins, and Joseph W. Beach, comparative literature and English; William H. Emmons, Clinton Stauffer, and John W. Gruner, geology; David O. Swenson and Norman C. Wild, philosophy; Henry E. Erickson, John T. Tate, and, a little later, Alfred O. C. Neir and John H. Williams in physics; Samuel C. Lind, physical chemistry; William Anderson and Harold W. Quigley, political science; Thomas Sadler Roberts, natural history; Ross C. Gortner and Clyde Bailey, agricultural chemistry; E. C. Stakman, plant pathology; Roy D. Blakey and Alvin H. Hansen, business school; J. B. Jesness, agricultural economics; John E. Anderson, child welfare; Jean Pickard, balloonist; Eugene Ormandy, conductor of the Minneapolis Symphony Orchestra; Bernie Bierman, named all-American coach in 1935, who led the Golden Gophers to several Big Ten and national championships. There were also many others, not to mention the up-and-coming secondary members of the staff.

The campus was teeming with students engrossed in these and other subjects. Student-faculty relationships were fostered through such activities as concerts, art exhibits, theater, convocations, seminars, lectures, sports, dancing, and dining clubs.

This was, indeed, a saturated solution of talent, furnishing pleasing prospects for a family with three girls to educate. Jeanne, the third, had arrived ten years earlier.

Pediatrics in 1930 was not one of the leading departments on the campus, not even in the medical school. There were six full-time people on the staff: myself, Drs. Mildred R. Ziegler, Albert V. Stoesser, Arild E. Hansen, Willis H. Thompson, and one full-time secretary. Dr. Chester A. Stewart was professor, "part-time" in charge of the outpatient department. There were four interns. Twenty-five years later seventy-six were on the payroll.

Building the Variety Club Heart Hospital was one of the particularly rewarding efforts to develop the Department of Pediatrics at the University of Minnesota. This addition to the University Hospital, conceived by one of our clinical teachers, Dr. Morse J. Shapiro, was devoted to the intensive investigation and ideal treatment of children and adults with heart and vascular disease. The pediatric service of forty beds, where children with all forms of cardiovascular disease could be cared for and studied intensively, greatly enriched the clinical material available for teaching and research. Construction of the hospital and then its expansion were made possible by the teamwork of members of the medical school faculty and administration, particularly Ray Amberg, and the Variety Club of the Northwest. This effort was at that time the most extensive single charitable undertaking by any of the Variety Club chapters.

A parallel development equally satisfying to me was the help of the American Legion Division of Minnesota in building up our own department. At the end of World War II, the leadership of the Legion group wanted to make a charitable contribution in memory of the men who had served in the war. They established an endowed Heart Research Professorship in Pediatrics with a gift to the University of more than $500,000. It was first occupied by Dr. Lewis Thomas. Since 1954, the chair has been held by one of my own students, Dr. Robert A. Good.

Another important addition to our department was the McClure metabolic ward for teaching and research on pediatric problems of greatest interest to me personally. It was achieved through an initial contribution by Katherine Esgen McClure, whom I had interested in the metabolic problems of children, and a subsequent, very substantial contribution to the university by Silas McClure, who had become a personal friend. The first director of the new metabolic clinic and ward was Dr. Robert A. Ulstrom, another of my students.

I have often been asked why it was that so many of my students became teachers. I do not know. Dr. Whipple imparted his love of teaching to me, and it may be that some of my satisfactions in the field were likewise communicated to others. I made a conscious effort to search out individual abilities and encourage self-confidence and initiative. Responsibility was delegated as soon as anyone was ready for it, which resulted almost invariably in increased interest and effort.

This technique was not reserved for the professional staff alone. All the people in our department were responsible for its success—secretaries, technicians, nurses, custodians—everybody was made to feel necessary and was aware of the mutual respect and personal interest which prevailed.

It is only natural, even within the same discipline, that one may turn to teaching and another away from it. But the successful teacher has done his part when he discovers the potential scholar and then provides adequate incentive and complete freedom to develop natural capacities through his own enterprise.

Writing is a part of teaching, a means of "sharing your knowledge." The first time one has a paper published is an exciting event. This happened to me in 1917 with S. Hanson as co-author. The paper was on the "Nondependence of the Protein Quotient in the Blood Serum upon the Rapidity of Metabolism, with Special Reference to the Non-effect of Antipyretics, Sodium, and Thyroid Extract" (a most impressive title for budding scientists). Two years later I had two more papers published as co-author with Dr. Whipple. During the next twenty-five years more than 150 papers appeared under my name, most of them with co-authors.

My most satisfying writing job was connected with editing the Brennemann-McQuarrie *Practice of Pediatrics*, an eight-volume work.

In 1935 I was made a member of the editorial board of the *Journal of Pediatrics*, the official publication of the American Academy of Pediatrics. This association was very pleasant. In 1948 the Academy decided to publish its own journal; hence, it was possible to be one of the founders of *Pediatrics*. I also served as associate editor of *Metabolism*, *Quarterly Journal of Pediatrics*, *GP*, *Postgraduate Medicine*, *International Medical Digest*, *The American Practitioner*, *Journal-Lancet*, and *Archives of Physical Medicine*. It was very satisfying to serve as editor of the *Symposium on Potassium Metabolism* inasmuch as the metabolic significance of potassium as an important cation was just emerging not only from the biochemical viewpoint but also in clinical medicine. In the presentation of the Porter Lectures at the University of Kansas, which were published in book form in 1944 as *The Experiments of Nature and Other Essays*, opportunity was provided to cite the ever-presenting evidences found in nature to observe new scientific facts. Nature by means of mutations brings forth new life-patterns, the study of which is unequalled food for scientific thought. Along the line of writing, it was particularly rewarding, though sometimes time-consuming, to go over manuscripts with younger colleagues. However, such experience made it possible to learn to know the man, and perhaps to stimulate his own thinking and help him to attain his full potentialities.

Professional Societies

For any physician, professional associations or clubs are important. The oldest of the specialized pediatric groups is the American Pediatric Society.

It was organized in 1888 and was one of the earliest specialty societies established in the United States. In the beginning, membership was restricted to outstanding men in the field of diseases of infants and children; later, men in professional and investigative positions were included. I was pleased to be elected to membership early in my career, and to serve as president in 1952–53. I greatly treasured my association with this group.

In time it became apparent that a professional society was needed in which younger men could find fellowship in the early stages of their professional lives. Realizing that what was needed was primarily a teaching organization, a number of us established the Society for Pediatric Research. Active founders were Drs. Kenneth D. Blackfan, James L. Gamble, Daniel C. Darrow, Samuel Z. Levine, L. Emmett Holt, Jr., James D. Trask, George Guest, Joseph A. Stokes, Jr., Edwards A. Park, Grover F. Powers, S. W. Clausen, and myself, among others well known in the field. Our first meeting was held March 23, 1929, and the original name given to the organization was Eastern Society for Pediatric Research. At the third meeting it was decided (by one vote!) to drop "Eastern." The purpose of the organization was to foster pediatric investigation and to provide opportunity for younger men to present their work. Membership was of two types, active and honorary, the former being limited to those individuals actively engaged in clinical or laboratory investigation in pediatrics.

Later some of us felt that even the two professional associations were not sufficient. Thirty-five pediatricians met June 23, 1930, in the library of Harper Hospital in Detroit and founded the American Academy of Pediatrics as the organization to speak for all members of the profession: teachers, scientists, practitioners. The purposes and aims were formulated at the first annual meeting held in Philadelphia, June 12 and 13, 1931. Drs. C. A. Aldrich, Hugh McCulloch, Clifford G. Grulee, Thomas B. Cooley, A. Graeme Mitchell, Bronson Carothers, Samuel Amberg, Isaac A. Abt, and Borden S. Veeder, among others, participated.

Naturally, believing as I do in the importance of full and free exchange of knowledge, I affiliated with a number of other professional associations devoted to scientific pursuits. I was made an honorary fellow of the American College of Dentists and belonged to the American Institute of Nutrition, American Society for Clinical Investigation, American Physiological Society, American Heart Association, and others. My memberships in foreign societies included the British Paediatric Association, Société de Pédiatrie de Paris, Canadian Pediatric Society, Chinese Medical Association, Mexican Pediatric Society, Cuban Pediatric Society, Pediatric Society of Peru, Brazilian Pediatric Society, The Horse Shoe Club (British), and the Instituto Brasil-Estados Unidos.

In addition to these many far-away contacts, I always wanted to participate in medical and scientific affairs in my immediate community. At the University of Minnesota we organized the Interdepartmental Seminar Series in order to be acquainted with the progress of the studies of those in other fields. On more than one occasion I had traveled half-way across the country to some meeting at which I had been invited to speak, and, hearing a colleague on my own faculty also present a paper, we would simultaneously say something like, "That was a very fine presentation. I would like to hear more about your interesting studies." And I always attended meetings at the local level—for example, the Society for Experimental Biology and Medicine, Northwestern Pediatric Society, Minnesota Pathological Society, Hennepin County Medical Society, and the Minnesota Heart Association.

Extra-curricular Activities

My social consciousness led me down many paths.

In the early 1930's the retirement program of the University of Minnesota was very good, but those were depression years and the outlook was bleak. It was becoming apparent that some sense of security beyond the university retirement program required sustained action. Compulsory saving by unified action seemed to be the answer. We formed an investment group among the faculty members to pool our resources for buying stock, get sound economic advice, and save on commissions. This was a comparatively new concept at the time. Investors Diversified Services made it possible to work out a plan for supplementing income. The original thought was for security primarily, however, as it turned out, the investments yielded almost as much as the so-called wizards obtained, although on a smaller scale.

Another organization which I helped found was a protest against the barbaric and useless custom of extravagant funerals. The death of a child had set me thinking.

The youngster had nephrosis. Over $2,000 had been spent for transfusions, oxygen, and general care of the child. The family was poor. In fact, they did not have sufficient funds to buy bread and milk for the surviving children. When I talked with the father a few weeks after the child died, I discovered that not only had they spent all their insurance money on the funeral, but they had gone into debt. My heart rebelled. Never, I decided, would I be a party to this custom.

The "no funeral" society—or Memorial Society, as it came to be called on the suggestion of Dr. John M. Adams—was started, and soon we had one thousand members. Although our belief was that there should be no elaborate funeral service, and that the body should be cremated, the type of service and disposal of the remains was optional. The organization is still active in Minneapolis, and similar ones have been established elsewhere.

Always a believer in peace, I developed an enduring interest in furthering international friendships and communication among all the peoples of the world. One rewarding experience for the entire family was a sojourn in China, where I taught as a visiting professor at the Peking Union Medical College for half of 1940 under the auspices of The Rockefeller Foundation. In 1947 I went to Japan and did a survey of post-war medical education, also for The Rockefeller Foundation. Then in 1953 I was privileged to make an extended visit to South America in the company of one of "my boys," Dr. Mauricio da Silva, who acted as my interpreter and guide while I lectured in Brazil, Uruguay, Argentina, Chile, Peru, and Panama.

Pediatric Grand Reunion

In 1954, from September 23 through 25, more than two hundred pediatricians from all parts of the United States, many accompanied by their wives, gathered in Minneapolis for a pediatric grand reunion, at which I was honored. This was my twenty-fifth anniversary at the school. The Northwestern Pediatric Society convened for its annual meeting at the same time and in connection with it. These sessions were the first ones held in the new Mayo Memorial Building.

One of the greatest satisfactions for a teacher is seeing one's pupil succeed. Of the twenty-four papers presented during the reunion, twenty-one were contributions of former students, residents, or interns whom I had helped to train. It was exhilarating to renew associations with the authors.

Particularly gratifying, too, was the announcement of a McQuarrie Fund. More than $50,000 had been contributed "to be used to further the education of young scientists and to provide lectureships, fellowships and scholarships." At long last the initial scholarship that promoted my own medical education was being repaid.

Out of this reunion came a book of the papers presented, *Essays in Pediatrics*, edited by Robert A. Good and Erling S. Platou. The "Essays" were written and the book printed without my being personally involved in any way.

These had been twenty-five wonderful years—filled with hard work, some triumphs, some disappointments, and some of the interdepartmental frictions and rivalries found in any live, growing school. In our own department, though, harmony with co-operative effort was the prevailing mood.

It was difficult indeed to cut the ties that had bound me to the pediatric department for so long. Compulsory retirement was still three years away, but warning health signals were beginning to appear, personal ambition and vigor were decreasing, and the size and complexity of the department were increasing. So as soon as voluntary retirement age arrived, I asked to be relieved, and Dr. John A. Anderson was chosen to fill the vacancy.

Honolulu Interlude

In 1956 we moved to Honolulu where the post of director of medical education at the Kaukeolani Children's Hospital had been offered me. It turned out to be a particularly challenging experience.

In Honolulu there is no medical school. Yet Hawaii is the focal point in the Pacific where many people and races intermingle. It is uniquely located to serve the Pan-Pacific area as a center for sharing the knowledge of our own land and for learning more about treatment and cure of the diseases particularly prevalent in the Orient and Asia.

The several months spent at the Peking Union Medical College and later in Japan convinced me that an international medical center in the Pacific area would provide tremendous opportunity to extend medical education throughout the world. Now my missionary zeal was afire.

I believed that if a good teaching program could be established, a medical school would be the logical outgrowth of such a plan and that the hospitals in Honolulu could furnish, or would attract, enough material for teaching and research.

Much time was spent trying to enlist the support of medical and other leaders in founding such a center, and a committee was formed to study the feasibility of the plan. I was strongly urged to remain in Hawaii at the Children's Hospital and to explore the possibility of a liaison relationship with the University of Hawaii, which would, in turn, be conducive to the formation of a medical school. Unfortunately, at that time there was a noticeable imbalance between the intellectual and the physical climates in Honolulu. The stimulating atmosphere of Minnesota was missing. In its stead was a feeling of delightful relaxation, induced, no doubt, by the almost perfect climate of Hawaii. We failed to sell the idea of a Pan-Pacific medical center. But the need remains and, I believe, will someday be realized.

Children's Hospital of the East Bay

The new year, 1958, presented another new situation—directing the research program to be started at Children's Hospital of the East Bay in Oakland, California.

In teaching, as in life, we have a "family tree"—a chain of ancestors and a chain of offspring. In California I had both. A number of my former professors and classmates were still there, as well as many of my own students, and some of my students' students.

Dr. Arild E. Hansen, who had been a professor of pediatrics on our staff at the University of Minnesota, and who had left us in 1944 to head his own department at the University of Texas, had trained there a young physician named James L. Dennis. Dr. Dennis had been appointed medical director of the Children's Hospital of the East Bay. It was largely on his urging that I agreed to join his staff in Oakland.

Here was another opportunity to start a medical center, this one specifically for children. Oakland is part of the San Francisco metropolitan complex with Berkeley adjacent, where the main branch of the University of California is located. Shipbuilding caused the East Bay area to mushroom during the war. Afterward many families remained. It is teeming with children. The first-rate hospital, recognizing the need for basic research, was planning the first research laboratory in Northern California devoted exclusively to children's diseases. Intellectually and physically, the climate was far more stimulating than in Honolulu.

After serving as research director for a year and a half, we decided that retirement could come in stages. Our friend Arild was persuaded to assume the directorship, and I acted as research consultant.

Dr. Hansen played another role in my life, for it was he who made the introduction and presented the Howland Award of the American Pediatric Society, May 8, 1958, in Atlantic City. This award is given to members of the Society who have made some special contribution in the field. The number of my students who became full-time teachers, scientific investigators, professors, or otherwise carried on the so-called "McQuarrie tradition" seemed to be the chief accomplishment to qualify me for this award. It was indeed a great honor, for which I was most grateful. No man could fail to cherish such recognition.

Another treasured honor was the award of an honorary Doctor of Science degree from Northwestern University, conferred September 29, 1959, at the centennial celebration of the founding of the medical school.

Such experiences are very humbling, for awareness that some contributions have been made only places in bolder relief all the unfinished tasks that remain.*

* Irvine McQuarrie was a man of gladsome disposition which was not disturbed by the difficulties and problems of a strenuous life—a man with the highest ideals and a teacher who got close to his pupils and gave them the feeling that they belonged in his family. McQuarrie was thirty years of age when he got his M.D. at Hopkins—definitely more mature than the average student, and finances continued to demand attention.

It is inspiring to remember that in the face of attractive opportunities to practice or to head the department of pediatrics in the Ford Hospital in Detroit, he held true to his program to be a teacher and an investigator. His pupils as leaders in pediatrics establish his standing as a teacher more than any words coming from his friends. His published papers speak for his rare ability in his chosen fields of research.—George H. Whipple.

JAMES HOWARD MEANS, M.D.

Experiences and Opinions of a Full-Time Medical Teacher

The name of the journal *Perspectives in Biology and Medicine* appeals to me strongly, for it indicates the main channels of my professional life—"biology and medicine"—what a happy juxtaposition of terms! And "perspectives," yes, indeed—from the vantage point of the early seventies one can perceive in true perspective those things that have had deep meaning for him as he has made his journey.

Medicine is, of course, far older than biology. It started in magic, and in Jesus it rested on faith. However, I came first to biology, and, for me, medicine emerged from that. It all began, I suppose, from childhood natural history, an interest which was nurtured by my father, who, though not a trained scientist himself, had science deeply at heart. His was undoubtedly the first important intellectual influence in my life. The actual life of any individual is the resultant of those forces that tend to hold him together and those that tear him apart—the impact upon him of persons, events, or ideas combined with the native equipment he has to withstand or to profit by them.

At first, my adventures in natural history were no more than collecting and classifying specimens. Then came a little dissecting. At fourteen I came upon *The Origin of Species* and read it through with rapt attention and excitement. It was my first encounter with a great scientific generalization—namely, biological evolution through the natural selection of spontaneously occurring variations, or survival of the fittest. Darwin called this

Dr. Means was Chief of Medical Services at the Massachusetts General Hospital, where he practiced and encouraged others in the traditions of inquiry, teaching, and service of this great hospital of Harvard Medical School—which made it an exciting place to work and study. He continues to devote much energy to making the best medical practice available to the most people with the least barrier between the service and those served.

a theory, and for a time it was violently attacked by both scientists and theologians. It has stood the gaff, however, and now, a century after it was first promulgated, it can properly be called a law. During this century, moreover, knowledge of its modus operandi has been greatly extended. I certainly have made no original contribution to this field, but it has fascinated me increasingly, and, as the years have flown by, it has provided me with a line of reference for many things that I have always found enlightening and sustaining. I was gratified to discover recently that Julian Huxley has said that "without some knowledge of evolution one cannot hope to arrive at a true picture of human destiny." I am sure this is true (1).

The next important intellectual impact came from meeting the late William T. Sedgwick, professor of biology at Massachusetts Institute of Technology. Since I was a well-to-do Bostonian youngster, it was routinely assumed that I would go to Harvard College. I did, but between "prep" school and college, because my father was a friend of Sedgwick, I had the privilege of spending a year (1902–3) in the latter's biology department at MIT. This was when I was seventeen years old, and it was a fateful year for me.

What Sedgwick did in a way to stir the imagination of his students was to present biology to them as one comprehensive basic science. The boundaries of zoölogy and botany faded away, and a single science of life emerged. I do not believe that many, if any, colleges of liberal arts were doing this sort of thing for their students at that time. Zoölogy and botany were taught as separate subjects, often by separate departments.

Sedgwick, when I studied under him, was using a textbook, *An Introduction to General Biology* (2), which he and Edward B. Wilson had first published in 1886. It was the second edition (1899) that I used, and it is no exaggeration to say that, because of its effect on the direction of my thinking, it became for me one of the great books. The word "general" is the significant one in this title. A new and prophetic concept of the nature of a basic science was implied in it. The classical type of naturalist had searched the earth for new species of plants and animals. He described and classified them. More importantly, he compared them one with another, and in his comparative work he approached basic principles. The theory of evolution itself, of course, emerged from this background. But the modern biologist has, for the most part, a very different orientation. He chooses species for his research which will best serve to advance his ultimate purpose. The fruitfly, the sea urchin, the squid, the guinea pig, the rat, the frog, the hydra, and many others have become popular laboratory species (or genera) because they are good means to ends, not because they have any interest merely as species. Of course, in the comparative fields, species may be selected for study because they have accomplished some extraordinary adaptation, and it is the adaptation itself and not the species as such that the investigator wishes to study. In medicobiological research, species are selected for study because they constitute a threat or offer a benefit to man. Polio virus can be taken as an example of a threatening one and *Penicillium* as one offering a benefit.

New horizons opened in my year with Sedgwick. I met bacteria for the first time, at least to observe them personally. Protozoa I had already encountered but had no insight into their part in the total concept of life. Particularly intriguing to me at this time, because of their bearing on evolution, were some studies in embryology and comparative anatomy. I learned of Haeckel's theory that ontogeny is a repetition of phylogeny and observed some of the evidence for it. This, as far as I was concerned, disposed for good and all of any special creation theory of the origin of species.

From being a special student at MIT, I entered Harvard College in the fall of 1903 as an ordinary Freshman and graduated with the class in 1907. This, of course, was following the line of least resistance, but it worked out satisfactorily for me. In retrospect, I find it somewhat difficult to discern the precise nature of my motivation at that point. I am quite certain that when I entered Harvard College I had already determined to go into medicine. As a child, I had hoped to become a naturalist (old style). In MIT for a time I thought of a career in pure biology (new style). Somehow this goal got changed from pure science to the applied, but the truth is that I do not now know why. I have no regrets, however. I do know that Sedgwick approved of this choice, but I am sure he made no attempt to influence me in the matter. The choice, whatever occasioned it, was mine.

Harvard College in those days was enjoying the free elective system of President Eliot. The idea was to offer the student a magnificent and variegated educational menu and, with very few restrictions, let him make his own free choices. If he chose an idiotic assortment of subjects, that was his his loss, not the college's. I made several mistakes in selection, and it may be helpful to some newcomers if I mention them. First, having chosen medicine, I was all too eager to use the free elective system to prepare myself for it as thoroughly as possible. I did not altogether neglect the wonderful opportunities for liberal education that Harvard then afforded, but I might have had more of it if I had not loaded up with some subjects which were largely repeated in the medical school. Specifically, I have for years regretted that I did not study more mathematics and modern languages.

Harvard had on its faculty of arts and sciences then a galaxy of stars representing all the important branches of liberal learning. I studied under a number of them. Philosophy was particularly strong—George Santayana, Josiah Royce, William James—and in psychology, which was then included in the department of philosophy, there was Hugo Munsterberg. I can see and hear them all in my mind today. It was a thrilling experience. Robert M. Yerkes gave a course in experimental psychology which I found stimulating. Barrett Wendell in English was intellectually titillating. The grand old man of geology, Nathaniel Southgate Shaler, was a fine example of the great nineteenth-century natural scientist. But perhaps the most significant of all my teachers in Harvard College, certainly from the point of view of my eventual discipline, was a young instructor, Lawrence Joseph Henderson. He himself had been graduated from the college nine years ahead of me, and he introduced me to biochemistry in a way to fire the imagination.

Harvard Medical School came next. It was easy to get into in those days. All that was necessary was to get credits in the prescribed subjects plus a Bachelor's degree and then turn up the day the school opened and sign on. The school was in a period of transition at the time I entered. Through a history then extending over a century and a quarter, it had had its ups and downs. In 1870 a new, young, and vigorous president of Harvard University named Eliot carried out a drastic reformation, making the medical school a part of the university in a way it had never been before and greatly improving its educational standards.

A "wonderful" new building (Boylston Street) was occupied in 1883 and by 1900 was already inadequate. A movement had begun for something even more magnificent, and this culminated in the opening in September, 1906, of the Longwood Avenue quadrangle, which is still in use today. It was in September, 1907, that I started my medical career on this campus.

The buildings were truly awe-inspiring, but it takes more than bricks (in this case marble) and mortar to make a great educational institution, and the fact was that the new and glamorous Johns Hopkins Medical School in Baltimore had for fifteen years or so been putting the older medical schools in the shade. To meet this challenge, Eliot began to strengthen the faculty and wisely started by getting a new dean. The man chosen was Henry A. Christian, a Virginian, then in his early thirties. He was imported from Hopkins with the idea, I am sure, that he would develop a Hopkins-like medical school at Harvard. I first met him in my second year at the autopsy table of the Carney Hospital in South Boston. He had been given an attending job there to take care of his clinical needs until the new Peter Bent Brigham Hospital should be built, of which he was to become chief physician. He was forthright and approachable and became and remained a loyal friend throughout his life. "The boy dean," we medical students often called him. He was ardently in love with teaching, and I think I caught some of my interest in this from him, even though I never served directly under him.

The first professorial personality that made a vivid impression on me at Harvard Medical School, he who gave the first lecture I heard there, was Thomas Dwight, professor of anatomy. A short, round-shouldered, heavily bewhiskered individual, a convert to and devout member of the Roman Catholic church, as well as a passionate student of gross human anatomy, he sounded off by saying to us, "Gentlemen, man is very like the higher apes except that he has an immortal soul, but we won't take that up in this course." Taking my cue from Professor Dwight, I may say that I too have a religious life, as well as a love life, and a recreational life, but in this "perspective" I shall confine my remarks to my professional life.

The first-year curriculum at Harvard Medical School in 1907–8 was highly compartmentalized. The medical faculty in its wisdom let not its anatomical left hand know what its physiological right hand was doing. The student studied any of the so-called preclinical sciences intensively for a few months, then took an examination in it, after which, if he passed, he was free to forget the subject, for all the faculty cared. There were no final general examinations in those days. Some students then, and since, have found this situation frustrating. They could not see what it had to do with the practice of medicine, which was their goal. I did not find it so. My original interest in biology was still running strong, and these subjects were all part of biology, and I reveled in them. At that stage I thought seriously of making one of these disciplines my career but did not have any particular one in mind. My interest was hovering about in a certain field but had not settled on a particular flower.

I have tried in retrospect to identify any yen or penchant I may have had at that time for doing research myself. Nothing concrete emerges. I was aware of certain pieces of research going on about me (there was actually very little compared with today), and they fascinated me, but I did not get caught up in any of them, as students sometimes are nowadays. My focused interest in research was to come some years later. I had in mind then to become an acquisitive scholar rather than a creative one.

Of teachers who inspired me in my preclinical years, I would put at the top Henderson, already encountered in college, and Walter B. Cannon, professor of physiology. Henderson expounded the laws of mass action and the role of reversible chemical reactions in the maintenance of a steady pH in the blood. Cannon was studying, for the first time by means of X-ray, the movements of the alimentary canal and the influence of the involuntary nervous system and emotions upon them. The work of both these brilliant investigators was basic in its approach, but also their findings later came to have great meaning and deep significance in clinical medicine. I think we students sensed this to some degree even then. Cannon became a lifelong friend, and one of my priceless possessions is a presentation copy of his wonderful book *The Way of an Investigator* (3), published in 1945 just before he died, in which he wrote me a heartwarming sentiment. Otto Folin, professor of biochemistry, was another teacher whose impact was considerable. For me he was the prophet of metabolism, especially protein metabolism, and from him I first learned of the amino acids, from which all proteins are made. When I hear today of the intricacies of the the protein molecule, my mind goes back to Folin. The evolution of our knowledge of this subject since I first heard of it from Folin is commensurate with the evolution of the protein molecule itself.

The transition from the preclinical to the clinical years (third and fourth) in medical school involved almost as great a change in direction as that from college to professional school. The teachers of the first- and second-year subjects and those of the third- and fourth-year subjects constituted two distinct groups with quite different viewpoints, and there was limited communication between them. The clinicians brushed off the preclinical scientists as mere laboratory men who knew but little of medicine, and the scientists looked upon the practice of medicine as largely unscientific guesswork. The whole manner of life of these two groups was different. The preclinical scientists were in the mold of college teachers on campus. They were full-time, salaried people. There were no full-time clinical teachers in those days—or salaries either, for that matter. Some small token honoraria were given by the university but nothing by the teaching hospitals. These men taught and attended hospital patients for love or kudos, or a mixture of the two, and made their livelihoods in private practice. Any degree of unanimity in a faculty so constituted I am sure was hard to come by. This gap was, of course, later to be closed by the development of the "middle estate" in medicine—namely, the full-time academic, salaried clinician. Little did I foresee in my student days that my own lifework would come to fall in this category.

The clinical years, when I encountered something new, different, and challenging—the patient—enthralled me no less than the medical sciences. Our contact with the patient, however, was far more tenuous than it is for the medical student of today, but we knew no better. From the modern point of view, the third year then was dreadful. Five afternoons a week we had to attend three, sometimes four, hour-long lectures, one after another. Not only general medicine and surgery but half-a-dozen or more specialty subjects were fired at us. No patients were shown at these lectures. It was a matter of verbiage or oratory, or something in between, without correlation of the several subjects. At least it can be said that we were offered a lot of information which at a later time we could, to some degree, digest. The mornings were better—then we saw patients. For an hour each day they were shown to the whole class in hospital amphitheaters by the great men of the clinical staff. These were worthwhile exercises. I remember some of them vividly. The first time one saw a patient with a disease previously known only through lecture or textbook, it made a deep impression. Certain of the teachers also stirred up a bit of hero worship. One would like to become such a great clinician as the professor. We also had the opportunity in these third-year mornings to visit outpatient clinics in small groups under the direction of younger instructors and talk with and actually get our hands on patients. In the afternoon lectures the emphasis was on diseases, but in the mornings we were concerned with history-taking, examination, and diagnosis; in other words, at last we got to the problems of the individual patient. Usually there was very little time left over for the discussion of treatment. That one had to get by osmosis.

The fourth-year curriculum in those days at Harvard was entirely elective. A wide choice of clinical and preclinical subjects was offered. This freedom was abolished soon afterward. The fourth-year student could walk the wards of hospitals but not in any such responsible role as that enjoyed by the clinical ward clerk of later years. We were taken around as if on a Cook's tour by an instructor who showed us interesting patients and quizzed us on them a bit, but we were actually observers, not participants in the casework process. Only the department of obstetrics gave us any responsibility worth mentioning, and it gave us plenty. We delivered babies in the slums of Boston and learned what it was like to be alone in the small hours with two or more lives in our hands. (Yes, I had one case of twins.) It was a professionally maturing experience and packed with a lot more than just obstetrics. For my fourth year I elected two months of pathology; the rest of the time was spent in clinical subjects. In retrospect, it seems that it would have been better to have included some preclinical science. I can recall practically nothing being said to us about research or research careers in the third and fourth years at Harvard Medical School. The whole current was flowing strongly toward the practice of medicine, and nearly all of us got caught up in it. Thus we came to the doctorate in medicine.

The next step was the internship. Although not then legally necessary in all states, it was by custom considered mandatory, except for the rare medical graduate who expected to do no clinical work, such as those intending to make careers in preclinical sciences. There were none of these in my class that I can remember. I was fortunate to secure an internship at the Massachusetts General Hospital. It was sixteen months of straight medicine arranged in four steps of four months each with ascending responsibility. There existed then neither medical students with ward responsibilities nor residents. Under the visiting physicians who made daily rounds, the interns reigned supreme. It was a thrilling experience, but it led, of course, only to practice. When it was completed, the world was the young doctor's oyster. He was free to open an office and erect his sign—at least he was when he had passed state board examinations and received his license. This was what I fully expected to do when I started my internship, but destiny was to decree otherwise.

Because it bears upon the mores which have interested me increasingly as I have seen them undergo radical changes, I will mention here that in its notice of examinations for interns which MGH posted in my day, it was stated conspicuously that "no married need apply." Married medical students or interns were almost unknown. Those were the days when a man was not supposed to marry until he could support a wife in the manner in which she was accustomed to live. Now she is more likely in medical circles to support him. I am not passing judgment on which custom is better. They are, however, very different. We were married to our work, and a wife would have been considered a nuisance.

The esprit de corps among the house staff at MGH was very high, and I believe that it still is. I shall quote the late France W. Palfrey on this subject. He was a decade ahead of me on the house staff, and in 1938 he wrote as follows:

> I hope it is true that the tradition of thoroughness and meticulous attention to every detail, small as well as large, which immediately impressed itself upon all who entered in my time, has continued unimpaired. This tradition was so universal and unquestioned that it seemed inherent in the hospital itself, undoubtedly from its beginning. It was first instilled into the new interne by the senior officers of his service, but it was maintained by the public opinion of the whole house staff, who were united in resenting any lowering of its standards; a slow mentality or irresponsible conduct off duty were condoned, but any slackness on duty was the cardinal sin. The visiting staff seemed to play no part in this unless by example. Clearly it was a self-perpetuating spirit within the hospital which I have not seen equalled elsewhere [from F. A. Washburn, *The Massachusetts General Hospital: Its Development, 1900–1935* (Boston: Houghton Mifflin Co., 1939), p. 176].

Our chief concern in this internship was to care for the patient in the best possible way, and, according to our training, to make a diagnosis was the first step to be taken. We wanted our diagnoses to be scientifically accurate, and to miss something was gall and wormwood to us. Also, to fail to get autopsies in fatal cases placed an intern to some degree in the doghouse. To treat a patient without a diagnosis, although sometimes that had to be done, was just not good medicine. We began to appreciate the importance of basic and preclinical sciences and the necessity of resting practice on sound theory. We heard but little of formal research until later, but each clinical case was approached in an investigative spirit. Because my contemporary and fellow intern George R. Minot was so meticulous in asking all patients precisely what they ate, he was later to discover the cause and cure of pernicious anemia. Even as an intern, he had the insight that faulty diet might be a major factor in the production of that disease.

The picture of illness as I saw it in my intern days was very different from what it is today. For one thing, the patient population of the medical wards was much younger—an average age of thirty-five years in 1912 as against sixty years in 1949. We had far more patients with infections and fewer with degenerative diseases than is the case nowadays. Typhoid abounded and pneumonia also in its old, classical, full-blown state, unaltered by any specific therapy and often complicated by empyema. Tuberculosis and syphilis were frequent, and acute inflammatory rheumatism in adults. Also, in young adults we often saw acute nephritis with dropsy. For none of these diseases except syphilis did we have any specific remedies, unless you call salicylate such for rheumatic infections. We did have serum for meningococcus meningitis, which may have done good in some cases. Nevertheless, we loved caring for all these people, especially the typhoids, and we did it in the grand empirical manner, which meant meticulously thorough bedside observation and application of such non-specific therapeutic agents as were available. Diagnosis was always under scrutiny—indeed, a subject of constant debate among the house staff—and was changed or added to whenever an indication arose. Nursing was more to the fore than it is today. There were more dedicated career women in it then, and collaboration between them and the house staff was very effective.

Such was the situation in the spring of 1912 when, into this somewhat complacent medical elite, strode David Linn Edsall. Certain wise men on the faculty of medicine had imported him from the University of Pennsylvania via Washington University, St. Louis, to become a salaried professor of medicine at Harvard and chief of one of the two medical services at MGH, a job comparable to that of Christian, previously mentioned, and comparable to none other at Harvard up to that time. These two men were the founders, as far as Harvard was concerned, of what I have called earlier the "middle estate" in medicine, the full-time clinical teacher, whom Simon Flexner was to characterize in his presidential address to the Association of American Physicians in 1914 as "the latest evolutionary product of the modernization of medical education." A year or two later Edsall and Christian were joined by Harvey Cushing in surgery. Edsall altered the course of my career by at least 45° and made an impact on me equal in magnitude to Sedgwick's. At once Edsall began the development of a full-time academic clinic by building up the educational and investigative functions of medicine. I was fortunate enough to be able to watch this revolutionary process from its beginning, and in a gradually increasing way I was able to participate in it. At the time Edsall arrived I was halfway through my internship.

One of Edsall's earliest actions was to get fourth-year Harvard medical students into the medical wards of MGH with certain direct responsibilities in the care of patients. They came for the first time as "clinical clerks." The institution of the clinical clerkship had been imported from Britain and established at Johns Hopkins by Osler. In Boston it was introduced more or less simultaneously by Edsall at MGH, and by Christian at the then new Peter Bent Brigham Hospital. The innovation of the clerkship was really a milestone in clinical teaching. It made the fourth-year student an integral part of the ward team and gave him an experience far more stimulating and maturing—because it carried responsibility—than anything theretofore. At the same time, attendance of third-year students in outpatient clinics, also with some supervised responsibilities, was made obligatory.

Edsall began to build his full-time clinical staff by picking out some of the interns he found on duty at the time of his arrival at MGH and sending them upon graduation to other places to get some exposure to research. Having persuaded me to become one of these, he sent me first to the Carnegie Nutrition Laboratory in Boston to learn the use of a certain apparatus designed by F. G. Benedict to measure the exchange of gases in the lungs, from which could be calculated the respiratory metabolism. This was a field he himself was interested in, and he hoped I would become so too and do some work in it. After a few months of this, I went abroad. That was in the early summer of 1913. Paul D. White went with me; he was en route to work in cardiology with Thomas Lewis in London, and I was headed for Copenhagen to study under August Krogh in circulatory physiology.

Before settling down with these masters, White and I made a quick tour together and glimpsed the great hospitals in London, Paris, Berlin, and Vienna. We also attended an international physiological congress in Groningen, Holland. I am sure that, so far as research went, I was quite a greenhorn at this point, nor do I know that White was much better.

Nevertheless, we were both tremendously stimulated by the great men we met at this congress and by the wealth of original work on fundamental problems presented there. It was a mind-opening experience.

After this tour, White went to London, and I settled down for several months in Copenhagen. It was a stirring experience to work in the laboratory of August Krogh. Through the years this great physiologist took in a succession of American pupils. I was one of the earlier ones. Everything was very intimate. The pupil was taught some methods by the professor himself and then became an actual assistant in the professor's experiments. Krogh was working on the volume of the blood flow in man at the time I was with him. He was using a method that he had devised with J. Lindhard which depended on measuring the rate of uptake of nitrous oxide gas in the lungs. I at once concluded that here was a procedure that could properly be used in clinical cases which might throw new light on the morbid physiology of the circulation. I decided to use it for that purpose on returning home. It seems to me now in retrospect that I was at that time preparing for clinical research by acquiring some methodology rather than by really coming to grips with basic principles. This may not be the best approach to such a career, but it is at least an approach, and it was the one Edsall led me into.

After leaving Krogh, I visited the physiological laboratory at Cambridge. In Copenhagen I had read of Joseph Barcroft's work on blood gases and decided that I would like to observe it personally. Barcroft was very cordial to me and taught me the use of his apparatus and a bit about its scientific usefulness. It gave me yet another instrument with which to plow the field of respiratory and circulatory physiology.

Thus provided, I went home and back to MGH, arriving there in December, 1913. I did not then suspect it, but this hospital was to be my base of operations for the next thirty-seven years. Edsall got me fixed up as a research fellow with a stipend, a minute laboratory, and said in substance, "Now do some research." So I got the equipment I had imported—Krogh's and Barcroft's—together with a Benedict Universal respiration apparatus already acquired by Edsall—set up, calibrated, and in working order. Then I bethought me what use I would make of them. I was somewhat in the situation of a small boy with a new tool kit. Problems must be found which could be attacked by the methods at hand. Obviously, imagination was needed, but mine was not outstandingly well developed at that time. The clinical investigator is by definition one who aims his inquiries at the problems of sick people. But his evaluation of morbid processes as he observes them in patients must always be in terms of how they differ from what is found in healthy persons. The studies I was prepared to make lay in the fields of the physiology of the respiration, circulation, and metabolism of energy as derived from the measurement of the respiratory gases. I did some probing in all these.

The three and one-half years between getting back from abroad in 1913 and being called to active military duty in 1917 constituted a distinct chapter in my life. It was a time of self-scrutiny and appraisal, of finding what precisely were my major professional interests and capabilities. If research was to be an important component, what line should it take? Also, there were the questions of teaching and care of patients, both quite dear to me, and I had no desire that research should deprive me altogether of either.

During this period I made three warm friendships which through the years have been deeply satisfying and stimulating. These were with Louis Henry Newburgh, Eugene Floyd Du Bois, and Joseph Charles Aub. Newburgh, who had finished his internship at MGH in 1908 and then gone abroad for further study, I found back at the hospital when I returned in 1913. Newburgh's first love was research, but, to eke out a living, he had also to do a bit of private practice. He invited me to join him in certain research projects, and this I did most happily. He introduced me to my first animal work, and together, in the physiological laboratory of Professor William T. Porter at Harvard, we made observations on the state of the respiratory mechanism in experimental pneumonia. In those days the only treatment for pneumonia—a very common and often fatal malady—was symptomatic, so we thought that the more we could learn about the nature of the functional disturbances it caused, the better we could treat them symptomatically. At the hospital we worked together on blood flow in patients with respiratory and cardiac difficulties. Newburgh deepened my understanding of what research in medicine is all about, and his devotion to it was contagious. Although after World War I he went to the University of Michigan and spent the rest of his professional life there, we maintained communication until he died in 1956.

Some of my work at this time turned more toward metabolism than respiratory and circulatory physiology per se, and I developed increasing interest in diseases of the thyroid because it became apparent that this endocrine is the dominant one regulating the metabolic rate. It was because of this interest that I met Du Bois. I was attracted by him in the first place when he read a paper on basal metabolism at the meeting of the American Society for Clinical Investigation ("Young Turks") at Atlantic City in May, 1914 (4). This was right up my alley, for I had already been making determinations of the metabolic rate with the Benedict apparatus, to observe what factors affected it— either conditions of disease or applied agents such as drugs. Du Bois was very cordial and asked me to stop at his laboratory at Bellevue Hospital, which of course I did. That was the beginning of a fruitful relationship which has lasted ever since, its intellectual binding force being our common interest in the metabolic rate in all its connotations.

The question uppermost at that time was how to derive the norm. Prior to meeting Du Bois, I had, together with W. W. Palmer and J. L. Gamble (5), found a parallelism between the basal calories per unit of time and the excretion of endogenous creatinine in the urine in normal subjects. F. G. Benedict had expressed the belief that basal metabolism is determined by the total protoplasmic mass of the body, and Otto Folin had taught that endogenous creatinine excretion is an index of total protoplasmic mass. Therefore, it seemed reasonable to determine whether any significant relationship existed between these two functions. Our results suggested that such was the case.

Endogenous creatinine excretion might have become the point of reference for judging the normality or abnormality of the basal metabolism, had not Du Bois soon after devised a more convenient one—namely, the surface area of the body, together with an easy way of determining it. This method has been universally used in clinical calorimetry ever since. In 1916 I spent three weeks with Du Bois, working in the Russell Sage calorimeter room at Bellevue, learning the techniques of the respiration calorimeter, participating in the "runs" on certain patients, and serving several times as subject in the calorimeter myself. This experience was, like that with Newburgh, highly educational to me, and its benefits have endured.

Aub, the third man who entered my life significantly at this time, had finished his MGH internship in 1915. He was eager for an experience in research, and I suggested that he go to Bellevue and work with Du Bois.

He did so for a year and then returned to the MGH as one of the early medical residents. He and I then worked together on certain metabolic problems until the spring of 1917, when the country's war effort claimed us both. Thus ended this formative period of our research lives.

Of my war service, nothing need be said here except to note which parts of the total experience were professionally rewarding. A considerable amount of administrative work seemed at the time a complete loss professionally. For twelve months I was adjutant of a base hospital in France, and for eight I had odd jobs in England—embarkation medical officer, ward medical officer, and for a brief time medical consultant. As I look back, it seems clear that these experiences were more valuable professionally than I had thought at the time. They were good training in human relations. Medically, the high spot was the influenza epidemic. I have not seen the like of it before or since. Its fulminating course, high mortality, early anoxemia, extreme moisture in the lungs, and watery bloody sputum made a unique picture—nothing at all like classic pneumococcus pneumonia. Our helplessness in treating this disease was appalling. The experience was one I shall never forget. It is as vivid in my mind as though it had occurred but yesterday.

When the war was over and people resumed their peacetime activities, events began to move fast on the academic front at MGH. Edsall had become dean of the faculty of medicine at Harvard, as well as being professor and medical chief at the hospital. He had converted a suite of old administrative offices into research laboratories close to the medical wards. He had collected funds bit by bit from hither and yon. There were no government or categorical disease society handouts in those days. Young men were rallying round—George R. Minot, Paul D. White, Reginald Fitz, Arlie V. Bock, and others. Lines of research were crystallizing—hematology, hemodynamics, metabolism, endocrinology, cardiology, and so forth. After the war, Aub went to work full time with Cannon at the medical school. Newburgh had already gone to Ann Arbor. The edifice of the full-time teaching clinic at MGH was well under construction.

When I returned to civilian status, I got fully into the way of life of the middle estate in medicine and accepted the idea that I would stay in it. Edsall got me a modest salary and instructorship in medicine and in 1921 an assistant professorship. The patterns of activity in such a milieu were forming. The three essential functions of medicine—practice, teaching, and research—all had to be served. The philosophy was that full-time clinicians had to participate in all these. One could be neither a well-grounded clinical teacher nor a well-oriented clinical investigator unless he was also exposed to the mellowing influence of some direct responsibility in the care of patients. So Edsall assigned me certain ward duty as early as March, 1919. Making rounds with house staff and ward clerks became one of my well-loved activities, and hardly a year has gone by since that I have not done some of it. Edsall also believed that having private patients did something to broaden the clinical teacher's viewpoint in a way that public hospital work alone could not do. He got permission for the full-timers to see a limited number of private patients at the hospital and to care for them in the newly opened private pavilion (the Phillips House). For this purpose I was allotted a Pullman-drawing-room-sized "office" to make my headquarters for all purposes of my job, including seeing an occasional private patient. It took some faith to see a doctor in such a place. It was more like a monk's cell than a doctor's office, and, as it was next to the place where the hospital stored its liquor, there was always a slight aroma of the barroom about it.

A policy question arose about just how much private practice the so-called full-timers should be allowed to do. Edsall consulted the trustees of the hospital about his own case, and all he could ever get out of them was that they considered him a gentleman and they hoped that he thought they were! The policy finally arrived at was that the amount of private practice should not be more than was consistent with doing a fair measure of full-time work. It was more a moral than a legal issue. Through the years it has undergone some modifications. How the private practice of the full-timers was to be paid for was also a problem. At Johns Hopkins Hospital—where, with abundant aid from the Rockefeller Foundation, the major clinical departments had been put on a strictly full-time salaried basis as early as 1913—"the professor and his staff consisting of associate professors, associates, assistants, etc." (6), agreed to accept no fees at all from patients. They were expected to live on their salaries. They could take care of patients privately, but the fees collected for such service went to the hospital and were applied to departmental budgets.

Edsall considered such a policy unsound. Inherent in it was the danger that the full-time staff member could be exploited by the institution and forced to make a substantial contribution to the departmental budget by caring for private patients. It was possible, although not inevitable, that such a system could lead to serious encroachment on the academic services of the full-time people. He arranged, therefore, that the full-timers collect their own fees for the small amount of private practice performed by them. This policy became known as the "Harvard full-time system."

Another policy followed by Edsall from the beginning of his service was based on the belief that, for ideal clinical teaching, full-time salaried teachers should work side by side with volunteer staff physicians who made their living in private practice. He believed that each could give the student something which the other could not so well. The organization of teaching and research was in the hands of the full-time staff. Clinical teaching was shared by the two groups without any distinction.

In 1923 Edsall resigned from his professorship and hospital appointment in order to devote all his time to being dean at Harvard, of both the faculties of medicine and public health. A joint committee of school and hospital got busy to find a successor. I was in no position to know what was going on and was rather astounded when, in the autumn of 1923, the job was offered to me. Although I had some misgivings about my competence for it, here it was in my lap; and, launched as I was by then in full-time medicine, I would have been a fool to refuse it. Thus I became the Jackson Professor of Clinical Medicine at Harvard and Chief of Medical Services at the hospital. These two constituted one job. Edsall left me a young but vigorous university clinic with great growth potential. Just before he resigned, he had obtained a grant from the Rockefeller Foundation sufficient to reconstruct the medical half of the Bulfinch building (the original MGH) and to add an ample ell in the rear. I had the opportunity to work out the plans for this reconstruction and new construction with the director of the hospital, Dr. Frederic A. Washburn, and the architect. The confines of the old building imposed some restrictions, but not serious ones, and it was possible with the money at hand to get an adequate edifice which for many years served the needs of the teaching clinic well. I wish some of the young people today who think they cannot do any research without the utmost in luxurious laboratories could see the facilities we then made good use of. As a matter of fact, a bit of this sort of thing remains in the cellar of the Bulfinch, where some very high-grade scientific work is being done in rather sorry quarters.

As the renovations would take the better part of a year, it was decided, the plans being completed, that I should take a semisabbatical year. I sailed to England in April, 1924, to spend six months. This period I devoted to what Osler used to call "brain dusting." I made ward rounds repeatedly with the heads of the several full-time professorial units in the London teaching hospitals, observing their methods of teaching as well as their care of patients. I visited their research laboratories and their outpatient clinics. I had particularly happy times with Francis Fraser at St. Bartholomew's, Arthur Hurst at Guy's, Arthur Ellis at the London Hospital, and Hugh MacLean at Thomas's. And there were many others.

I visited Cambridge several times and renewed my friendship with Barcroft. Also, I met Sir Gowland Hopkins and discussed with him the likelihood of there being many cases of multiple subclinical avitaminoses. At a meeting of the Physiological Society at Cambridge, I was impressed by the free way in which investigators tore each other's work apart, with no apparent ill feeling. We could learn something from them about healthy scientific disputation. Also at this meeting I saw Julian Huxley demonstrate that the Barcroft blood-gas apparatus could be used as a metabolimeter for studying protozoa. I was interested in respiratory metabolism myself and was familiar with the Barcroft apparatus. And I was rather put out that I had not been bright enough to think up this application for myself. David P. Barr, who was abroad for a reason similar to mine, brushing up for his full-time professorship of medicine at Washington University, attended this meeting with me.

Other visits during this sojourn in Britain were to Sheffield to see the Mellanbys' work on rickets, oatmeal, and vitamin D; to Edinburgh and Glasgow; and to Bristol, where I attended a meeting of the Association of Physicians of Great Britain and Ireland. Altogether, this British interlude was delightful and intellectually refreshing. It produced new friendships and brightened old ones, and in subsequent life these overseas bonds have been especially rewarding.

Back in Boston in the autumn of 1934, I at once took up the full duties of the job to which I had been appointed. As it turned out, I held it uninterruptedly for the next twenty-seven years—that is to say, until the university's retiring rule ended the connection in June, 1951. I shall treat this period, which has been the *pièce de résistance* of my professional life, as a whole.

It is necessary to speak of my own attitude toward this job and my concept of its nature. The primary, all-inclusive objective, begun by Edsall, was to promote the development and evolution of a modern university medical clinic of the best quality possible. I use "university" here in a spiritual rather than organizational or pedagogical sense. The place must have the ethos of a university.

Although the objective was essentially the same as Christian's at the Brigham Hospital, the problem at MGH differed sharply, in that, instead of creating everything *de novo*, one had to deal with a venerable institution and mold it to a modern purpose. When I took over, the hospital was already 103 years old and the medical school 150. There were plenty of intrenched mores which had to be dealt with understandingly if peace was to be preserved. There was also a sizable group of volunteer staff physicians without whom we could not have carried the customary patient load. It was very necessary that the morale of these physicians be kept high by making their conditions of work rewarding to them. Several in this group and on the staff, all senior to me in years, had been my teachers. All these men supported me handsomely in everything I wanted to do as chief and thus earned my profound gratitude.

I visualized my own role in this milieu as chiefly integrator and curator. I felt it should be the duty of the chief to maintain an environment in which creative scholarship in medicine could flourish, high standards of practice (both scientific and ethical) would prevail, and the learning process would be enhanced at all levels by the very nature of the place itself. There was no call, as I saw it, for dominating leadership—*geheimrath* medicine—in an American university clinic. If the chief could establish conditions that would attract able people and, having got them, keep them content in their work and promote their growth, his main function would be fulfilled. This was my concept of the task in the beginning, and this was the policy I followed throughout my tenure. All I can say now is that the clinic was a distinguished one during that whole period and that there was a minimum of animosity among its members. At least I may claim that I did not hold it back!

There are several categories of people in the community of such a clinic

—full-time and part-time staff physicians, house-staff physicians, undergraduate medical students, and occasional graduate students—and their recruitment and the relationships among them are important matters. Then, of course, there are patients, and they are very important too; the whole affair exists for them.

The undergraduate students were assigned to us by the dean's office at the medical school. They were split about equally among the Brigham, the Boston City, and the Massachusetts General. At the present time, the Beth Israel Hospital also has a share. The other categories of people mentioned above we selected for ourselves. Choosing interns I always regarded of primary importance. These were the people by whose performance in later life the merit of the clinic would be judged. The objective was always to secure the most promising from among the total lot of candidates that came up for the oral examination. The medical school of origin was not a factor in selection unless it was known to be an inferior one. The candidates were in competition with one another for jobs, and the hospitals were in competition with one another for candidates. This competition I always felt was wholesome, provided that no element of skulduggery ever got in. The examination committee could agree at once on the desirability or undesirability of some of the candidates. Over others we often had long and penetrating disputations. The "promise" we sought was not identifiable by any one pattern. Moreover, the decisions represented value judgments of intangible attributes subjectively arrived at by each member of the committee for himself. Sometimes it was tough going to arrive at a consensus.

The residency was something else again. As indicated earlier, there were no residents when I was an intern. Edsall cautiously put in a medical resident in 1913. Walter W. Palmer was the first incumbent, Paul D. White the second. Their time was largely free for research, although they were available to advise the interns on request. From that simple beginning the impressive residential hierarchy of the present time has gradually evolved. When I took over, I increased the teaching function of the residents considerably, with regard to both the undergraduate medical students—"the clinical clerks"—and the interns they supervised. They still had a portion of their time for research. In 1930 I added, somewhat in the Hopkins tradition, a "chief resident." He became the kingpin of the medical house staff, and through him I had an excellent liaison and contact with all house-staff and student affairs. He tied the whole service at these levels into a closely knit, smoothly running enterprise. The house-staff program eventually became a four-year one—or longer if, as often happened, an extra year for study elsewhere were interposed. Through the years the chief residents have been a distinguished line of progeny. Most of them have remained in full-time medicine. Several are professors of medicine and heads of university departments. Some are in full-time research positions. A few have gone into private practice but have maintained some research and teaching activities on a part-time basis. Of those who did not go all the way through the chief residency, many have stayed in full-time medicine after completing house-staff training in some other clinic. The main point I want to make about the house-staff system is that it has evolved, not exclusively, but par excellence, into a breeding ground for the middle estate in medicine.

A few points need to be made about the permanent staff also. Edsall started with a corps of old-style volunteer physicians plus a skeleton force of full-time people. As time went on, more funds for full-time salaries from both the hospital and the medical school gradually became available. Also, a new category of workers, research fellows, made its appearance—and has grown prodigiously of late. It was my duty as chief to harmonize the activities of these several categories so that patients would be well cared for, students would be well taught, and good research would be done. My policy was to avoid compartmentalization and administrative interference as much as possible, although some of both was inevitable. I tried to get as many physicians as possible, of all categories, involved to some extent in the care of general hospital patients.

In the private pavilions, originally, private doctors took complete responsibility for their private patients. So long as they did not commit mayhem and get found out doing it, their work was supervised by no one. Gradually house staff was introduced into this area, thus exposing the work a little more to view and thereby elevating its standard. In sharp contrast, there is in general wards and outpatient clinics of a closed-staff teaching hospital what amounts to group practice provided by teams of doctors. Under such circumstances, it is absolutely necessary to have all responsibility for the care of patients so clearly defined and placed that there never can be any confusion about who is responsible for whom and for what. To this end, a member of the senior staff was placed in charge of each medical ward for stated blocks of time. While on such a tour of duty, he had final and continuous responsibility for every patient admitted to his ward. He had the allotment of house staff and fourth-year students—clinical clerks—assigned to his ward to help him. He performed his function chiefly through the daily visit or ward round, which became an exercise of central importance from the point of view of both medical care and medical education. The surgeon's pinnacle of professional activity is in the operating room; the physician's is in the teaching hospital, at the bedside during the ward round. I assigned staff physicians to ward duty without regard to whether they were full-time or volunteer. Their responsibilities and functions on the wards were the same regardless of their status. I assigned some of this duty each year to myself. The apportionment and integration of responsibilities in the care of patients among all members of the team, from clinical clerks up, by the visiting physician made the ward round an occasion at which all involved could give of themselves in service and receive in understanding and learning. The doctor-patient relationship and the teacher-student relationship had to be established fully, but in such fashion that neither jeopardized the other in any way. This integration became a vital responsibility of the visiting physician. The maintenance of these standards was always one of my major concerns and interests. I should like to stress the generalization that the presence of medical students and the surrounding atmosphere of learning inevitably improve the care of patients.

And so we come to the third great function of the university clinic, research. For two reasons, despite its importance, I shall not elaborate here on the research done during my conduct of the MGH medical clinic. For one thing, lack of space precludes it, and, for another, I have just had published a book entitled *Ward 4* (7), which gives a perspective of this matter. I hope some of my present readers will care to have a look at it. *Ward 4* is the ten-bed research ward which I founded in 1925. It is now called the Mallinckrodt Ward in honor of Mr. Edward Mallinckrodt, Jr., its chief benefactor.

The strong pillars of research during my time were Joseph C. Aub, Chester M. Jones, Walter Bauer, and Fuller Albright. Their labors are sketched in depth in the book. Antedating them all, and myself also, was Frederick T. Lord. This volunteer physician, who graduated from the internship in 1901, served on the outpatient staff from 1903 to 1912 and on the visiting (wards) staff from 1912 to his retirement in 1934. As already mentioned, he was one of my teachers, to whom I owe much. The point I wish to make about him is that, despite a very active private consulting practice, he did all his hospital assignments with the utmost devotion, and, in addition, throughout his career he found time to carry on a series of researches entirely his own. These had to do chiefly with bacterial infections of the lungs—pneumococcus, actinomyses, and tuberculosis. When I was a student, Dr. Lord had a cubicle in the pathology building, and when Edsall first got some rooms for medical department laboratories, one of these was Lord's. For diligence and dedication to a scientific objective in medicine, I have seldom seen his equal. His practice, moreover, lay in the same field as his research. He made them complementary to each other.

Similarly, I saved some of my own time for clinical research, and the subject of this remained what it had been before World War I—the thyroid. To use academic terminology, if internal medicine was my field of dispersion, then the thyroid was my field of concentration. At the present time, in spite of two retirements, I still am keeping actively involved in matters thyroid. This may be called my "medical hobby."

The development of special clinics closely tied up with research laboratories has become a frequent pattern at MGH. It has been by means of such hookups that much of our long-term clinical investigation has been accomplished. In them we find physicians, surgeons, clinical specialists, and basic scientists joining hands to solve problems of mutual interest. It is significant that this type of activity has attracted an ever increasing number of professional visitors both from home and from abroad. There is educational, as well as investigative, value in it. We got such an affair—the Thyroid Clinic and Metabolism Laboratory—going in a small way before World War I. It gained impetus after that war and has grown steadily ever since.

The thyroid studies dear to my heart from the beginning are fully described in other publications, so I shall not go into any detailed description here. *Ward 4* has a chapter on them. Also, the Prefaces to the two editions of my textbook, *The Thyroid and Its Diseases* (8), give a narrative of the enterprise from its inception. Here I shall merely indicate the evolution of our thinking on thyroid problems and the broadening of our approach to them. The direction of this evolution was from practical to basic, but always related to the patient.

At first, I merely collected patients and measured their metabolism, which contributed a quantitative flavor to the otherwise empirical character of clinical observation. It was analogous to taking the body temperature or blood pressure but more specifically related to a certain function—that of the thyroid. The type of study made in the beginning was on the effect of treatment in various types of thyroid disease, e.g., Graves' disease, myxedema, etc. We used the BMR as a measuring stick of thyroid function in observing the effect of certain therapeutic agents. Other clinicians, notably Edward P. Richardson, first full-time chief of a surgical service at MGH, and George W. Holmes, chief roentgenologist, joined forces with me in clinical observation and study of patients. After World War I, the activity began to attract young full-time workers—research fellows—who acquired additional methods and delved deeper into the morbid physiology of the thyroid, striving to find the explanation of symptoms and the effects of therapeutic agents by exploring at basic levels the processes involved in the function of the thyroid. Early in the game we studied quantitatively the effect of subtotal thyroidectomy in Graves' disease and determined a curve of decline in metabolic rate which later we compared with one obtained from patients treated with iodine instead of thyroidectomy. The curves were essentially alike, from which we concluded that both procedures acted by cutting off the flow of hormone from the thyroid—in the first instance by removing most of the factory, in the latter by somehow blocking the production or delivery of its product—thyroid hormone. My first research fellow in this work was Harold N. Segall, of Montreal, and the second was M. Paul Starr, then of Chicago.

Very early our thoughts became centered about iodine and the fact that the thyroid parenchyma has a specific need for this element unlike that of any other cell in the body. In brief, the biochemical hormonology of the thyroid became a center of interest. In 1928–29 I sent one of my most gifted residents, the late William T. Salter, to work at University College, London, under the tutelage of Charles R. Harington, the synthesizer of thyroxine. Salter came back with techniques for producing various fractions of thyroglobulin—the thyroxine-containing colloid of the thyroid acini—and, together with J. Lerman, he assayed them on patients with myxedema. The patient with untreated myxedema thus became a priceless *Versuchsperson* for us, and we were constantly on the watch for them, picking them up even on the streets! From all this work it became evident not only that any substance possessing thyroid-hormone-like activity must contain iodine but that its calorigenic activity is related to the relative amount of iodine it contains. The curves of response to physiologically active substances and the corresponding curves of decay were worked out.

Scientific inquiry is likely to progress by fits and starts. The advent of a method that opens new territory may lead to rapid exploitation. Radioactive isotopes, which became available for biological and medical research in 1937, offered such a method. They were a bonanza for investigators of the thyroid. Iodine could be made radioactive, and its passage could thus be traced by means of radiation detectors or counters not only through the thyroid but through the entire body. Those of us in the thyroid study group at MGH got this information from the late Karl T. Compton, former president of MIT. This was early in 1937. Almost immediately, with his collaboration, a joint research enterprise was set up by the physics department of MIT and the thyroid clinic of MGH. It was a sound interdisciplinary partnership and has continued with ever broadening scope. The whole metabolism of iodine, in both health and disease, is being worked out by means of radioiodine. Moreover, through the years radioiodine has been found useful in diagnosis and treatment also, and the indications for its use in these fields have been thoroughly determined.

Other techniques came along in rapid order—antithyroid drugs, pituitary thyrotropin, tissue culture of thyroid cells, chromatography. They were all put to good use by members of our thyroid study group to attack basic problems of thyroid hormonology such as these: How is thyroid hormone made in the body? What actually is the thyroid hormone? How is its rate of manufacture regulated? How does it act upon target cells? R. W. Rawson, who was with us from 1941 to 1948, studied particularly the pituitary-thyroid relationship and various factors which affect this servomechanism. John B. Stanbury, who has taken a leading part in the research activities beginning in 1948, the year he was chief medical resident, has actively explored the biosynthesis of all the iodinated amino acids found in the thyroid—and is still at it. Each step in the process appears to be promoted by a particular enzyme, and when there is a defect in the process, as in certain sporadic cretins, its location can be pinpointed. Sometimes the same defect will be found in several members of one family, which introduces to thyroid studies the consideration of biochemical genetics—also being applied to the problem of the etiology of Graves' disease.

On visits in 1958 to the thyroid laboratory, I found the investigators actually working inside target cells to observe the action of thyroid hormone at the protoplasmic level—a far cry from merely measuring the BMR of the whole person, which is where we started in 1914.

As time passed, the thyroid study group developed friendships and scientific correspondence with investigators in several other countries. With the Latin-American countries, especially Argentina, we had particularly constructive exchanges. These came to full flower in 1951, when we inaugurated a long-term study of endemic goiter jointly with members of the faculty of medicine of the University of Cuyo at Mendoza in the Argentine Andes. The results of this study were published in monograph form in both English and Spanish (9). We also had enlightening associations with various British workers, notably Sir Charles Harington, Rosalind Pitt-Rivers, E. E. Pochin, Selwyn Taylor, Raymond Greene, and others. We were especially intimate with the medical clinic of the University of Leiden through Professor A. Querido. Also, we made good scientific friends in the Scandinavian and other countries. I should like to stress how valuable such exchanges are, not only scientifically, but as instrumental in promoting friendships among scholars in different countries which can constitute at least one binding force in this dreadfully divided world.

Another compelling concern of mine was that both students and staff should at all times be thoroughly conscious of their humane duties toward patients. I always had the inspiring co-operation of Ida M. Cannon, for many years chief of social service at MGH. She had deep insight into the meaning of illness to the patient and a powerful urge to impart this understanding to the medical student. As early as 1913, with Edsall, she had started a weekly medicosocial conference for students, which for a number of years I conducted with her. Later, Dr. Edward L. Young and the late Drs. John P. Monks and William W. Beckman ably took turns doing likewise with her. The ward clerk would present the medical aspects of a case he had taken, and then the social worker, who had visited the patient's home, would give her angle. Students were very resistant to this sort of exercise in the early years, thinking it irrelevant to their medical objective. But gradually this attitude gave way to real interest and recognition that the social component could be as important as the biological in diagnosis and treatment. The interest of the house staff also became aroused, and very effective teamwork with the social workers developed.

In 1948 a signal event occurred. We brought the parson into the medical education picture. My ward team one day on rounds put a difficult question to me which I evaded by saying, "This is not a medical question but one in moral philosophy. I will get you a moral philosopher." The Rev. Willard L. Sperry, dean of the Harvard Divinity School, answered this call. He was received with spontaneous enthusiasm. The amphitheater was packed with house staff, students, social workers, and nurses. Even some of the visiting staff turned out. Sperry's message made a lasting impression (10). It was evidently one long wanted. But I do not believe that, had it been offered in 1912, there would have been any such response. Recognition of the nature of patients' moral and spiritual needs had increased markedly in that interim.

Psychiatric insight of physicians in routine care of patients has also grown apace in this same period. There was hardly any in my intern days. When, in 1934, MGH installed a psychiatric service close to the medical services, progress was accelerated.

It should be clear by now that I have an enduring interest in medical education. I have practiced it at the hospital. I have disputed about it in the sanctums of the medical school and elsewhere. Reform and improvement of the curriculum have always challenged me. Even as a fourth-year student, I participated in a memorial to the faculty giving the students' opinions on how the curriculum could be improved. Nothing came of it! In 1921 and 1928, I sat on special committees which achieved great reduction in the number of third-year lectures and, in 1928, the introduction of some good clinical work in the third year. This gain for teaching by the case method over didactic lectures was all to the good, but many other changes were badly needed.

No further reform was accomplished until 1942. Then we were in the midst of an accelerated program imposed by World War II. Also, we were thinking of postwar problems and opportunities. In 1942 Dean of Medicine Charles Sidney Burwell appointed a new committee on curriculum reform with me as chairman. We struggled manfully for a year and a half. It was tough going. The representatives of some of the departments clung to their relative autonomy. No one was eager to relinquish hours. It was interesting that the preclinical departments were, on the whole, more resistant to change than the clinical. Their spokesmen seemed fearful that the virginal purity of their disciplines might be violated.

We did identify some principles upon which we thought reform should be based but had little success in getting them applied. Perhaps the most important of these was that the curriculum badly needed integrating both horizontally and vertically. It was believed, for example, that the learning process would be facilitated for the first-year student if he could learn how the kidney functions concurrently with how it is built, instead of four months later. Similarly, it was thought that patients could be shown early in the course to bring alive certain basic principles; and, conversely, that preclinical science could be brought to the bedside in the clinical years to enhance the understanding of diagnosis and treatment. Some of us felt that the progressive stages in undergraduate medical education could be identified as (*a*) normal human biology, (*b*) abnormal human biology, and (*c*) practical applications—medicine, surgery, and psychiatry. Several medical schools, notably Western Reserve and Colorado, have been making good progress along such lines, but it was only recently that Dean George Packer Berry got something of the sort going at Harvard. It should not be forgotten that experiments must be tried in education as well as in anything else if better methods are to be reached through evolution.

Of other educational activities in which I participated at the medical school, choosing students and choosing professors were perhaps the most important. The admissions committee of a medical school today has a big job. When I sat on Harvard's, the method of free discussion of each candidate (after inspection of credentials) until a consensus was reached was probably as sound as any.

Professors were selected by ad hoc committees, and I sat on several. I recall an amusing incident when a successor was being sought to Cannon in the chair of physiology. Three questions came up which indicate the thinking at that time: Do we want a physiologist? What is a physiologist? Is Landis a physiologist? None of these was answered, but Eugene M. Landis, who had been a professor of physiology and later of medicine elsewhere, was chosen.

Of course, through the years I also took part in discussions of many policy problems, in faculty meetings and, more intimately, on the school's administrative board. A good deal of time at such meetings was spent on necessary, humdrum routine, but occasionally a real battle was joined on some issue, such as the admission of women to medical school, and then the meetings became enjoyable.

Something needs to be said of my extramural activities. The American Society for Clinical Investigation I joined in my youth and was at one time its secretary. This was stimulating for the young clinical investigator, and I made many important friendships there. I had the good fortune to be elected a member of the Association of American Physicians in 1919, and its meetings have been among the most rewarding experiences of my professional life. In thirty-nine years I have missed only four, twice because I was attending those of the daughter society, the Association of Physicians of Great Britain and Ireland, and I have been secretary, councillor, and president (1942) of the association. I have always enjoyed presenting and discussing papers for this forum of physicians and basic scientists. The association's programs document the history and the advance of scientific medicine over nearly three-quarters of a century. One can see here clearly the action of survival of the fittest on new forms of therapy—drug and other—that appear, usually with great acclaim and an explosion of papers, and in five or ten years, or less, may have disappeared. On the other hand, if they possess genuine merit, they survive and find their proper level of interest. The same process applies to ideas, theories, concepts, and technology.

The American Goiter Society has been an activity of more recent years. It is very useful in helping me keep up to date on my "hobby," the thyroid. I was president of this society in 1948.

I joined the American College of Physicians in 1928 at the request of its newly elected president, Charles F. Martin, dean of medicine at McGill, and immediately became a member of its board of regents. The college is essentially a great postgraduate educational enterprise for its thousands of internist members. Martin wished to elevate its standards and did. In 1938 I was president of the college, and then the fun began, because I made some statements which infuriated the stalwarts of organized medicine (11). All I said was that I believed that the American Medical Association should allow freedom of speech and expression of minority opinion in its legislative body and publications. I thought they should encourage a "loyal opposition." I was immediately attacked in both the lay and the medical press with quite a show of emotion. It was from this experience that my interest in the public affairs of medicine began to grow. To make a long story short, I have continued to think, talk, and write on the subject of getting better medical care to the American people at a price they can afford. I get satisfaction from this sort of activity because I believe it may contribute to the development of a more enlightened public opinion on problems of the distribution of medical care. I have even felt that it was my duty to air these opinions (believed to be liberal), because my academic position made me immune to punishment by organized medicine in a way that private practitioners are not. It is not possible to elaborate here on my views on the public affairs of medicine, but that has already been done in my 1953 book, *Doctors, People and Government* (12). At the moment it is sufficient to state briefly the conclusions I have reached on these matters. This paper would not be a true "perspective" of me without them.

In the first place, I will say that my experience through the years leads me to believe that the behavior of organized medicine in social, political, and economic matters is reactionary. It is guild behavior. It seeks to preserve and promote the special interests of doctors. It is like labor-union behavior. It intrigues me nowadays to see the mine workers and organized medicine at odds with each other over the miners' medical program—the pot calling the kettle black. Second, I regard "fee for service," to which the organized profession clings desperately, as outmoded and not conducive to fair and even distribution and provision of medical care. I also regard the slogan "free choice of doctor" as emotional and unrealistic (13).

I think we must experiment in the provision of medical care just as we do in education, in order, by survival of the fittest, to evolve something better. I think the most promising plan at the moment is group practice combined with prepayment of all costs, the benefits to be paid solely in service. Under such a plan, welfare agencies, voluntary or tax-supported, will have to meet such portion of premiums as patients cannot meet themselves. Plans of this sort should ideally be operated by non-profit disinterested bodies with both lay and professional people in their membership. The best example of what I have in mind is the Health Insurance Plan of Greater New York. I would, however, like to see a further step taken: namely, such a plan tied to the medical education process. I can best illustrate this notion by quoting from a recommendation I circulated two years ago to key people in the Boston area:

On the theory that medical practice, medical education, and medical research are inherently interdependent, and that the medical schools with their affiliated teaching hospitals are the fountainhead of all of them, it is proposed that there be set up for Greater Boston a comprehensive prepaid voluntary medical and hospital care plan for any individuals or groups that wish to join it, which will make use of the area's three medical schools and six of their affiliated hospitals, and also the health departments of the universities and colleges. It is proposed also that in the operation of such a plan the functions of practice, teaching, and research be correlated in so far as possible at all levels of operation.

It is not suggested that the plan be applied exclusively to all patients of the organized staffs of the hospitals involved. It is believed that it can coexist smoothly with other methods of providing medical care. It is expected, however, that if it proved its worth, it might ultimately become the prevailing method. Nor is it suggested that the plan be confined to the teaching hospitals. It is to be desired that gradually others, and of a variety of sorts, be fitted into it.

So far the doctors have resisted any such development.

There are, of course, other extramural activities, but I cannot dwell on them. During World War II, I served as chairman of a committee of the National Research Council on clinical investigation. I was very happy to find that my friend Newburgh was a member of this also. We served together. We had the duty of evaluating proposals for research projects of possible military value and making recommendations to higher authority. In the early 1950's I served four years on the National Advisory Health Council of the National Institutes of Health.

I have also served as teacher of medicine at several other medical schools, among which I prize especially a month in 1949 at New York University as Stieglitz Visiting Professor; two months at St. Luke's Hospital, Tokyo, in 1955; and a month at St. Bartholomew's Hospital, London, in 1956. I have lectured at many medical schools in the United States and abroad and given papers or talks to state and county medical societies, student medical societies, and lay groups and have participated in a variety of postgraduate medical courses about the country.

A delightful thing about the travels involved in such activities is that one is constantly meeting former residents, interns, or students, and the interest, even affection, which they display is heart-warming. Often they are responsible for the invitation to go to the place in question. They often have attained distinction there. One takes pride in the progeny of the parent clinic.

There is one highlight which cannot be left out of this picture. Partly social but intensely professional, the Medical Exchange Club of Boston, a dinner club, has been meaningful to all its members through the years. Started in 1920, it is still going strong. The membership is held at about a dozen. Those who depart this life are mourned, but their places are filled with the most suitable young successors we can find. Once a month except in summer we dine at one another's houses. "Exchange" signifies intellectual exchange. We aim to have among our members a nice balance of clinical and basic disciplines. We dine well, we talk well—at least we think we do—and we learn something at each meeting. We can count two Nobel laureates in our membership—the late George Minot and the very much alive John Enders. A. Newton Richards is a very loyal honorary member; so are Ernest Goodpasture and Philip D. Wilson. Formerly they were active members. Among our dead are Watson Sellards, Elliott Cutler, Kenneth Blackfan, Cecil Drinker, George Wislocki, Frederick C. Irving, and others. Our living include some good minds also. Francis M. Rackemann is and always has been the shepherd of this flock (secretary). He alone keeps it going and duly buries its transactions in the deepest depths of Harvard's medical archives. "The Fecundity of Aggregation," said Cannon—this is it.

But now I come to an important milestone in my life—my retirement by Harvard. For many years I knew that I would be through July 1, 1951, if I lived that long—that is to say, to the age of sixty-six. I prepared myself in advance by developing a philosophy of how to deal with postretirement years and extra years which the lengthening life-expectancy in our country is offering. I had seen enough friends and patients meet retirement the wrong way so that at least I knew how not to do it. Sudden transition, I became convinced, from a full life to an empty one invites degenerative disease and discontent, and a life all of play and loafing is an empty one. The way to health and happiness as one ages, I am sure, is to work as hard and for as long a time at something which gives deep satisfaction as the good Lord will let him. I had resolved, therefore, to get myself a new job as soon as I retired.

Through the kindness of a former intern of mine, Dana L. Farnsworth, I was able to get a very good one. As a full-time man, I had accumulated very little in the way of private practice and had no desire to start one at the age of sixty-six. So, when Dr. Farnsworth, who was then chief of the medical department at MIT, offered me a position as physician, I accepted with alacrity and thereafter had six extraordinarily happy years in this new environment. It is amusing that, having been a student at MIT before ever I went to Harvard, I ended up there fifty-three years later as a salaried physician. Between the two connections I had also collaborated with MIT people in research and had served on the advisory committee to visit the medical department.

My duties at MIT were essentially practicing internal medicine as a member of a medical group. I took my turn, with my fellows, in charge of bed patients—students chiefly, but some faculty and employees, in the infirmary and also on outpatient duty. Dr. Farnsworth had started a routine health survey of faculty members and asked me to take it over. This was a fascinating experience because, while I made the periodic medical checkups called for, I likewise made friends with a group of brilliant people in many different disciplines. In fact, I got a free liberal education of a most unique and delightful kind from these gentlemen. Instead of taking lunch every day with a flock of doctors of medicine, as I had for many years, I began to eat this meal at the Faculty Club with the companionship of scholars in nearly every field but medicine. It was thrilling. Before retirement I had supposed I would be homesick for MGH, but I never was. Indeed, I am glad I left it because I never could have been content there on a reduced job, exposed always to the possibility of making difficulties for my successor. My successor is Walter Bauer, formerly my resident, and I love him dearly. The last thing I want to do is get in his way by haunting my old job. Actually, he has been extraordinarily kind in asking me often to come back on special occasions, and we have thus preserved an active and happy relationship.

I had not supposed that I would have any educational occupation at MIT, but indirectly I did. If there were no medical students there, at least there were a few premedical, and I had the opportunity to interview them for medical schools and sometimes to counsel them as well. And I continued to interview medical candidates for Harvard. This experience put into my head the notion that if MIT is already in premedical education, why should it not go partway into medical—namely, through preclinical sciences up to the level of the third year of medical school? It seemed to me that MIT, with its excellent basic sciences and adequate humanities, could without too much trouble take on a further educational commitment which would be the equivalent of the first two years of medical school. In 1956 I agitated for such a project, and some genuine interest seemed to develop among the leaders of the institute. I also published a paper in the *Technology Review* (14) in which I attempted to draw an analogy between engineering education and medical education and use it as an argument in favor of MIT's taking up the latter. Nothing happened for two years, but then I was invited to submit a more detailed proposal, which I did, after some traveling to interview certain experts. So far as I know now, the matter is still being considered, and I wonder whether the plan will ever materialize. I hope it may, because I believe that it would offer something new and different in medical education. It would give an opportunity to obtain a better integration of liberal and professional education for persons going into medicine and a smoother flow of education from the high-school level to the clinical years of medical school. It would get MIT into the equivalent of a two-year medical school, although it is not desirable to call it that. I would rather compare such a program with the British, in which students matriculate for medicine at Oxford or Cambridge and stay there until they enter a London teaching hospital for their clinical years. I would expect that under such a plan a small group of very carefully chosen students would be educated for careers either in full-time medicine or in the sciences basic to medicine. I would hope that the graduates would be truly productive scholars in medicine.

It was while I was at MIT that I paid the visits to St. Luke's, Tokyo, and St. Bartholomew's, London. The latter really represents my farewell to clinical medicine, at least my last active hospital appointment. To walk the wards of this fabulous hospital, haunted by the shades of so many of Britain's medical great, clothed with all the responsibility of a full-time clinical teacher, was a heart-warming valedictory experience. My title was "Temporary Director of the Medical Professorial Unit," and it was for the month of May, 1956. I owe this opportunity entirely to my friend and host, Dr. E. F. Scowen, the permanent director of the unit, and I am profoundly grateful to him for it.

While I was at Bart's, I had an American opposite number in surgery, F. A. Simeone, once of Harvard and MGH, now of Western Reserve. On one occasion our hosts had a delightful little dinner party for us, and we were both invited to enrol as "perpetual honorary students of the Medical College of St. Bartholomew's Hospital." I consider this a very great honor because it carries the direct implication that I am still capable of learning!

In June, 1957, I resigned from MIT and thus entered my second retirement. My appointment was an annual one, so they were under no obligation to keep me. Although they very cordially asked me to stay a year or two longer, I thought it much smarter to leave while they felt that way rather than to stay until the time they would have wished me to leave. I am sure that the service at MIT did much to promote both my bodily and my mental health, and I am very thankful for it.

Now in my second retirement I seem to be still able to keep pleasantly busy. I greatly enjoy writing—I even enjoy thinking. That is why I consented to write this "perspective." And I have a list of other things I want to write that will keep me going indefinitely. I also still attend the weekly thyroid sessions at MGH and occasionally other exercises, grand rounds, and that sort of thing.

For the last few years I have been the secretary of my Harvard College class of 1907, and I am making gerontologic studies of the class, trying insidiously to give them hints about how to make their extra years as good as possible.

At this time of life I have been able to do more general reading. I will mention but one item, Julian Huxley's *Evolution in Action.* It filled in for me the whole gap since the *Origin*, read sixty years ago. I had said in my Kober Lecture at Georgetown in 1955, concerning the nature of research:

> In the long view, progress through research discloses itself as an evolutionary process. We may draw an analogy between the research performed consciously and with intent by man, and unconscious research on the part of nature. As man sets up experiments to find new truth, so does nature, in the case of living organisms at least, make experimental types through the process of mutation, and test them out in the struggle for existence. Thus we believe has the evolution of species come about, and in similar fashion has man acquired new knowledge and learned to improve his ways of approaching his objectives. As does nature, under an irresistible drive to procreate, force life to adapt itself to every environment, no matter now inimical, capable of supporting life at all, so does man under his drive to know, inquire into and explore every region of his cosmos to which his sensibilities and his intelligence direct him.

After saying that, I became aware of a much broader but compatible statement which Huxley had made in his book just mentioned. He carries biological evolution one step further, namely, to "psychosocial" evolution, which belongs only to man. He ends by pointing out that the "unity and sweep" of the whole process of evolution characterize all of life. I find this a convincing and noble concept.

I will now bring this "perspective" to a close by putting in a plug for the middle estate in medicine, where, after all, my life has been spent.

The middle estate in medicine is where the three functions of medicine—research, teaching, and practice—are most sweetly blended. And if, to be sure, it is those who follow exclusively a single scientific beam who make the most signal advances, it is also true that their contributions may long lie fallow unless there is development by those whose field of competence is described by a wider angle. Consider penicillin. After Fleming discovered it, nothing further happened for thirteen years until Florey proved its medical value and put it into clinical use and A. N. Richards got it into mass production, thus revolutionizing medicine throughout the world.

The full-time clinicians make and maintain teaching clinics which are the germinative centers both of new knowledge and of the people who create the forward march of medicine. None but those who love medicine and strive for excellence should go into this field.

REFERENCES

1. J. Huxley. Evolution in action. New York: Harper & Bros., 1953.
2. W. T. Sedgwick and E. B. Wilson. An introduction to general biology. 2d ed. New York: Henry Holt & Co., 1899.
3. W. B. Cannon. The way of an investigator. New York: W. W. Norton & Co., 1945.
4. E. F. Du Bois. Proc. Am. Soc. Adv. Clin. Invest., **6**:28, 1914.
5. W. W. Palmer, J. H. Means, and J. L. Gamble. J. Biol. Chem., **19**:239, 1914.
6. A. Flexner. Medical education. New York: Macmillan Co., 1925.
7. J. H. Means. Ward 4. Cambridge, Mass.: Harvard University Press, 1958.
8. ———. The thyroid and its diseases. 1st and 2d eds. Philadelphia: J. B. Lippincott Co., 1937, 1948.
9. J. B. Stanbury *et al.* Endemic goiter. Cambridge, Mass.: Harvard University Press, 1954.
10. W. L. Sperry. The ethical basis of medical practice. New York: Paul B. Hoeber, 1952.
11. J. H. Means. Ann. Int. Med., **11**:1925, 1938.
12. ———. Doctors, people and government. Boston: Little, Brown & Co., 1953.
13. H. R. Hansen. Minnesota Law Rev., **42**:527, 1958.
14. J. H. Means. Bull. Georgetown Univ. Med. Center, **9**:4, 1955.

GEORGE HOYT WHIPPLE, M.D.

Experimental Pathology—as Student and Teacher

An invitation to write an autobiography takes away some of the doubts which arise when an individual considers this very personal piece of business. Others share with me the propriety of this move. If anything which I can say will prove of some value to young workers in this wide field, then the pleasure more than compensates for the effort.

I was born (1878) in Ashland, a small town in north-central New Hampshire in the lake district. I feel very fortunate that I grew up in the country. As a result of this environment, I became interested in wild life and camping, also hiking, snowshoeing, skating, bob sledding, canoeing, fishing, hunting—all this was an essential part of my life. My physical development and stamina were favorably influenced by these factors. A continuing interest in hunting, fishing, and camping has carried throughout my life and I feel sure has increased my capacity for work, study, and teaching.

My father and his father were general medical practitioners. My mother's father, George Hoyt, was a businessman in Ashland. My father and maternal grandfather died when I was two years old and my Grandfather Whipple a year later. My two grandmothers were both intelligent, determined women who ran their households very competently. Grandmother Hoyt, with whom we lived, took large responsibility for my development and discipline. My mother had great interest in my education and was determined that it be of the best type.

I have no memory of any conscious decision during my growth period

As a young man, Dr. Whipple studied tropical diseases in the Canal Zone when General Gorgas was in command. Later he discovered and refined the potent liver extract treatment for anemia by experimental work with dogs. He built up from the ground the University of Rochester School of Medicine and Dentistry, where he actively continues work although retired as its Dean.

to become a doctor. No one tried to influence me; yet, when I was asked what I intended to do, I always replied that I was going to be a doctor. This was true in grade school, preparatory school, and college. Grade-school work went along at an average pace, but in the last year there were disciplinary troubles. This resulted in a transfer to high school in Tilton, New Hampshire, commuting daily by train. That year's work was quite satisfactory and prepared me to enter Phillips Andover Academy.

Preparatory school life was wholly given to classwork, as we lived in Andover. Mathematics, physics, chemistry, and biology were very interesting. Greek, Latin, German, and French courses, as they were then taught, were largely memory tests and were most difficult for me. If any good came from these struggles with languages, perhaps it was stern training in doing uninteresting but necessary tasks. The summers of this period were spent earning money in a drugstore and various summer hotels. I sometimes think I learned as much during the summer work periods as during the school terms.

At Yale, my courses were more diversified. Again, I enjoyed the science courses and endured the foreign-language courses, which demanded very long study periods. When the minimum of these language courses was completed, life became much brighter. In my Senior year (1900), I came in contact with an unusual man who exerted a strong influence on me—Lafayette Mendel. Work with him in biochemistry was exciting and never to be forgotten.

In college I became deeply interested in athletics—rowing and gymnastic work especially—a member of the gymnastic team, and oarsman on house and class crews. I planned to teach athletics for a year or so between college and medical school, as I was almost entirely self-supporting. I spent a year at the Holbrook Military Academy in Ossining, New York, where I taught mathematics and sciences and had charge of the athletic and gymnastic training. I found time to study Gray's *Anatomy* and learn much of the bones, muscles, vessels, and nerves with the new vocabulary. This year matured me, and I was able to take full advantage of the medical school training which began the following year at Johns Hopkins. The summers of this period were spent working on summer steamers which operated in Sunapee and Squam lakes in New Hampshire. This type of work was strenuous, interesting, and rewarding.

My mother's interest in my medical training had much to do with my final decision to train at Hopkins. She had read much about its opening, plans, and methods and thought the school plan was ideal. She urged me to be sure that my college training would qualify me for Hopkins. She was aware that many of my college friends were to study medicine at Harvard, Yale, Columbia, and Pennsylvania.

Soon after taking up my work at Hopkins in 1901, I realized that I was happier than I had ever been in my life. The work was most interesting, and to me there were no unpleasant tasks. My student associates were friendly and stimulating. Dr. Mall and Warren Lewis took charge of the dissections and left us free to do much or little as we chose. My earlier study of Gray's *Anatomy* at Holbrook helped me to qualify as student instructor the second year, the added income being most welcome. I also came to a better understanding of Dr. Mall, who subsequently urged me to work as an assistant and study abnormal human embryos.

Because of my training with Mendel and Chittenden in biochemistry, I reviewed this work with Walter Jones and acted as student assistant in his biochemistry course. He was an unusual teacher, with rare wit and interesting stories. I assisted him with some of his research study of nucleoproteins, but the chemistry was beyond me and I acted merely as an extra pair of hands and a good listener.

Physiology at first did not rouse my enthusiasm in spite of the superlative lectures of Dr. Howell. Yet, a few years later, I found my research interests in that realm and now might be termed an experimental physiologist. There seems to be no line of demarcation between physiology and pathology or pharmacology and biochemistry—all to the benefit of these related subjects.

Pharmacology with Dr. Abel was enjoyed by our class. He was spontaneous and unpredictable, a lovable person. Because of my work with Walter Jones, I was fortunate in attending several of Dr. Abel's afternoon teas, where his associates came to understand and learn from Dr. Abel, the investigator. Loevenhart was very helpful when I brought research problems to him for advice and aid at a later date.

Bacteriology and pathology were taught in one department under the direction of Dr. Welch, whose lectures were masterpieces. I enjoyed bacteriology, but pathology stood out as the subject which meant the most to me. Everything in pathology was superlative—autopsies and histopathology alike. We were fortunate to see much of MacCallum, Opie, Banting, and Marshall. I was able to do some extra work for MacCallum dissecting out parathyroids from autopsy material.

Medical students during this period, as a rule, lived in homes within walking distance of the school—a few in fraternity houses close to the school. Life in these private homes was pleasant, as most families treated the students as relatives. There were no dormitory noises and distractions. There is nothing like a quiet home environment for hard study. Boarding houses left something to be desired, but their frugal menus could be supplemented in various ways. In my senior year I took meals at a clubhouse (Pithotomy) with a group of friends, many of whom enjoyed occasional vacation cruises on the Chesapeake.

Our class looked forward with great expectations to our contacts with Dr. Osler, and we were not disappointed. Many believed him to be the greatest clinical teacher of his generation, and I am among that number. His personality was magnetic, and a smile would make a friend for life. Clinical diagnosis came with rare insight. He loved students, both junior and senior types, and enjoyed having a fringe of them at hand for his rounds on the wards. He was very proud that he was largely responsible for first bringing the medical student into the wards for active teaching and diagnosis. His large clinics were never to be forgotten, and he usually added important points because of his knowledge of pathology, often presenting autopsy material. He enjoyed having the fourth-year medical student groups at his home for Saturday suppers which resembled seminars, including some of the interesting clinical material of the week plus a discussion of medical history, often with rare books from his large library to point up the reviews. He always attended the school historical meetings, usually taking part in the discussion—an added opportunity to learn from him. He frequently came to the autopsy table if a case of his was being examined and added to the review and discussion—often toward the end of his morning teaching rounds.

When he decided to accept the Regius Professorship at Oxford, it might be said that the school and hospital went into mourning. We felt most fortunate that he completed our clinical teaching courses in 1905, before he left Baltimore—we said he graduated with us.

We had valuable contacts in medicine with other fine teachers: Drs. Thayer, McCrae, Futcher, Hamman, Henry Thomas, Campbell Howard. Our outpatient training was gained during our third year and left us in rather a confused state, as we were supposed to cover all the specialties along with medicine, surgery, pediatrics, neurology, and psychiatry. During the fourth year, we were in the hospital and attended to patients assigned individually in medicine, surgery, and obstetrics.

Surgery gave us little of the satisfaction which we derived from medicine. Dr. Halsted did not conduct student rounds, which were the responsibility of the resident surgeon. Dr. Halsted held a weekly surgical diagnostic clinic for the whole class, but, as a rule, this was a bit over our heads. Dr. Finney and Dr. Walker did splendid teaching in the surgical outpatient clinic. Dr. Cushing introduced our class to experimental surgery on the dog—a fine course designed to train students in aseptic surgical operative technique.

Gynecology was a total loss, as we were not permitted to enter the wards for gynecology. There were no general clinics. We were privileged to see Dr. Kelly in the operating room but nothing of what he did. He talked to our class more about religion than medicine.

Obstetrics was a complete contrast to gynecology. The clinic and wards were open to students, who took active part in obstetrical deliveries, both in the hospital and outside. Dr. Whitridge Williams we admired, and we accepted him and his staff as good teachers who were interested in student training.

Medical students at Hopkins often had opportunities to enjoy home visits with many of their teachers. I was most fortunate while junior and senior house pathologist in such contacts with the Cushings, Futchers, Thayers, Finneys, and especially Dr. and Mrs. Henry Thomas.

During these four busy years, a moderate amount of athletic activity was enjoyed. At that time, graduate students could participate in undergraduate athletics. I played football until a knee was injured. Orthopedic care was inadequate, and recurrent injuries followed in the succeeding years—an educational process! Baseball in the spring brought me into college grounds and country-club fields within a hundred miles of Baltimore. Handball during the winter at the YMCA improved my physical condition.

During the summer periods in medical school, I earned money as pilot on a summer steamer on Squam Lake and as medical camp counselor. This complete change in summer environment and physical activity did much to build up physical and monetary reserves for the following winter program.

During our senior year there was much debate relative to internships. Like all students, I had changed my mind relative to my future goal—surgery, medicine, pediatrics. Finally I decided on pediatrics, in which subject we had had but little training, but decided to take further basic training in pathology. MacCallum offered me a junior position in pathology, with the understanding that I would spend much time on pediatric pathology and go on the following year in clinical work, probably in New York. After an interesting year in pathology, I asked Dr. Welch about a second year in the department. He said he would be glad to give me the opportunity, but he stated another year would anchor me in pathology—an accurate prediction. So plans are ever subject to revision as interests develop, which points up the futility of a program reaching many years into the future.

The two years in pathology after graduation were most interesting and rewarding. Everything was enjoyed—autopsies, surgical pathology diagnosis, teaching, and study of special cases for publication. At this time, much of the autopsy work was done without gloves, and pathologists frequently developed superficial skin lesions of tuberculosis with enlarged regional glands, also occasionally skin lesions due to the spirochete of syphilis or to staphylococci or streptococci. These occupational hazards I was fortunate to escape. When I look back at the dirty autopsy room at Bay View where numerous examinations of persons dead from advanced ulcerative tuberculosis were made, I realize that I must have had a high resistance to the tubercle bacillus. It seems likely that this was due to a continuing exposure at age ten, when two sickly young people lived in our house and a year or so later died of pulmonary tuberculosis—"consumption." My sister developed a "scrofulous" gland which was drained, but I showed no obvious lesions—probably pulmonary foci were present.

We had the privilege of examining many unusual surgical specimens sent in from other areas for Dr. Welch's opinion. Our diagnosis having been made, we listened to the decision of the supreme court (Dr. Welch) and thus learned much from our mistakes. I remember one shocker—a specimen vomited by a young woman and examined by many so-called experts—diagnosis of various types of malignancy and operation advised —Dr. Welch's opinion—a cat's placenta showing some digestion—diagnosis, psychotic patient.

Research during these two years was largely histological—study of unusual abnormalities in autopsy material. This included a rare case of "Intestinal Lipodystrophy" (1). I was able to observe some of MacCallum's research and give a little manual aid. Teaching of second-year medical students continued my own education. We learned to lecture and prepare reports by practice. Student nurses and graduate students gave further opportunity for training.

Toward the end of this second year, an interesting opportunity in Panama was presented. A chance to learn tropical disease pathology was stressed, but the salary was much larger than my salary at the school. I believed enough money could be saved to finance a trip abroad. Dr. Welch granted me a year's leave for this work.

I am confident that the year in Panama was a valuable experience. Much contact with tropical disease resulted—amoebic dysentery, malaria, beriberi, leprosy, filariasis, and intestinal and other parasites. Reports dealing with hookworm and anemia, also blackwater fever and malaria, were published. Dr. Darling, head of the laboratory, was working on histoplasmosis, then thought to be due to a parasite but later proved to be a fungus infection.

I was fortunate in making contacts with General Gorgas. On inspection trips along the Canal Zone, I saw the master of public health in action. He was an extraordinary man who carried through on any program and overcame obstacles seemingly without difficulty. He could talk over any group of local officials to his way of thinking, and they finished by doing what he wanted while believing it was all their own plan. He was fond of evening rides on horseback, an excellent horseman, and was often accompanied by his daughter and younger men on his staff. He never assumed the attitude of the executive army general. At home and in the field he was direct, friendly, and generous to young men like myself. After this experience, I could understand his conspicuous ability to retain the loyalty of his staff and to control the health problems in a notoriously difficult tropical area.

During this year there were ample opportunities for exercise: tennis, swimming, riding, and especially baseball. In fact, exercise was a necessary part of a healthy life in the Canal Zone. The officers' quarters and dining hall were excellent. During this year we took quinine daily at breakfast, but, in spite of this, I had a malarial attack on the return trip. In New York while under treatment for this malaria, I made my first contact with Allen Whipple—a friend over the years. We decided we were "cousins."

The years 1908–14 in the Department of Pathology at Hopkins gave me further training and expanding opportunities for research in a friendly and stimulating climate. MacCallum and the other seniors in the department had gone to be directors in other schools. Winternitz and I, under Dr. Welch, carried the responsibilities for teaching and autopsy work. I moved into the hospital as resident pathologist and enjoyed all the associations with the various clinical resident staffs.

Research work developed in the Hunterian Laboratory, divided between surgery and pathology. Dr. Cushing was most active at that time on the surgical side. Some joint problems developed. Late in 1908 an interesting paper on chloroform poisoning was read by Howland and Richards at a medical school meeting. Liver necrosis was produced. I decided to produce these lesions in dogs, with the confident expectation that liver cirrhosis would result and could then be given careful study. This illustrates the fact that research programs often do not evolve as planned but that the results may be of some interest in other directions. We found that we could never produce any significant liver cirrhosis by repeated chloroform necrosis and injury of the liver. This organ in the normal dog can repair rapidly and completely with no residual scars. This work was taken up with John Sperry, and attention was given to this repair of the liver cells. Fibrinogen changes in the blood due to liver necrosis were recorded. Jaundice develops in chloroform poisoning, and this was studied in considerable detail with John King. Gradually our interest in jaundice expanded, and the various paths of escape of bile pigment from the liver were investigated.

The summer of 1909 was spent in Heidelberg, working in the laboratory of experimental medicine with Morowitz in Krehl's department in the university. Morowitz was a very vigorous and stimulating laboratory investigator. Otto Warburg was a junior in the laboratory at that time. This experience was very valuable and enabled me to understand many details of laboratory functions—some good, some not. The visit was too short to complete any significant laboratory experiments. Some crew rowing on the Neckar River was much enjoyed, and weekend trips made into Switzerland with some mountain climbing. Nürnberg and other old cities were visited.

Back at Hopkins, research problems developed in relation to chloroform poisoning in maternal, placental, and fetal tissue—also in pups in the three weeks following birth, when they are resistant to chloroform poisoning. Experimental pancreatitis interested several of my associates, including Goodpasture. A careful study of intestinal obstruction and closed intestinal loops in dogs was carried out. Studies of possible toxic factors were reported with Stone and Bernheim.

Relative to the teaching in pathology, Dr. Welch planned to give many of the lectures, but his numerous commitments in New York and elsewhere frequently meant that Winternitz and I had to give an emergency lecture. We soon divided the whole lecture series equally between us, as a fixed responsibility. It was an illuminating experience to prepare a talk and then to listen to Dr. Welch give one of his superb lectures covering the same subject. This improved our technique and kept us free of any feeling of superiority as teachers. Amusing happenings were not infrequent, and one may be mentioned to illustrate the friendly informality of the teaching. Dr. Welch would always be smoking a large cigar in his office, and when he went into the nearby classroom he disliked to throw away a half-smoked cigar, so, routinely, he tucked it into his vest pocket. One fine day the cigar set fire to his vest, and he was evolving a cloud of smoke—great excitement, disrobing, water, and so on. He then went on with the lecture. Later in the day, the class decided he must have a metal cigar case, and purchased it. The subsequent presentation was indeed difficult and left one responsible class official *speechless*—it all resolved into laughter, but Dr. Welch enjoyed it.

A second trip to Europe was made in the spring and summer of 1911. I decided to stay several weeks in the laboratory of pharmacology in the University of Vienna under the distinguished Professor Hans Meyer. Much of the work in his laboratory could be designated "experimental medicine." My stay in Vienna in Meyer's laboratory was most profitable and educational in many ways. Drs. Wiechowski and Froehlich were friendly and helpful. I was able to participate in many teaching courses and research problems. I learned a new and simple technique for operative production of an Eck fistula in the dog, which was of great service to me later in my research work when the Eck fistula was used constantly—new instruments and a simple aseptic operation. I think Hans Meyer was a bit disappointed that I did not finish up any research problem for publication. He was kind to his staff, and we frequently enjoyed his hospitality at home dinners followed by informal seminars.

Opportunities to hear fine music and to attend operas were frequent and enjoyed. I took trips to Budapest, up the Danube, to Munich, and to the Dolomites during this visit. I lived in the home of a family all unable to speak English, so my German speaking and reading came along rapidly. On the return trip I paid a visit to Dr. Osler in Oxford. As usual, his hospitality took in friends and students from the States and Canada—a memorable visit and my last glimpse of this remarkable man.

Diseased states associated with abnormal blood coagulation were studied in the clinic at Hopkins, as well as at the autopsy table. Various coagulation factors were investigated, including fibrinogen. Dr. Howell, then working with normal coagulation factors, gave me valuable assistance. He welcomed me into his laboratory on Sundays when we could work without interruption. His work was always carried out with meticulous accuracy and frequent repetition. He was an inspiring teacher to all his junior associates, and I strove to measure up to his accurate simplicity as my own research interests matured.

Icterus was studied further by Hooper and Whipple, using the Eck fistula, also a rapid change of hemoglobin to bile pigment outside the liver (2). Liver function was investigated, and this brought us into co-operation with Rountree in pharmacology. Lipase was studied at this time as related to liver injury.

San Francisco

In 1913, my engagement to Miss Katharine Waring was announced, and we planned to live in Baltimore after our marriage in the late spring. During this spring (1914), a proposal came to me from President Benjamin Ide Wheeler, of the University of California in Berkeley. Following a bequest, a new department of research medicine was to be established in

San Francisco as a part of the medical school. I was offered the position of director of the Hooper Foundation for Medical Research and professor of research medicine. At first, this proposal did not appeal to me, but the more I thought about it, the more was my interest roused. My friends could see no good in it and said I would be crazy to accept. The opportunity to develop a new department in which research was the primary objective was the strongest factor in this decision. I liked what I had heard about the University of California and its medical school. My fiancée was in sympathy with the new development, and acceptance followed.

It was indeed difficult to say good-bye to Hopkins, where I had spent so many happy years and numbered very many close friends. After our marriage in June, Katharine and I went to Lake Winnipesaukee, New Hampshire, for a month's camping with canoe and tent. When World War I broke out, I suspected it would cause me much trouble, but not the half of it, in equipping a new laboratory.

We arrived in San Francisco in August, 1914. We lived for the first year in a residence district close to and above the World's Fair tract, which we visited frequently. During the first month, we never saw the sun because of heavy fog. We never became resigned to these cold fog banks over the city in the summer time. Commuting across the city by streetcar was time-consuming and unpleasant; therefore, we moved over to Parnassus Heights, close to the medical school and hospital tract. The following year we occupied a home built on our specifications in Forrest Hill. The house was about one-half mile from the Hooper Foundation and commanded an inspiring view out over the Golden Gate and Bay region.

An old veterinary building, back of the medical and dental buildings, was assigned to the Hooper Foundation. This building was much more suitable for this project than appeared at first sight; three floors in a building about 90 feet long, yellow brick exterior with large skylights in the roof over the third floor. A large room in the basement was used for autopsies coming from the university hospital. The top floor was reconstituted with new partitions only 7 feet high because of the skylights. These new small rooms served admirably as laboratory space for research in experimental physiology, bacteriology, and parasitology. A chemical laboratory was located on the second floor; small animals were kept on the ground floor, and a new animal house for dogs was constructed on the hill slope back of the main building.

Equipment and chemicals were very scarce, but I was given the opportunity to scout through the attic stores of various departments in Berkeley. Dr. Gay (bacteriology and pathology) was most helpful, and I found many pieces of apparatus formerly used by Professor Jacques Loeb, which were life-savers for us. Chemicals and glassware were picked up here and there through the friendly interest of the purchasing department and various university departments in Berkeley.

I came in contact with union labor for the first time when union carpenters were refitting the third floor. An animal caretaker in the new animal house needed a small shelf for food cups. He proceeded to saw a piece of board and nail it on the wall. This was observed by a union carpenter, who reported it to his boss, who promptly came to me with a threat of a strike if this man of ours again used a saw and hammer as reported. I was a bit shocked at this threat, but fortunately called an officer of the Buildings and Grounds Department in the University in Berkeley. He advised me to comply with the "request," as the union could tie up this needed construction indefinitely and cripple our research program.

President Wheeler, during our preliminary discussions (1914), assured me that the medical school would be united in a year or so. After the earthquake and fire in San Francisco, the preclinical departments of the first two years had been moved to Berkeley and housed in "temporary" buildings. The war prevented any thought of immediately returning these departments to Parnassus Heights in San Francisco. Meanwhile, these departments of anatomy, physiology, and biochemistry became so happily associated with the science departments of biology, physics, and chemistry that they resisted any attempts at removal from Berkeley. In fact, these departments all worked vigorously for the plan to move the University of California Hospital in San Francisco over to the Berkeley area. All this pulling and hauling promoted friction and impaired the joint effort of the clinical and preclinical teachers to train adequately the medical school classes. Bacteriology, pathology, and pharmacology were moved to Parnassus Heights some years after I left, but, even today, this cleavage is troublesome. There are parts of biochemistry in Berkeley and San Francisco—not a united department. The only solution, apparently, is a new medical school in Berkeley with its own teaching hospital.

The most important business was the appointment of members of the professional staff, and President Wheeler left this wholly in my hands.

Dr. Charles Hooper (no relation to the donors of the Foundation) had worked with me in Hopkins, and I felt quite happy when he decided to go along with me in this new venture—a loyal and able young man. Two seniors were appointed early in 1915. Dr. Earnest Walker, recently back from the Philippines, continued his investigations in tropical diseases—amoebic dysentery, leishmaniasis, and leprosy. Dr. Karl Meyer was only recently appointed a member of the Department of Pathology and Bacteriology in Berkeley. Dr. Gay disliked to see him cross the bay to join with us in various investigations related to the bacteria responsible for dysentery, typhoid, and bovine abortions. Walter Alvarez carried on his experimental observations on the smooth muscle of the intestinal tract during the forenoons and did clinical work elsewhere in the afternoons. A number of able part-time workers and volunteers soon took up work in the laboratory—Frank Hinman, Jean Cooke, William Kerr, and others. Frieda Robbins began her work in the laboratory in 1917 and continued over the years in San Francisco and Rochester as a loyal and able associate.

Student fellows were first appointed in 1916 and were a very important addition to the laboratory staff. I soon found during the first year, 1914–15, that I missed the active teaching of students. Through the interest of George Corner, who was in the Department of Anatomy in Berkeley, several first-year students were recommended for this type of work with research opportunity. In addition, these student fellows saw a good deal of autopsy material. They were paid a reasonable salary, and, at the end of the year, they returned to their routine medical training with a wider experience and improved rating. These student fellows after graduation developed as professors and leaders—Harry Smith, pathology at the College of Physicians and Surgeons; Stafford Warren, radiologist, physicist, and dean, U.C.L.A. Medical School; Francis Smyth, pediatrician and dean, University of California Medical School; Irvine McQuarrie, professor of pediatrics, University of Minnesota; Elmer Belt, surgeon and historian, U.C.L.A.; Nelson Davis, Rockefeller Foundation, International Health Board; and others.

As I look back over those first years in San Francisco, it is quite obvious that my marriage and assumption of family responsibilities plus the problems of a new department were stabilizing factors. My research program was sharpened in focus, and my drive was strengthened. Long hours in the laboratory were a pleasure, but I was told that I was neglecting recreation and exercise. There was not enough time to do what I desired, and I had not learned to "leave some work for next year."

My work on icterus and bile pigment metabolism in the dog was continued with Hooper. Bile pigment output was influenced by diet in bile fistula dogs, and hemoglobin, obviously, was a factor. Eck fistula dogs were included in this program. We decided that it was necessary to study hemoglobin production as a part of the bile pigment study. So it may be said that our experiments with liver injury (Hopkins) led us into the bile pigment studies, and, in logical sequence, we took up our anemia studies to find out more about *new hemoglobin production.* It soon became clear that diets were important factors in the production of new hemoglobin in anemia. We reported some of these experiments before the Physiological Society, with abstracts in the *American Journal of Physiology* in March, 1918.

Hemoglobin production under the stimulus of anemia was studied intensively in 1918. Diet factors were most important, and *liver* emerged as the most important diet agent (3). Various extracts of meat and liver were tested.

It should be mentioned that Dr. Hooper wished to test a liver extract on anemic patients, especially pernicious anemia. His extract was an alcoholic, fat-free preparation and was given subcutaneously to three pernicious anemia patients, and there were remissions and improved hemoglobin levels. The clinicians laughed him out of the wards and told him these were spontaneous remissions and were of no significance. Hooper was a very shy, sensitive young man, and this unfortunate attitude of the clinicians caused him to quit this clinical work. It was most unfortunate, as his extract almost certainly contained the potent B_{12} factor from the liver and the clinical liver therapy might have been discovered in 1918. It is tragic that he made no published record of this material, its preparation, and its effect on clinical cases. This story illustrates an important principle that a junior worker should never be turned back by self-styled experts or critics. The critics should be helpful, and the junior should persist in spite of various thoughtless comments.

Work on plasma protein regenerations was initiated with Kerr and Hurwitz but was not continued at that time because of pressure of other work. Shock was studied during the war period, with attention given to therapeutic factors (Smith and Belt). Extensive studies in blood volume were carried out in association with the work in experimental anemia and shock. Roentgen-ray injuries of the mucosa of the intestinal tract were studied in animals (Warren and Whipple, 4).

When the United States entered World War I, there were many serious changes in all universities. The desire to participate in the war operations and to leave enough teachers to carry on the necessary university work called for many difficult decisions. Professor John C. Merriam gathered a small committee to review carefully the personnel of the various university departments. I served on this committee, which tried to keep heads of departments and older men in the university work and release younger, physically competent men for army service. A medical unit was formed and departed for the war area. Many large groups of medical officers were sent out to the Hooper Foundation for training in pathology and clinical microscopy under Rusk, Cooke, and Whipple. Lectures in these and other subjects were given at various large army camps and hospitals in the Bay region.

Influenza struck California in 1918, and many able teachers and investigators were lost—Dr. Marjorie Foster in the Hooper Foundation. Everyone had the disease. Dr. Walker had a depression of many weeks following the influenza. I developed a severe bronchitis and bronchopneumonia (postinfluenzal) which left a badly scarred lung following organizing pneumonia. Convalescence was slow and associated with some depression After this, my physicians (Moffitt, Kerr, and Alvarez) put me on a strict regime, including regular exercise and work periods. Summer camp periods in the Sierras did much to bring about complete recovery.

Antivivisectionists were numerous and active. Antimedical and related groups were strong in Southern California and numerous in the Bay region. They constantly made trouble for the Hooper Foundation and were given militant support by all the papers of William Randolph Hearst. Efforts to persuade the city administration to prohibit all vivisection within San Francisco were frequent and demanded our attendance at hearings. Stanford was equally involved, and thus I became well acquainted with Dr. Ophuls, dean and professor of pathology. A year or so later, this antivivisection attack was transferred to Sacramento, and finally a bill to prohibit vivisection was put on the state ballot. This was a grave matter which called for all-out efforts by the medical schools, laboratory investigators, and physicians. Two bills were finally defeated, but much time and effort were needed all over the state—talks before conventions, women's clubs, chambers of commerce, farm associations, parent-teacher associations, and so on. In a sense, it was educational for the speakers but wearing and time-consuming.

The Hooper Foundation is a department in the medical school of the University of California. Dr. Herbert Moffitt was dean during the first six years of the Hooper Foundation and also a trustee. On many counts I felt grateful to Dr. Moffitt, not only as an associate of the advisory board, but as his patient and friend. He was always most generous and helpful. It came as a surprise when in 1920 I was invited to succeed him as dean.

This experience as administrative officer of the school was valuable to me and put me in close contact with the president's office in Berkeley and many able heads of science departments and deans of other schools (agriculture, education, and so on). Meetings in Berkeley were time-consuming, as the trip from San Francisco and return consumed at least three hours and it seemed that relatively little was accomplished by such large committee efforts. I was convinced that small committees were better functionally. Perhaps I understood that old saying that best of all was the committee of three, of which two were out of town.

Budgetary problems were difficult at that time and included the Hooper Foundation, as well as all the medical school departments in Berkeley. I saw something of the politics of this aspect of a state university as worked out in the State Capitol in Sacramento.

At that time, many university departments boasted that they would do nothing in research that had any practical application—only *pure research* was worthy of university effort. Fortunately, this attitude has been modified.

I learned something of research aid derived from industry when Dr. Meyer became involved in the acute botulism problem which injured the California packing companies. As a result of this experience, I was convinced that modern industry was conscious of the progressive work going on in universities and was willing to co-operate loyally toward solution of many problems. This enlightening experience, probably in part, was responsible for the friendly and mutually advantageous association of the Department of Pathology in Rochester with the Eli Lilly and Company, starting in 1928.

"Split schools of medicine" were the rule on the West Coast. This means that the preclinical departments were associated with some university science departments, while the teaching hospitals were elsewhere, perhaps in the same city or county, but miles separated these departments and hospitals to the great disadvantage of all concerned. This cleavage always means differences of opinion, friction, and waste of time, energy, and money—nothing can be said in its favor, except, perhaps, that time is conserved for the clinical part-time teachers and associates.

Rochester

In the spring of 1921 I was happy and busy with my work in the Hooper Foundation and medical school. I had not been interested in proposals coming from medical schools in the East and assumed without question that my future lay in California. We had heard of a new school being started in Rochester and that some appointments had been made. A letter came from President Rush Rhees inviting me to visit Rochester, but I was extremely busy, and a visit meant at least two weeks' time. Therefore, I sent my regrets.

President Rhees, a few weeks later, appeared in San Francisco and called on me in the Hooper Foundation. We had a pleasant informal visit, and he sat in on a short advisory board meeting in the old medical building. In further conversation, Dr. Rhees explained in detail the plans for the new medical school. The original proposal came from the General Education Board of the Rockefeller Foundation, through Mr. Abraham Flexner. Mr. Flexner gained the interest of both Mr. Eastman and Dr. Rhees, and finally it was decided that five million dollars would be given by the Rockefeller Foundation and four million by Mr. Eastman, plus one million for the University Hospital from the daughters of Mr. and Mrs. Henry Strong (Mrs. Gertrude Strong Achilles and Mrs. Helen Strong Carter). No appointments had been made. The school was to be a part of the university. There was no old medical school in Rochester to complicate the problem. The dean would have the support of President Rhees in constructing a modern school with its hospital and an adequate full-time staff, everything to measure up to the highest standards. The funds were in the Treasurer's Office drawing dividends and seemed adequate to build and operate a school with its teaching hospital.

I liked President Rhees on our first contact. This liking deepened into lasting friendship over the years. We never had any disagreements, and our contacts were always most pleasant and stimulating. One of the trustees of the Hooper Foundation, Mr. Henry Pritchett, when I asked him about Rush Rhees, said that, in his opinion, Rhees was in the top group of university presidents at that time. Dr. and Mrs. Rhees visited our home in San Francisco and gave us confidence that their friendship would be an important part in making contacts in Rochester.

President Rhees reviewed with me many of the problems inevitable in a new school. I explained to him that I could never be completely happy as dean unless I could find time for teaching and continuing my research work. I assured him that I believed this could be done if the Dean's Office was separate from the Department of Pathology and was operated by an able executive secretary. Further, that much time could be spent in community effort and in organized medical meetings. I said I was willing to take the criticism to the effect that I was selfish and lacking in civic concern if he would understand and approve. This plan he did approve and never tried to intrude local problems, though at times, with a smile, he would mention such criticisms. I felt sure of his support and knew that he approved of the operation of the Dean's Office.

New schools of medicine are established rarely, and opportunities to take responsibility at the very start are unusual, to say the least. The endowment seemed generous and adequate for construction and maintenance. Perhaps it is not wise to attempt a detailed analysis of all the factors involved in this proposal. At least it would be a test of leadership and would give a chance to build, from the ground, a new school with the very best young teachers and students and with the necessary laboratories for research in all departments. Co-operative teaching and research would be inevitable with a united hospital and school. All this carried visions and excited thrills.

The decision to accept came without much debate, and my friends in San Francisco were understanding and sympathetic. Tearing up roots in California was not pleasant. Many, many good friends and co-workers on the medical staff in San Francisco would be seen only rarely. Clearing up research work at the Hooper Foundation presented difficulties. Dr. Frieda Robbins remained in the Hooper Foundation for a year and was generously granted space in the laboratory and animal house to carry on our long program of research in experimental anemia and hemoglobin production in dogs as influenced by diet and other factors. In 1922, Dr. Robbins took up her work in Rochester without serious interruption.

Our departure from San Francisco was in mid-September. At Washington, I put Katharine, Hoyt, four years, and Barbara, two months, on the train for Charleston, South Carolina, to visit with her family for a month while I went to Rochester to prepare for their arrival.

For the first few days in Rochester (September, 1921) I was a house guest of President and Mrs. Rhees and enjoyed their friendly hospitality. My office was set up in the Eastman Building on the Prince Street Campus. This office, fortunately, was adjacent to the small administration building where Dr. Rhees had his office. Consultation was easy and frequent—always valuable and stimulating. Dr. Rhees had the curiosity of an investigator and true scientist. His questions were numerous and always to the point and constructive. He was truly a great president, and his wisdom was a large factor in the development of the medical school within the university. He gained and held the interest of Mr. Eastman, Mr. Flexner, and other influential people, both within and outside Rochester.

Many important decisions now called for prompt action. The first was the location of the medical school. It was suggested that it be constructed on the university campus, but it took little study to show that the site was completely inadequate. Other sites in the city were then studied. President Rhees, Mr. Eastman, Mr. George Todd, and the trustees agreed that the university and medical school should be relocated to insure adequate space for growth. It was thought that the medical school and hospital would be better served in a separate but adjacent land tract. The sick patients and hospital business, if within the campus, might be unpleasant to the university students and staff. Discussion of the present location of the medical school brought forth numerous objections, in particular, that the hospital must be in the center of the city to command adequate patient supply. It was pointed out that the patients would travel considerable distances if the clinical care was of a high order of excellence—examples: University of California, University of Chicago, Mayo Clinic, and so on.

The old Oak Hill golf club tract and the adjacent Crittenden tract are located at the southern edge of the city, on the east bank of the Genesee River. The Crittenden tract was reasonable in cost and gave sufficient space for the medical school and hospital and related future developments. It was made up of farm land plus a tree nursery. The Men's College was to move to Oak Hill and the Women's College was to remain on the old university tract. The Lehigh Valley Railroad tracks separate the university and medical school tracts and might seem to be an objectionable feature. There were advantages—heavy construction material was easily delivered, and the large power plant which served both tracts was operated at minimum expense because of proper construction and gravity delivery of coal direct from freight cars.

One important decision relating to the medical school was never debated, as everyone agreed that the school and its teaching hospital should be under one roof—I had seen enough of the "split medical schools" to be able to supply all needed arguments for a united school. At this time, the Vanderbilt Medical School at Nashville was making plans for a new building program (Canby Robinson). It is of some historical interest to note that Vanderbilt and Rochester evolved the same general plan for these buildings, working independently. Essentially, this new plan consisted of two major axes, about 100 feet apart, extending north and south and two other axes of similar type pointing east and west. Such a central unit can be expanded in any direction and shows no long, naked corridors. Elevators are located at the intersections of the axes. Related clinical departments and hospital wards can be placed on floors adjacent to the various related preclinical departments. A few steps will take students or teachers from one department to any other department, and joint research problems are inevitable, to the benefit of everyone. A common dining room or rooms and kitchen can serve economically students, doctors, nurses, and personnel. This common dining room is also important to establish good morale, particularly for students and faculty, with its friendly climate.

In a sense, 1921–22 was a sabbatical year for me—no teaching, no autopsy work, and a good deal of wandering about, as visits were made to many medical schools. Study of medical teaching and methods in use in various schools was combined with a search for promising young teachers. Architecture was noted, and various types of building construction and present cost were studied. A Harvey Lecture was given January 7, 1922 (5), "Pigment Metabolism and Regeneration of the Hemoglobin in the Body." A physiological review was published, "The Origin and Significance of the Constituents of the Bile" (6).

My office in the Eastman Building was soon functioning, with Miss Laura Olmsted (Mrs. Albert Dunson) as secretary. I was fortunate in my neighbors in that building—Dr. John Murlin and Dr. Henry Matill, recently appointed to carry on the Lewis P. Ross Department of Vital Economics in the university. It was also pleasant to make the acquaintance of the professors of biology, chemistry, and physics, whose advice was valuable. The friendly interest of the university faculty and trustees was of the greatest help to the new dean as the medical school and hospital programs were elaborated. The closest possible integration of the university, the medical school, and the community was our goal.

The most important decisions obviously related to staff appointments. Consultations were frequent with President Rhees, Dr. Winford Smith, director of the Johns Hopkins Hospital, Dr. Richard Pearse of the Rockefeller Foundation, and many others in New York City, Baltimore, Chicago, St. Louis, Cleveland, Boston, and elsewhere.

Dr. Nathaniel W. Faxon accepted the position of hospital director in May, 1922. He had been trained under Dr. Frederic A. Washburn at the Massachusetts General Hospital. He did not come to Rochester until November, but was in consultation relative to plans and blueprints from the time of his appointment.

Two other early appointments were decided, Dr. George Corner and Dr. Walter Bloor in anatomy and biochemistry. I had known intimately these two men in the faculty of the University of California School of Medicine and had no hesitation in giving them my most enthusiastic recommendation to President Rhees. Invitations went to Dr. Corner in May, 1922, and to Dr. Bloor in June, 1922. We felt happy to receive their acceptances. Dr. Faxon and Dr. Bloor, for a short time, occupied office space in the Eastman Building with me before we moved to the Research Laboratory on the Crittenden site in late November, 1922.

Up to the summer of 1922, four heads of departments had been appointed: Dr. Bloor, Dr. Corner, Dr. Faxon, and Dr. Whipple. This group, together with President Rhees, discussed other appointments on many occasions. As senior appointments were made, these men, when available, participated in the discussions relating to future appointments, and in this way the advisory board grew to be the Administrative Committee of the School and Hospital. In October, 1922, Dr. Stanhope Bayne-Jones accepted the appointment in bacteriology, coming from the Department of Pathology and Bacteriology (William G. MacCallum) in Johns Hopkins Medical School. Dr. William S. McCann accepted his appointment in medicine in December, 1922, coming from the Department of Medicine (Warfield Longcope) in Johns Hopkins Medical School. Dr. John J. Morton, Jr., was appointed in surgery in May, 1923, coming from the Department of Surgery (Samuel Harvey) at the Yale Medical School. Dr. Karl M. Wilson was appointed in obstetrics in September, 1923, coming from the Department of Obstetrics (Whitridge Williams) at Johns Hopkins Medical School. Dr. Samuel W. Clausen was appointed in pediatrics in February, 1924, coming from the Department of Pediatrics (William McKim Marriott) at Washington University in St. Louis. Dr. Wallace O. Fenn was appointed in physiology in May, 1924, coming from the Department of Physiology (Walter Cannon) in Harvard Medical School, and Dr. Stafford L. Warren was appointed in radiology.

The next important step related to the "Research Laboratory." It was decided to construct a small building on the school and hospital tract—a relatively simple, two-story structure—to house the growing staff over two or three years while the main building was constructed, equipped, and finally occupied. This building was called the Research Laboratory and later became the Animal House. It was built between August and November to supply rooms which were occupied late in November, 1922. It gave ample space for Dr. Faxon, Dr. Whipple, and other members of the hospital staff and school faculty to work on the plans for their departments.

As Faxon and I talked over the hospital and school problems, we agreed that the hospital with its patients must be under the same roof with the school. Further, as the plans matured, we also agreed that the standard units should have the same width and floor-ceiling heights. This was contrary to the standard construction at that time. This uniformity made for economy and speed of construction, as concrete forms could be used over and over again. Concrete construction was used because of lower cost and possible delays if a steel frame was used. Experience showed this plan to be sound. Test pits showed quicksand of 10–20 feet in thickness below a layer of clay of 10–15 feet in thickness. Rock and boulders were found at 30–50 feet depth. This complication necessitated concrete pile foundations which were well driven, and there has been no sign of settling or cracking of the structure over the years.

As blueprints began to flow from the architect's office, we had many pleasant discussions with Mr. Eastman. He said many times that plenty of medical schools and universities had demonstrated how *much* could be spent on construction, exterior adornment, and interior furnishings; for his part, he would like to see how *little* could be spent while assuring excellence of construction and function. The architects naturally wished the new structure to be a monument and memorial. The trustees and others participated in the debate, which became lively and, at times, a bit warm. The simple type of building was branded as "Late Penitentiary," "Factory type," and so on. President Rhees took a neutral stand. Finally, Mr. Eastman took a firm stand for simplicity and settled the debate with Mr. Lawrence White, the consulting architect. I was happy at this decision, as I had worked in very simple buildings at Hopkins and at the Hooper Foundation and knew that such laboratories were satisfactory and that the upkeep was minimal. The savings from proposed exterior decorations of the main buildings alone were of the order of one to two million plus inevitable delay.

Mr. Eastman was sincerely interested in the blueprints as they took form. He never looked at them without making constructive suggestions, as described elsewhere (7). He was an expert in the prevention of explosions and fires in industrial buildings (film manufacture, Eastman Kodak Company) and suggested invaluable protective devices for the school and hospital plant.

I had been told by many experts that the plant could not possibly be completed for student training inside of five years. As our staff began to gather, we all felt the urge to get under way at the earliest possible moment. The architects co-operated loyally, and, with no strikes and no serious mishaps or faults of co-ordination, we were able to start our first class of medical students in four years (September, 1925) and open the hospital five months later (January, 1926).

It seems clear that Mr. Eastman's interest in medicine came through dentistry. He had had trouble with his teeth during his young adult life, probably because of inadequate dental attention. In Rochester, his mouth got excellent attention, and properly adjusted dentures brought his mouth into a healthy state. This was responsible, in part, for the Eastman Dental Dispensary under Dr. Burkhart. It was Mr. Eastman's first venture into the realm of public health.

During the discussions relative to a school of medicine, it was his suggestion that a combined school of medicine and dentistry be established. Mr. Eastman was interested in education of the highest order in dentistry as well as in medicine. If the dental students were to be associated with the medical students in their initial basic science work, obviously they must have had the same quality of training. It was specified, therefore, that three years of college training, including two years of chemistry, one of physics, and one of biology, be the minimum requirements for both medical and dental candidates. When the school opened in 1925, it was expected that there would be a significant number of dental applicants. There were no dental applicants of any sort for the first two or three years and only a very few inadequately trained applicants during the first five years (1925–30). The young men and women who were training for dentistry preferred to go for their training to the established dental schools requiring one or two college years, or even less, and they were not interested in the Rochester school.

After this experience, the whole question was re-examined. It was suggested that *graduate dentists* be offered scholarships for *graduate* instruction and opportunities in teaching and research. They would have training adequate to gain Master's or Ph.D. degrees but not M.D. degrees. This experiment was supported by the Rockefeller Foundation and subsequently by the Carnegie Foundation. It has been continued successfully since its beginning, and, of that group of graduate dentists, a very high percentage subsequently occupied senior positions as professors, deans, and investigators in dental schools in various parts of this country and abroad (8). It has been a successful experiment, totally different, however, from the original plan. Mr. Eastman was satisfied with this development, although he was disappointed that no undergraduates turned up for training.

The university hospital was named in honor of Henry Alvah Strong and Helen Griffin Strong, whose daughters gave a very generous gift toward its construction. A memorial tablet is placed in the main lobby. This lobby was designed to be a comfortable waiting room for patients and visitors to give them a pleasant impression and induce a friendly climate, rather than the cold and dreary atmosphere too frequently found in large hospitals.

As plans took shape for the Strong Memorial Hospital, they roused the interest of the health officer of the city of Rochester. The university, the School of Medicine and Dentistry, and the city owe a great debt to Dr. George W. Goler. He saw visions and was a crusader who, as a health officer, was ahead of his time. He was not popular with city politicians, but they respected him. Dr. Goler was interested in a municipal hospital about to be built on Waring Road, but he saw at once the great benefits to be gained by its construction as a part of the school and hospital plant. As soon as Dr. Goler presented his plan of uniting the municipal hospital with the university hospital, it received enthusiastic support from all persons concerned, including Mr. Eastman and Mayor Hiram Edgerton. It was so obviously advantageous both to the university and to the city that the plan advanced very rapidly, and a contract was drawn up by Mr. Walter Hubbell, a distinguished lawyer and University of Rochester trustee, covering the relationships between the municipal and university hospitals. This was a model contract which has been copied subsequently and, on request, sent to many hospitals in all parts of the country. The union of these two hospitals has fulfilled all the hopes of the persons concerned, and there has never been any significant friction. In fact, the city officials and the university trustees have remained enthusiastic about this co-operative effort.

In general, the laboratory space for all departments was of uniformly simple construction. The monolithic concrete floors made possible room walls of single-brick thickness, which could very easily be taken down and put elsewhere—flexibility. The steam pipes were run on outside walls, and all other pipes on the inside walls and left exposed. The concrete ceilings and gray brick walls were not painted. This all was in keeping with the plan to hold maintenance cost at low levels.

The total space needs had been estimated for each department, and, fortunately, all heads of departments were at hand to plan this floor space according to their ideas of teaching and research. There was discussion as to the total space needs for the school, as some consultants believed that somewhat smaller wings would be adequate. On this point Mr. Eastman's opinion was against construction space shrinkage. He felt that if the school was successful, the demand for space would soon fill it—a prophetic vision.

Research Programs

When Dr. Bloor and I moved to the Research Laboratory on the Crittenden tract, we promptly developed space for research. Dr. Bloor had his work on lipids in progress. Dr. Robbins brought the anemia colony from the Hooper Foundation and installed these forty dogs in the laboratory. Dr. Robbins had been working with me on anemia due to blood loss, and several papers had been published (3) dealing with diet influences on the production of new hemoglobin. *Liver* was shown to be most potent in the formation of hemoglobin in these anemic dogs (9). In the anemia experiments from 1923 and subsequently, various factors were better standardized. The anemia level was kept as constant as possible. The hemoglobin produced and removed was accurately estimated; blood volumes and hemoglobin levels measured accurately by standardized dyes and hemoglobin samples. A basal diet was worked out to supply all requirements but to permit minimal formation of new hemoglobin. It was soon shown in experiments with these standard anemia dogs that bread, milk, fish, and grains were poor in hemoglobin-producing factors. Visceral tissue of beef, sheep, pig, and chicken was quite potent—liver, especially.

Plant Construction

Excavation for the main building was begun in April, 1923, and pile driving began in May. Work on the concrete skeleton went on rapidly, and structural questions came into the offices of Whipple and Faxon at all times. We spent much time in boots and raincoats exploring all parts of the growing structure and were able to make savings and improvements by this supervision. It is to be remembered that construction work began long before completion of interior plans—this presented difficulties but saved much valuable time and, with the active co-operation of the architects, was carried through successfully. The concrete skeleton with floors was almost completed during the summer and fall of 1923.

Construction of brickwork began as soon as weather permitted in 1924. Plumbing and steam and water pipes were installed. The power plant was built during 1924 and took up the heating load in November, so that interior finishing of the main building could proceed rapidly through the winter, 1924–25.

The Nurses' Dormitory was begun in February, 1924, and the Staff House in September, 1924. The Staff House gave adequate space for the resident staff of both the Strong Memorial and the Municipal Hospital. There were also resident juniors of the preclinical departments, and this experiment proved its value in promoting better understanding and co-operative work between the clinical and preclinical departments.

Equipment for the laboratories—tables, desks, drawers, cabinets, sinks, chemical tables, and hoods—all came from local dealers. The contractor doing the woodwork in the laboratories had unusually fine well-seasoned western white pine lumber, and this fixed equipment was exceptional. Today, after thirty-four years, the equipment is in excellent condition requiring rarely some minimal repairs or refinishing.

During the spring of 1924, Katharine and I were fortunate in accompanying Mr. Eastman on a camping and fishing trip and cruise in British Columbia, Canada. In subsequent years we also enjoyed his hospitality at his farm "Oak Lodge" in North Carolina, where quail shooting, riding, and camping were the order of the day. I took many pictures on these various trips which were recently written up, illustrated, and published through the generous help of Mr. Thomas Hargrave, Mr. Albert K. Chapman, and Mr. Donald McMaster of the Eastman Kodak Company (10).

Library space for reading room, for stacks, and for the office of the librarian were in the very center of the main building, convenient to all departments, thus eliminating the demand for department libraries. Telephone calls would bring needed reference volumes promptly to any department. The purchase of books began in 1921, Dr. Rhees having directed Mr. James F. Ballard, of the Boston Medical Library, to proceed with the purchase of complete sets of standard medical scientific journals, then available abroad at very reasonable prices. This was a most fortunate arrangement, as Mr. Ballard was able to purchase various complete sets which were very difficult to obtain in this country. This advantageous association continued through the period of rapid growth of the school library. Substantial gifts to the library came from Dr. Edward Mulligan, Dr. Goler, and Mr. Edward Miner.

Student Choice and Training

It is self-evident that the reputation and prestige of any medical school rests on the competence of its graduates and the clinical and research standing of its staff. The choice of teachers is all-important, but these teachers must train future teachers and investigators. The choice of students is equally important, as excellent prospects given good training will emerge as competent doctors and potential teachers. Inferior students can be given excellent training, but rarely will superior graduates be found in this group.

Much discussion of ways and means for the important choice of premedical candidates concerned the advisory board. Scholastic ability is essential to carry the tough medical training program, but the character and personality of the student were thought to be equally important. Health and determination are also important. In my opinion, the aptitude tests tell less than the academic record plus the evaluation of the student coming from senior science college teachers. Personal interviews also are important—single, but not group interviews—to gain some knowledge of the initial contact personality. "Would this person appeal to a sick patient and gain his confidence?"

This school was planned for small classes—laboratories, histology rooms, lecture rooms—initially fifty medical and twenty-five dental students. When no undergraduate dental candidates appeared, the medical candidates were gradually increased to sixty. World War II brought increased pressure and classes of seventy. Small classes and close personal contacts between students and teachers are most important for the best teaching.

Notices were sent out in 1924 that the first class for medical and dental students would begin work in September, 1925, and candidates were invited for interviews. The admissions committee did not always agree on candidates then or later, but many decisions were reviewed at graduation or later, with gradual improvement in method of choice.

It is not always appreciated that *graduate students* are as important and demand as much teaching supervision and more space than do medical students. Included in this group in Rochester are the graduate dentists working for graduate degrees (M.A. and Ph.D.), also the resident staff of the clinical departments, plus student fellows, special students, visiting foreign students, and exchange students. The preclinical departments have many graduate students working toward a Ph.D. degree. The total number of graduate students is close to the total number of medical students in this school. From this group emerge many able teachers and investigators.

Dean's Office

The Dean's Office began its development in 1925. During the construction period, the occasional bits of work relating to the Dean's Office were taken over by Miss Laura Olmsted—first in the Eastman Building, where she acted as secretary for Whipple, Bloor, and Faxon. In the Research Laboratory, she took over the small switchboard and continued as my secretary. When the Pathology Department moved into the main building, the Dean's Office was occupied by Mrs. Laura Olmsted Dunson. This office was separated from the Department of Pathology but located in the school, close to the student locker area and student entrance. The Dean's Office served all departments and cared for all student records, applications, student acceptance, alumni records, student problems of all sorts. The President's Report, school catalogue, budget, and miscellaneous details all were handled in the Dean's Office. Mrs. Dunson carried on this work effectively until her tragic death in an automobile accident in 1929.

Miss Hilda DeBrine then took over this difficult and demanding position and, with her able associates, has carried on over the years to the complete satisfaction of everyone, faculty and students alike. The dean and various assistant and associate deans (Bloor, Berry, Bradford, and Fenn) concerned themselves with matters of policy and acted as agents of the advisory board. Complex problems during World War II were resolved with the help of officers of the Army and the Navy, and veterans added many problems as they returned to take up medical training.

Department of Pathology

This department began to function in research in December, 1922. Space for this research was located on the ground floors in the southeast corner of the Research Laboratory.

Dr. Harry P. Smith was appointed senior assistant in pathology and began work in September, 1924, after a period of several months spent abroad. Obviously, the gross pathology of this period was comparative, related to the various types of animals kept in the Research Laboratory. Consultation with local hospitals brought some surgical and autopsy material for review. Dr. Whipple was elected president of the American Society of Experimental Pathology in 1925.

Department removal to the main building in February, 1925, was readily accomplished, and a surplus of laboratory space was enjoyed. Dr. Robert Kennedy joined the department in June, 1924, and Dr. William B. Hawkins in August, 1929. The first autopsy in the department was done by Dr. Whipple, on January 20, 1926. Since that time, the autopsy service has grown steadily up to the present level of 650–700 per year. The autopsy permission rate runs at 70 per cent, or above—a high rate for a large, active, general service of the Strong Memorial and Municipal hospitals.

This indicates hard work by the clinical staff and is usually accepted as an index of good hospital standing.

A Museum of Pathology developed early in the department. Miss Edna Fairman was the first, and is the present, curator, and its success reflects great credit on her skill and responsibility. This Museum of Pathology serves all departments, and its specimens are used for clinics, special meetings, and research. Files for lantern slides, photographs, microscope slides, index cards, and drawings are all available, as in a library, with the same ease of requisition.

A large service room for the preparation of histological sections was essential for the department. It prepares sections of all types for all school departments, except anatomy. This eliminates the demand for scattered, small histological units in various departments. Miss Harriet Feary has been responsible for this service preparation room since its beginning, and her ability and interest have been invaluable. Many junior technicians are trained for work elsewhere.

Teaching in pathology began in December, 1926, with a first class of twenty-three, much to the enjoyment of the department. The students saw many autopsies and much fresh autopsy material, with related frozen and fixed sections.

Our student fellowship program began with this class (Edward Manwell) and has continued regularly since then. These student fellows in pathology are paid a salary and live in the staff house, if desired. They participate in routine autopsy work, see much surgical pathology, aid in class teaching of pathology, and participate in research. At the end of the year, they return to the regular medical curriculum. These student fellows, in many instances, after graduation remain in pathology and research and go on to senior positions as teachers.

The Department of Pathology enjoyed co-operation with several able men of *chemical* training, appointed as associates in pathology. They brought unusual skill and vision to joint research problems in the department—Dr. Paul F. Hahn, Dr. Floyd S. Daft, Dr. Leon L. Miller, and Dr. Garson H. Tishkoff.

After the department moved into the main building (1925), the pace of research work accelerated, and publications appeared in increasing numbers. Work in experimental anemia in dogs was extended by Whipple and Robbins. Liver fractions and potent factors were investigated. Several lectures were given on anemia and related problems (11, 12). Muscle hemoglobin (myoglobin) was investigated in dogs (13) and shown to be influenced by exercise, anemia, and other factors.

Experimental anemia in dogs was continued, and a *liver fraction* potent in secondary anemia was standardized and shown to be useful (Whipple, Robbins, and Walden, 14). We enjoyed the facilities of the Eli Lilly and Company (Clowes and Walden), as they had prepared a potent liver fraction for pernicious anemia and were interested in liver extractives. Our association with the Eli Lilly and Company was very pleasant and enabled us to test liver fractions that could not be prepared in the Department of Pathology in Rochester. We were not interested in taking out patents for these liver fractions. Finally, an agreement was drawn up to further this work. We agreed to test and standardize certain liver fractions supplied by Eli Lilly and Company, and they put these fractions on the market for patients with secondary anemia. We were compensated by their aid in our chemical work and by stipends to further and expand our work in anemia. Over the years 1926–53, the budget in pathology was expanded at no cost to the university, and we set up a reserve fund which yields an income of more than $30,000 per annum. Our routine testing of these fractions was useful to us and no burden to our research program. Animals were constantly being standardized for research work, and these tests of liver fractions were a part of this basic standardization.

I served as President of the American Association of Pathology and Bacteriology in 1930. I received the William Wood Gerhard Gold Medal from the Philadelphia Pathology Society in 1934. *The First Decade* (15) records the events in the early history of the school and hospitals and supplies many details.

A Nobel Prize announcement comes to any individual with a shock which cannot be defined—disbelief, doubt and self-examination, excitement, curiosity as to the official protocol, and so on. But in Stockholm there is not the faintest doubt in the minds of the laureates that the occasion is of maximal importance to the court and the people—further, that long and careful study by experts precedes the award. It adds up to a most impressive ceremony with related entertainment and receptions by royalty and all important officers.

Because I am aware of many mistakes in published and spoken reports relative to the 1934 award to Minot, Murphy, and Whipple, I feel that a quotation from the official presentation (16) is in order:

PROFESSOR I. HOLMGREN:

Your Majesty, Ladies and Gentlmen,

The Caroline Institute has awarded this year's prize for Physiology and Medicine to three American investigators, . . . in recognition of their discoveries respecting liver therapy in anaemias. . . .

Of the three prize-winners it was WHIPPLE who first occupied himself with the investigations for which the prize has now been awarded. He began in 1920 to study the influence of food on blood-regeneration, the re-building-up of the blood, in cases of anaemia consequent upon loss of blood. . . . The method WHIPPLE adopted in his experiments was to bleed dogs, that is to say to withdraw from them a certain quantity of their blood, supplying them afterwards with food of various kinds. By that method he discovered that certain kinds of food were considerably superior to others, inasmuch as they gave stimulus to a more vigorous reformation of blood, that is to say stimulated the bone-marrow—in which the blood-corpuscles are produced—to a more vigorous manufacture of red blood-corpuscles. It was first and foremost liver, then kidney, then meat and next after that certain vegetable articles of food too, e.g. apricots, that proved in an especial degree to have a strongly stimulating effect. WHIPPLE'S experiments were planned exceedingly well and carried out very accurately, and consequently their results can lay claim to absolute reliability. These investigations and results of WHIPPLE'S gave MINOT and MURPHY the idea, that an experiment could be made to see whether favourable results might not also be obtained in the case of pernicious anaemia, an anaemia of quite a different type, by making use of foods of the kind that WHIPPLE had found to yield favourable results in his experiments regarding anaemia from loss of blood.

From 1927 to 1943, I served as trustee of the Rockefeller Foundation and its various divisions. Since 1936, I have been a trustee and member of the Board of Scientific Directors of the Rockefeller Institute. In 1929, I was elected to the National Academy of Sciences and in 1938 to the American Philosophical Society. I was awarded the Charles Mickle Fellowship by the University of Toronto, the Kober Medal by the University of Georgetown, and the Rochester Civic Medal.

An unusual type of anemia was investigated by Bradford and Whipple. It shows a racial tendency (Mediterranean people) and has many of the gross and histological abnormalities observed in hemochromatosis. The name "thalassemia" (Mediterranean anemia) was proposed (17).

Research in bile fistula dogs over long periods showed interesting abnormalities (Hawkins and Whipple). Plasma protein regeneration was again investigated after an interval of some years (Holman, Mahoney, and

Whipple). Diet control was an important factor. Blood plasma protein given by vein was utilized in the body metabolism in dogs. Infection and intoxication were shown to decrease the output of new hemoglobin in standard anemic dogs (Robbins and Whipple).

A Mellon Lecture was given, "Protein Production and Exchange in the Body, Including Hemoglobin, Plasma Protein, and Cell Protein" (18). Iron metabolism had interested various members of the Department of Pathology over the first ten years in Rochester. When radioactive iron became available to us, it was used as a tracer to investigate all aspects of the complex pattern of iron absorption and distribution within the body as modified by various conditions—anemia, iron-free diets, and infections. The life-cycle of the red cell was studied by Hawkins and Whipple.

"Plasma Proteins: Their Source, Production, and Utilization" was the title of a physiological review by Madden and Whipple (19). Plasma protein production was shown to be increased by casein digests, and the influence of sterile abscesses was studied. Simultaneous production of hemoglobin and plasma protein as influenced by bleeding, diet protein, and other factors was studied. Shock was investigated actively during the war period. Peritoneal absorption of red cells was demonstrated by the use of red cells labeled by radioactive iron.

Visits from foreign students were enjoyed during these years. They came from South America, Japan, English Isles, Middle Europe, India, and other countries. Visits of a year or more as research fellows often resulted in one or more co-operative publications.

During the summers of 1927–36, we enjoyed ranch camps in Colorado and Wyoming. Horseback riding, camping, fishing, and exploring occupied the family for about two months of the summer. We drove out and back, and, as the roads were quite primitive, adventures of all sorts were encountered. Camps on the Pine River in southwest Colorado were most frequently visited, and we explored the Cliff Dweller areas, the Grand Canyon, Jacksons Hole, Yellowstone and Glacier Park, and adjacent areas. During the late summers of 1937–57 I was fortunate in renewing friendship and starting salmon fishing in Cape Breton with Ned Park, then in pediatrics at Hopkins. This area was free of ragweed and gave me perfect freedom from hay fever and enjoyable out-of-door recreation.

In the fall, I was able to enjoy duck and pheasant hunting. My first hunting associate in Rochester was Dr. William Wallace, who had lived in the Lake area and knew the country well. We got others interested, and a small school group hunted pheasants pretty regularly in the country south of Rochester—Drs. Wallace, Stafford Warren, Bayne-Jones, Morton, McCann, and Whipple. Later, Mr. Willoughby Middleton, Mr. Frank Lovejoy, Dr. Fenn, Dr. Bradford, Dr. Pearse, Dr. Hilleman, and Dr. Pammenter joined us and enjoyed the shooting. My interest in pheasant shooting continues.

The Atomic Energy Project is an important part of the university and School of Medicine and Dentistry. Dr. Stafford Warren gained the support of Rochester industry for a powerful X-ray laboratory, in which heavy castings for military purposes could be tested to comply with government specifications. This was built in 1942, close to the power plant. In 1943, Dr. Warren organized the Atomic Energy Project, adjacent to this X-ray laboratory and extending east along Elmwood Avenue. The building was completed in September, 1943. Its staff was concerned with the manifold problems related to the atomic bomb—in particular, the testing of all radioactive factors for protection of personnel.

In 1948, a new Department of Radiation Biology was set up in the School of Medicine and Dentistry under Dr. H. A. Blair. A training program developed, and a new wing was built between the first atomic energy laboratory and the main school building—a modern laboratory building of seven stories, 150 feet long—completed in 1950. Special students (50–100) can be accommodated. Its large staff, trained in radioactive research, enables the school departments to develop research by use of labeled material. Proteins can be labeled by these radioactive elements, and joint problems in medicine and surgery, physiology, and pathology develop rapidly and expand this effective research technique.

Research work continued in pathology in the field of blood protein regeneration (Whipple, Robbins, and Miller, 20). Parenteral plasma protein maintains nitrogen equilibrium in dogs over long periods (Terry, Sandrock, Nye, and Whipple, 21). The use of radioactive lysine in studies of protein metabolism, synthesis and utilization of plasma proteins was demonstrated (22). Protein metabolism and exchange as influenced by constriction of the vena cava and experimental ascites were investigated. Conversion of plasma protein to tissue protein without evidence of protein breakdown and results of giving plasma protein labeled with C^{14} parenterally to dogs were recorded. Plasma protein labeled with lysine-E-C^{14} and its oral feeding and related protein metabolism in the dog were studied. Red cell stroma in dogs was investigated, and stroma protein was labeled with C^{14} lysine (23).

The placenta and protein metabolism, transfer studies using C^{14}-labeled protein, concentration of labeled vitamin $B_{12}Co^{60}$ in various organs and tissues of the dog in short- and long-term experiments were investigated. It was shown that B_{12} participates in red cell stroma production (24). Space did not permit adequate review of the research work as it developed over the years.

A monograph in "American Lectures in Pathology," *Hemoglobin, Plasma Protein and Cell Protein, Their Production and Interchange*, by G. H. Whipple was published in 1948 (25). A monograph, *The Dynamic Equilibrium of Body Proteins* by G. H. Whipple, was published in 1956 (26).

In February, 1945, Mrs. Helen Woodward Rivas of LeRoy made a generous gift to build a psychiatric clinic with suitable endowment to continue its maintenance. Dr. Romano was appointed head of this department and took up work in June, 1946. Construction was completed in 1948. This important department functions as a part of the School of Medicine and Dentistry, integrated closely with all clinical departments and the Municipal Hospital with its psychiatric unit.

A valuable gift "for research in Medical Science" was made in 1948 through the will of Mr. Ernest L. Woodward of LeRoy. Other large gifts came to the school (1942–57) from Dr. Henry C. Buswell, Mrs. Bertha Hochstetter Buswell, and Mr. Ralph Hochstetter, all of Buffalo, to further research work in urology, medicine, and other school departments.

Following World War II, there was a great demand for postdoctoral training in pathology, coming from veteran M.D.'s just released from service. The department took on twenty per year for this six-month training which was like that given to interns in pathology. In all, 74 veterans took this training. They were responsible students who did good work, and the department enjoyed giving them this training.

The department takes natural pride in its group of alumni. Some have become clinical teachers and attained senior grade in teaching institutions. We list the men who have spent one or more years in the department and subsequently have become heads of departments or professors of pathology in universities: Dr. Harry P. Smith, P. and S., Columbia University; Dr.

Sidney C. Madden, School of Medicine, University of California, Los Angeles; Dr. Louis J. Zeldis, School of Medicine, U.C.L.A.; Dr. Charles L. Yuile, School of Medicine, U.C.L.A.; Dr. Frank W. McKee, School of Medicine, U.C.L.A.; Dr. Russell L. Holman, School of Medicine, Louisiana State University; Dr. Emory D. Warner, College of Medicine, State University of Iowa; Dr. John R. Carter, College of Medicine, State University of Iowa; Dr. James B. McNaught, School of Medicine, University of Colorado; Dr. Richard M. Mulligan, School of Medicine, University of Colorado; Dr. Frank B. Queen, University of Oregon Medical School; Dr. Cyrus C. Erickson, University of Tennessee Medical School; Dr. Ralph E. Knutti, National Institutes of Health, Bethesda, Maryland; Dr. Lauren V. Ackerman, School of Medicine, Washington University; Dr. John B. Miale, University of Miami School of Medicine; Dr. Robert W. Coon, University of Vermont College of Medicine; Dr. William B. Hawkins, University of Rochester School of Medicine and Dentistry.

In conclusion, I would say that teaching and research represent the ultimate in pleasure and satisfaction in my career. Perhaps research may give a greater sense of accomplishment, but teaching carries greater personal happiness. This is of the order of the pleasure derived from patient contact or from boys' camp counselor experiences—a reaction, in part, like that of the parent or grandparent. The routine duties of a department are not unpleasant, nor are they exciting. It is essential that such routine does not demand too much time. Administrative duties are important and, at times, stimulating, but these tasks must not absorb too much time and energy, else the research program will wither away. I have been most fortunate in that teaching has been a part of my life ever since college graduation in 1900. The pleasure, if anything, has become greater as teaching experience accumulated. I believe a good medical teacher must be an investigator, philosopher and/or clinician. I would be remembered as a teacher.

REFERENCES

1. G. H. WHIPPLE. Bull. Johns Hopkins Hosp., **18**:381, 1907.
2. G. H. WHIPPLE and C. W. HOOPER. J. Exper. Med., **17**:593, 1913.
3. G. H. WHIPPLE, F. S. ROBBINS, and C. W. HOOPER. Am. J. Physiol., **53**:236, 1920.
4. S. L. WARREN and G. H. WHIPPLE. J. Exper. Med., **35**:203, 1922.

5. G. H. Whipple. Arch. Int. Med., **29**:711, 1922.
6. ———. Physiol. Rev., **2**:440, 1922.
7. ———. Planning and construction period of the school and hospitals, 1921–1925. Rochester, N.Y.: University of Rochester, 1957.
8. University of Rochester Dental Research Fellowship Program, Proceedings 25th year celebration. Rochester, N.Y.: University of Rochester, 1957.
9. F. S. Robbins and G. H. Whipple. Am. J. Physiol., **72**:408, 1925.
10. G. H. Whipple. George Eastman: a picture story of an out-of-doors man—camping, fishing, hunting. Rochester, N.Y.: Eastman Kodak Co., 1957.
11. ———. Am. J. M. Sc., **175**:721, 1928.
12. ———. J.A.M.A., **91**:863, 1928.
13. ———. Am. J. Physiol., **76**:693, 1926.
14. G. H. Whipple, F. S. Robbins, and G. B. Walden. Am. J. M. Sc., **179**:628, 1930.
15. The University of Rochester School of Medicine and Dentistry: the first decade, 1926–36. Rochester, N.Y.: University of Rochester, 1936.
16. Les Prix Nobel en 1934: The Nobel Prize for physiology and medicine for the year 1934, pp. 34, 35, Stockholm, Sweden: Imprimerie Royale, P. A. Norstedt and Soner, 1935.
17. G. H. Whipple and W. L. Bradford. J. Pediat., **9**:279, 1936.
18. G. H. Whipple. Am. J. M. Sc., **196**:609, 1938.
19. S. C. Madden and G. H. Whipple. Physiol. Rev., **20**:194, 1940.
20. G. H. Whipple, L. L. Miller, and F. S. Robbins. J. Exper. Med., **85**:277, 1947.
21. R. Terry, W. E. Sandrock, R. E. Nye, and G. H. Whipple. J. Exper. Med., **87**:547, 1948.
22. L. L. Miller, W. F. Bale, C. L. Yuile, R. E. Masters, G. H. Tishkoff, and G. H. Whipple. J. Exper. Med., **90**:297, 1949.
23. G. H. Tishkoff, C. L. Yuile, F. S. Robbins, and G. H. Whipple. J. Exper. Med., **102**:713, 1955.
24. W. D. Woods, W. B. Hawkins, and G. H. Whipple. J. Exper. Med., **108**:1, 1958.
25. G. H. Whipple. Hemoglobin, plasma protein and cell protein, their production and interchange. Springfield, Ill.: Charles C Thomas, 1948.
26. ———. The dynamic equilibrium of body proteins. Springfield, Ill.: Charles C Thomas, 1956.

RUSSELL M. WILDER, PH.D., M.D., M.A.C.P.

Recollections and Reflections from the Mayo Clinic, 1919–1950

Apologia

This is an abridgment of memoirs written in 1954 for the library of the Mayo Clinic. My retirement from the Clinic came in 1950.

As I review these memoirs, it annoys me to find so many personal pronouns. It was not my intention to make them autobiographical, but I was so much involved in what was considered that it had to be that way. I was the "Odysseus," in a sense, of this particular Odyssey—but an Odysseus who was fully appreciative of the advantages to a scientific life provided by the atmosphere of the Mayo Clinic, where there can be, and is, such intimate rubbing-together of shoulders and brains and where opportunities for helping one another are so many. It was in the Mayo spirit of "my brother and I" that I wrote, and the "I" part I begged the reader to put in lower case.

Exordium

In its early years the Mayo Clinic, having developed from the practices of the Doctors Mayo, was concerned primarily with surgery. Patients with diseases of all kinds were examined, but hospitalization was restricted, insofar as possible, to those for whom a surgical operation would be helpful. Other patients were referred back to their home physicians or elsewhere with reports regarding their examinations and suggestions as to therapy.

Then, in 1915, came the arrangement with the University of Minne-

Dr. Wilder's career spanned the exciting discovery of insulin and the subsequent painstaking efforts in laboratories and clinics to standardize its control over diabetes. He became a statesman of medical education and research by facilitating traffic in heuristic ideas as a professor, a consultant, and a member of scientific societies concerned with medical research. After he retired as Chief of the Department of Medicine at the Mayo Clinic, he joined the National Institutes of Health and helped plan and develop the Clinical Research Center. Dr. Wilder died December 16, 1959.

sota whereby the practice of the Mayo Clinic was to provide facilities for the training of graduate physicians in Rochester in the several specialties of medicine as well as in surgery. The Mayo Foundation for Medical Education and Research was established for these purposes as a part of the Graduate School of the University of Minnesota, and the necessity arose of extending facilities for bedside teaching in medicine and for clinical investigation.

This, in brief, was the explanation I was given by Dr. Will (Mayo) and Dr. Wilson for being asked to join the staff. I came in the early fall of 1919, having recently completed two years of service in the Army Medical Corps, preceded by a year of postgraduate work in organic chemistry at the University of Chicago, six months of clinical study in Vienna, and two years of teaching and clinical research as an instructor at Rush Medical College and as a resident in the Presbyterian Hospital of Chicago. As a resident in medicine, my duties had been general. They included assisting Dr. Rollin Woodyatt in the care of diabetic patients; furthermore, such research as I was then engaged in was principally in diabetes.

Activities of the 1920's

BEGINNINGS

Responsibility for the care of diabetic patients coming to the Mayo Clinic had been placed on Dr. David M. Berkman's shoulders. He, too, had recently returned from military service overseas. Dr. Berkman had established a diabetic service on the first floor of what was then the Stanley Hospital, a three-story building. He had twelve rooms, none of them large enough for more than a single bed. In one he had installed a diet kitchen, presided over by Miss Daisy Ellithorpe. She and Dr. Berkman, guided by Joslin's already famous text, *The Treatment of Diabetes Mellitus*, were weighing foods and meticulously following the then-popular "fasting" management of the disease.

My time at first was almost equally divided between the study of diabetic patients in the Stanley Hospital and general diagnosis at the Mayo Clinic. I was appointed an associate to Dr. George B. Eusterman, together with Dr. Berkman and Dr. Howard B. Hartman. Among some vivid memories of those days is one concerning a woman who had come from Winnipeg to the "Mayo Brothers." Most members of the staff were youthful in appearance at that time, and this patient had not come this long distance to be examined by "mere boys," as she called us. To my first question she replied, "Now when do I see Dr. Mayo?"

I learned some helpful lessons that year—one from a Norwegian country physician. He was in my examining room when I saw this particular patient, a farmer from nearby whose complaints baffled me completely—no appetite, bloating, belching, heartburn, some epigastric pain, but nothing on palpation and the stomach "negative" by x-ray. I was obviously puzzled, and my visiting physician, amazed I am sure at such ignorance in a member of the staff of the Mayo Clinic, told me to look at the patient's teeth.

"Can't you see the snoof?" he said.

A snuff chewer, of course! We had fewer of them at the Presbyterian Hospital in Chicago than we saw in Minnesota.

I also must record chagrin, occasioned not by ignorance this time but by youthful cockiness. I was fair at general diagnosis but really good in diabetes—so I thought. I used to point out to my students the so-called peaches-and-cream-like coloring in the cheeks of youthful patients who had chronic diabetic acidosis, the so-called rubeosis, on a background of yellow pigmentation due to carotene. On this day the light was good, and I had no doubt at all about the diagnosis. So I at once asked the patient about his diabetes. That was inept. He had come to "Mayo's" for a thorough examination, and my hasty diagnosis led him to tell me so emphatically and to leave the place forthwith.

Good lighting is essential to good practice. It was atrocious in some of the rooms in the rear of the first floor of the 1914 building. Once I was called to such a room to see a man who must have had the yellow skin of carotenosis, but it was not apparent in that light. The patient was one of those strange, but not unusual, personalities who refuse to divulge any information which may influence the decision of the physician. These people hold out, thus, for objectivity. This man had been diabetic for a year or more, but he did not tell us that. He had fasted, and so the specimen of his urine showed no sugar, but he did not tell us about the fasting either. I saw him late one evening. He was in a rush to leave and left without a diagnosis. A few weeks later I lectured on diabetes in some Dakota city and was asked to see this patient there. His physician could not understand how we had failed to recognize his diabetes at the Mayo Clinic. Nor could I. "Mehr Licht," as Goethe said. It cannot be overemphasized.

For some reason, no doubt readily understood by psychiatric colleagues, one remembers best one's errors and frustrations. I have always placed great emphasis on the training of the senses—all of them. My olfactory acuity for acetone in time became legendary. It later used to be said that I could sense the admission of patients with diabetic coma before I crossed the threshold of the front door of the hospital. Thus my chagrin was horrible on the occasion of one of Dr. Emanuel Libman's visits.

I had had a large experience with typhus fever in my student days, having been with Dr. Howard Taylor Ricketts in Mexico, and had had some part in the discovery of the micro-organisms in the blood, later named *Rickettsia*. Since then, although alert to the disease, I had not encountered typhus either in Chicago or in Rochester.

One day a colleague, knowing of my earlier experience, asked me to see a febrile patient who he thought might be suffering from typhus fever. I examined the man and noted a rash, but the spleen was large and the rash less hemorrhagic than it usually is in typhus. So I made a note to the effect that I suspected typhoid fever, not typhus, and I ordered a Widal test and culture of specimens of the blood and stools.

That very afternoon Dr. Rowntree escorted Dr. Libman through the hospital. A large group of physicians accompanied them, including Dr. Wilder. Dr. Libman, too, was cocky about his sense of smell. Having been interested in the then newly described Brill's disease in New York City, recently recognized as a form of typhus fever, he sniffed the air and pronounced the condition at hand, which I had thought was typhoid fever, to be typhus. Actually, results of the Widal test were positive for typhoid fever, as were results of culture of the blood, but these reports did not come in until after the great professor had departed. In the meantime, Dr. Wilder's reputation as a smeller was eclipsed.

EARLY RESEARCH

To begin some clinical investigation, I secured the services of one technician, housing her in an improvised laboratory in one of the tiny rooms of our Stanley floor for diabetes. The technician chosen was Carol Beeler, trained by Dr. Julius Stieglitz in the University of Chicago and then employed by Drs. Henry F. Helmholz and Samuel Amberg at Children's Memorial Hospital in Chicago. Carol was a find, although I had been advised against employing her, on the score of nepotism, because she was a sister of my wife. She was promoted some years later and left my immediate work group. Still later, in the 1920's, she was married to Dr. Geza de Takats, of Chicago, who has acquired eminence as a surgeon.

We accomplished something that first year in the Stanley Hospital. A study with Miss Beeler on chlorides and edema in diabetes was presented to the American Physiological Society (1), and a paper with Henry P. Wagener on the retinitis of diabetes mellitus (2) served to direct attention to a complication of diabetes which had been neglected but which now has assumed a place of great importance. Dr. Wagener, then a fellow in ophthalmology, later became renowned for his knowledge of the retina, and I take some pleasure in having had a part in arousing his interest in the manifestations of systemic disease in the retina.

The year 1920 was notable also as the first in which graduate students were assigned for a period of continuous duty and study on a hospital medical service. One of these was Dr. Waltman Walters. I recall that he fell in love with Phoebe Mayo then and was much disturbed about her being the daughter of the "Boss." He asked me what he ought to do about it. My advice was to go ahead and marry her, if she was willing. She was, and that was that. My only regret was that later this led to his transfer from a medical to a surgical fellowship, because his work in medicine had been excellent.

THE ROWNTREE GROUP FOR TEACHING AND CLINICAL INVESTIGATION

The same reason that had led to my employment by the Clinic—namely, to extend facilities for bedside teaching and clinical investigation—accounted also for the addition to the staff of Drs. Leonard G. Rowntree and Henry F. Helmholz. Dr. Rowntree came in April, 1920; Dr. Helmholz in January, 1921. Dr. Rowntree had been director of the Department of Internal Medicine at the University of Minnesota, and it was thought advisable to place a man of his academic significance at the head of the Department of Medicine of the Mayo Foundation. He was not made chief of medicine in the Mayo Clinic; Dr. Henry S. Plummer held that position. But Dr. Rowntree was given supervision of the training of fellows in medicine and direction of clinical research. The same responsibility in pediatrics was assigned to Dr. Helmholz. Dr. Samuel Amberg came with Dr. Helmholz.

Amusing now is Mrs. Helmholz' recollection of a condition she imposed before agreeing to move to Rochester. It was that if either she or Henry should fall sick, they were to return at once to Chicago. Her concern was occasioned by the very serious septicemia that had attacked Dr. Helmholz only a short time before in Chicago. She attributed his recovery, very correctly, to the solicitous and expert care he had received from Dr. Woodyatt. Woodyatt was like that. If a patient needed his attention, he gave him everything he had.

Dr. Rowntree brought Dr. Norman M. Keith from the Johns Hopkins University; Dr. Reginald Fitz from the Harvard Medical School; and, a little later, Dr. George Elgie Brown from Miles City, Montana, and Dr. Charles S. McVicar from Toronto. Clinical beds were provided for them on the second and third floors of the Stanley Hospital until, in the spring of 1921, all of us were moved into somewhat larger, but also temporary, quarters. An old hotel, rechristened the Olmsted Hospital, was remodeled for the purpose. The lobby on the first floor became a dining room for use by patients who were ambulant, and the front three rooms of the third floor were thrown together to make an adequate, although crowded, biochemical laboratory.

Here we remained until July, 1922, when the surgeons, who had occupied the older wings of St. Mary's Hospital, took over a newly constructed surgical pavilion adjacent on the west. We were then given their former space—after some remodeling of it—including the old operating rooms, converted into laboratories. Miss Beeler and I had the opportunity to move into the room which had been Dr. Charlie's operating room. It was challenging to do so, for the walls seemed to reflect the renown he had attained there.

The period at the Olmsted Hospital and the later period at St. Mary's Hospital were very satisfactory, from the standpoint of good fellowship. On paper we were one department. In practice, I retained considerable independence, although at first dividing the diabetic work with Dr. Fitz. Reg Fitz and I developed a close friendship in those days which lasted ever after. We worked in the greatest harmony, and I regretted more than anyone his decision, late in 1922, to return to Boston.

Reg Fitz had a funnybone. For our delight one time, he produced an excerpt, as he called it, from the *Almanach de Gotha,* on the Royal Family of Rochester: King William and Queen Hattie, the Grand Duke Charles of Mayowood and Grand Duchess Edith, Lord and Lady Balfour, the

Baron Rowntree and Lady Kitty, Sir William and Lady Braasch (née Stinchfield), Princess Daisy and Sir Henry Plummer, Princess Helen and Sir E. Starr Judd, Sir Melvin and Lady Henderson, and Dame Maud Mellish, who headed "Editorial" then but later married Dr. Louis B. Wilson. The rest of us were commoners. It was a perfect picture of society in that early period. We were "hired men of Dr. Will," as one staff member put it, and we liked it.

The Mayo Clinic then was small. There were forty-seven members of the staff in 1920, as well as forty fellows and twelve so-called courtesy registrants. Thus everyone, professionals and non-professionals alike, could be invited by Dr. and Mrs. Will to Christmas parties at their residence. Theirs were royal parties.

Research in diabetes at the Olmsted Hospital consisted mainly of a very elaborate study on the effect of protein on the basal metabolic rate and the carbohydrate tolerance of a severe diabetic patient whose name was Bessie Bakke. This was undertaken jointly with Dr. Walter M. Boothby, who assumed responsibility for the many determinations of the basal metabolic rate required in this investigation. It provided evidence in support of the high-fat diets that had recently been recommended by Petren, of Lund, and, independently, by Newburgh, of Ann Arbor. The report received high praise from Professor Graham Lusk, and "Bessie B." became historic, like "Cyril K.," a patient at the Sage Laboratory on whom extensive studies had been done under Lusk's direction (3). This was followed by further investigations, with Dr. Malcolm D. Winter, on "The Threshold of Ketogenesis," reported with him to the American Society for Clinical Investigation.

An observation which stemmed from the study of ketogenesis, for the development of which much credit is due to Dr. Helmholz and his associates, was the value of a ketogenic diet in the treatment of epilepsy. At an Atlantic City meeting, I had heard Gehelin's report of the benefit in epilepsy of periods of absolute fasting and was led thereby to look into the effect of prescribing a diet so designed that it would provoke ketosis—that is, a diet very high in fat and rigidly restricted in its content of carbohydrate. The results in a few cases were reported to the staff jointly with Dr. C. E. Baker (4), and, from then on, the pediatrists pursued the work with notable success, not only in epilepsy but, strange as it seemed, in infections of the urinary tract.

In October, 1920, came Mary A. Foley, who remained with us until her death in 1943. Mary Foley was a saint. She possessed a selfless personality, was devoted to her patients, and was always friendly, faithful, and loyal to her associates. She had been with the Army Medical Corps during the war and later was dietitian and instructor in dietetics at the Massachusetts General Hospital, Boston. Her appointment was director of dietetics of the Kahler Hospitals, meaning the Kahler, Colonial, Worrall, and Olmsted. Her early effort was devoted to the preparation of the very special diets required at the Olmsted and to instruction of the patients there.

I have mentioned the conversion of the lobby of the Olmsted into a large dining room where ambulant patients could be fed. The room was also used for group instruction of the patients. Miss Foley introduced such group instruction to supplement the individual teaching of the patients. She had had experience with this in Boston. She equipped this room with food models, charts, and a screen for the projection of lantern slides, and she and Miss Ellithorpe performed miracles there in the training not only of diabetic patients, who were increasing in number, but also of patients for whom other therapeutic diets were prescribed. Their instructions included demonstrations of weighing foods, using the Chatillon scales, thrice cooking vegetables, and washing bran to rid it of adherent starch.

Dr. Will, much impressed by these dietary arrangements at the Olmsted Hospital, called me to his office one day and asked whether we could provide a similar facility for other physicians of the Clinic and their patients. People learned better with their eyes, he said, than with their ears. He pictured a restaurant to which any member of the Clinic staff, indicating only in rough terms the diet to be given, could refer a patient for instruction. I thought it could be done and agreed to give it my support, provided that Miss Foley would take it on and provided also that all concerned would recognize that it would be expensive and need a subsidy of some kind. Dr. Will agreed to this.

By this time, June, 1922, the medical hospital services of Rowntree, Fitz, Keith, Brown, and Wilder were moving to St. Mary's Hospital. Miss Ellithorpe accompanied us, Miss Foley remaining behind to organize the Rochester Diet Kitchen. Space was provided in the three-story building on First Street opposite the Clinic, next door to and across an alley from the then recently completed Kahler Hotel and Hospital. The building had been occupied for a year or two by the Section of Therapeutic Radiology, and so it had been named the Curie Hospital. Here Miss Foley was established with rooms above for individual and group instruction of patients. The entire first floor was occupied by a restaurant with a seating capacity of one hundred and by the kitchen proper.

The Rochester Diet Kitchen was the first institution of its kind. It offered a unique service not only to patients and physicians but for teaching. In addition, Miss Foley continued to supervise dietetics in the Kahler, the Colonial, and the Worrall hospitals. In 1927 she had six assistants and, in addition, six young women impermanently attached for training. One of these was an English girl, Rose Simmonds, who had come to America in 1925 for such training on a Rockefeller scholarship. She first went to Dr. Elliott P. Joslin in Boston and then came to St. Mary's Hospital and the Mayo Clinic. Miss Simmonds later established a school for the instruction of dietitians in a hospital in London. She was a pioneer in England. She organized the British Dietetic Association and for many years was the editor of its journal. When King George V was in his final illness, she was called upon for advice and to oversee his diet.

In my war diary for February 28, 1941, I find this note: "Last night Eddie Rynearson, God bless him, staged a nice event. He was the public-health lecturer and arranged to have there in attendance many of the diabetic children from town, and Mary Foley. He then surprised us all by telling about a new diabetic camp, the Mary Foley Camp. Afterward, certain invitees adjourned to the University Club, where the dietitians had a party for us, and there Mary received a bouquet from the Board of Governors and a corsage from her 'male assistants.' " Her death two years later saddened all who knew her.

THE DISCOVERY OF INSULIN

In the fall of 1921 the first word came to us of insulin. Excitement prevailed. Without a background of experience such as we had had with the ineffective methods for the pre-insulin-era management of diabetes, the dramatic nature of that news can hardly be appreciated.

Never again was I to experience a thrill equal to that of being invited to attend the meeting in Toronto of a small committee of experts, called together by Professor J. J. R. Macleod to undertake an extensive clinical evaluation of the product insulin. The members of this committee, and later others, were supplied with insulin first from the Connaught Laboratories of the University of Toronto and soon thereafter from the Eli Lilly Company. Our first lot arrived in the early spring of 1922. Our hospital service then was in St. Mary's Hospital, but not as yet completely organized, so Dr. Boothby, with his customary kindness, invited me to use facilities on the tenth floor of the Kahler Hospital in a unit which he had recently set up for metabolic studies. Thus he and I joined forces again for these first studies of insulin.

In the autumn of 1922 we were honored by a visit from Dr. Frederick G. Banting, Professor J. J. R. Macleod, and their associates Mr. (later Dr.) C. H. Best and Dr. J. B. Collip. They told their story to the Mayo Clinic, and later that same evening I accompanied them to Chicago, where the lectures were repeated at the Institute of Medicine. This was an inspiring occasion, marred only by the obvious ill-will that had developed between Banting and Macleod. The former was determined, very justifiably, that the latter should not receive the lion's share of the acclaim for this accomplishment, and when Macleod talked for nearly ninety minutes, Banting took two hours, which was just too much for everyone, both in Rochester and in Chicago.

Our early investigations of insulin included an attempt at clinical assay. Under the conditions of the experiments and especially of the type of diet employed—namely, a pre-insulin-era formula, high in fat and very low in carbohydrate and protein—it was of reasonable significance. The average equivalent was 1.6 gm. of dextrose per unit. It was also found that a high intake of protein (3 gm. per kilogram of the patient's weight) greatly increased the insulin requirement in diabetes of severity.

The studies made with Boothby showed, for the first time, that insulin does not increase the rate of heat production and, therefore, that insulin is not a true calorigenic agent, like thyroxin or epinephrine. However, they also showed that when the sugar of the blood has been depressed by insulin to a level which provokes the symptoms of hypoglycemia, the rate of heat production increases abruptly, as if epinephrine had been injected at that point (5). I reported this at a meeting of the Harvard Medical Society and noticed that Professor Walter B. Cannon, sitting in the front row of the hall, was greatly interested. Sure enough, using dogs with hearts from which all nerve connections had been removed, he obtained the same tachycardia that we had observed, thus confirming our supposition that epinephrine is released when the level of the sugar in the blood decreases sufficiently. This is one means, as we had suggested, which the body uses to defend itself against an excessive lowering of the blood sugar.

Our clinical results with insulin were reported in three other papers (6, 7, 8). We then had given insulin to a hundred and fifty diabetic patients, with results that were exhilarating. We had had only three deaths, one attributed to pneumonia, one to pyonephrosis, and only one to diabetic coma. On the other hand, we had had more than twenty cases of diabetic acidosis, including four of actual coma, in which the patients had been restored. "More important, however," so I wrote, "than the dramatic results observed in cases of acidosis, are the improvements that are noted when insulin had been used as an adjunct in the treatment of the progressive cases of diabetes of several years' standing. A considerable proportion of our cases is made up of patients who had been previously trained in the dietary management of their disease, and who had faithfully adhered to restricted diets for two or more years. Despite the diet, the majority of these patients had lost tolerance until, at the time of their readmission, they were unable to keep themselves free from sugar, or safe from impending acidosis. . . . Such patients have gained from 20 to 30 pounds in weight, with proportionate improvement in strength and vitality, so that nearly all of them could pass for perfectly healthy persons within a few months of the institution of treatment with insulin. . . . A source of satisfaction is the record of cases complicated by severe infection, such as pneumonia, erysipelas, carbuncle, furunculosis, or septic gangrene. Two young children with severe diabetes have successfully passed through pneumonia . . . three patients with rapidly spreading, septic gangrene underwent amputations and convalesced from their operations uneventfully. . . . A patient with a pancreatic cyst underwent operation, developing most severe glycosuria and acidosis subsequent to the operation. He recovered with the help of insulin. Patients with such complications used to die. They now live!"

Insulin at that time cost five cents a unit in the market. However, the patients in our early cases received theirs gratis for a period of several years, thanks to the Eli Lilly Company. Barborka discussed in more detail our clinical procedure in the third paper of this series. That it was not without some merit would appear from the remarkable report made by Drs. Johnson and Rynearson (9). A farmer from the hinterland of Montana had adhered faithfully for twenty-nine years to the diet prescribed in those days—a diet providing only 40 gm. of carbohydrate, 50 of protein, and some 220 of fat. He had taken regular insulin in a dose of 30 units daily. His bread had been the washed-bran muffins he had learned to make at his first visit here in 1922. His vegetables had all been cooked in three changes of water. He was thirty-one years old in 1922 and sixty when he returned, yet examination revealed no abnormalities other than his diabetes—no retinopathy, a normal blood pressure, and no evidence of atherosclerosis, despite the high-fat diet, which included quantities of butter.

SURGICAL OPERATIONS ON DIABETIC PATIENTS

A surgical problem of great importance to the Mayo Clinic has been the care of diabetic patients requiring operations. In the pre-insulin era the hazards attending surgical treatment were considered by many to be prohibitive and, with the exception of minor procedures carried out for patients whose diabetes was mild, operation was discouraged. However, a conservative selection of patients, together with the expertness of the surgeons in limiting the amount of anesthesia and of trauma, had resulted in a very creditable showing at the Clinic before insulin became available. Berkman reported a mortality rate of only 7.4 per cent in 201 patients, covering in his report a period of four years prior to 1921.

The advent of insulin quickly changed the status of diabetic patients in respect to acceptability for surgical operation. After October, 1922, no patient was refused a necessary operation because of diabetes, and over the ensuing years the mortality rate among these patients was held to a figure very nearly as low as that prevailing in the Clinic for the same operations performed for the non-diabetic clientele.

These heartening data, to be further improved upon after the introduction in the 1940's of the sulfonamide drugs and the antibiotic agents, were attributed not alone to the availability of insulin but also to the complete co-operation obtained from the surgeons, anesthetists, nursing staff, and dietitians.

PREGNANCY AND DIABETES

The danger of pregnancy in diabetes had been extreme. Serious complications were avoidable when the disease was mild, but even at the best of institutions—at the Johns Hopkins Hospital, for example—25 or 30 per cent of pregnant women died in diabetic coma before or at delivery. The outlook after insulin became available improved rapidly, so that maternal deaths from acidosis or infection were practically eliminated. The infant mortality rate, however, which had always been high, continued to be high even after we had insulin. Counting abortions, stillbirths, and neonatal fatalities, it amounted to nearly 50 per cent. The same was true elsewhere, even in the leading diabetic centers. The abortions usually occurred about 4 weeks before term. Because of this and because of an observation made by others, and confirmed by our pathologists, that the pancreatic islets of such infants were often hypertrophic and thus presumably hyperfunctioning, two decisions were later arrived at: (*a*) to terminate the pregnancies at the earliest time by which viable infants could be expected, and (*b*) to begin feeding the infants immediately after their delivery to prevent excessive lowering of blood sugar levels from excessive production of insulin. Our improved experience with these policies was the subject of papers with Drs. Eloise Parsons and L. M. Randall (10) and of later reports by Randall and Rynearson (11).

The thought and study given to the problems of pregnancy and diabetes contributed to saving the life of an infant born in the Mayo family, a grandson of Dr. Charlie. Briefly, the child was delivered by Cesarean section prematurely, and, anticipating hypoglycemia, I arranged to observe him continuously myself, actually sleeping in the room for three nights in succession. The mother, then twenty-five years old, had been brought to us eight years before, at the onset of her diabetes, and had required insulin since then. She had lost three babies since her marriage in 1926. Once a miscarriage had occurred at the thirtieth week of gestation, and twice she had been delivered at the thirty-fourth week. One of these two infants was dead at birth, the other succumbed shortly after birth in convulsions. In the baby of the fourth gestation, convulsions developed 68 minutes after it was born. Thereupon, I gave dextrose by injection, and the convulsions stopped. Hourly feedings, reinforced with dextrose, were then begun, and no difficulty was encountered after that. The baby became a rugged man, with no diabetes.

DIABETIC CHILDREN

Appealing to me and binding me ever more closely to the Clinic with the passage of time has been the truly remarkable co-operation obtained here from one's colleagues. Whether this stems from an absence of financial competition or from the felicity of choosing for membership on the staff physicians who would work in harness well, or whether it was the example of Dr. Will and Dr. Charlie, who each referred so gladly to the other with the "my brother and I" that was heard so frequently, I cannot say. In any case, my debt of gratitude to many colleagues became very great indeed. From the beginning of the work on diabetes at the Clinic, the diabetic children were placed in the diabetic service of the hospital under the co-operative care of the Helmholz group and ours. This pleased me very much, for children are appealing, and diabetes rarely is so severe as it is in childhood.

What insulin meant to children in whom diabetes developed was forcibly recorded with Dr. Frank N. Allan (12). Frank came on the diabetic service in 1926. He was from Toronto, where in 1923 and 1924 he had worked in physiology with Macleod, studying in particular the differences in the effect of insulin in normal and depancreatized dogs.

Juvenile diabetes, as was pointed out in the paper I wrote with Allan, was almost always fatal in the era before insulin. Careful treatment might prolong the life of the child, but the longest course seldom would exceed four years. Between 1919 and 1922, thirty-two diabetic children had been cared for by our service. One child was moribund on arrival; two others died under our eyes in spite of all that we could do; twenty died at home within a year or two; nine survived to benefit from insulin in 1922.

In the next six years, with insulin available, the children treated numbered 167, and, of this number, 147 were known to be alive in 1928, and only 17 had died. Moreover, almost all the deaths might have been prevented. One child had died in Rochester, the others at home, months or years after their treatment at the Clinic. In several of these cases the use of insulin had been discontinued because someone had advised against it. In those days some physicians "did not believe in insulin," and many had not yet learned to use it properly.

HYPERINSULINISM

That excessive lowering of the level of blood sugar (hypoglycemia) represents a serious hazard in insulin therapy was discovered early by Banting and Best. Indeed, in one of Banting's papers, credit was given to Dr. Frank C. Mann and Dr. T. B. Magath of the Mayo Clinic for their lucid description of the symptoms of the hypoglycemia induced by total removal of the liver. This, Banting wrote, enabled him and Best to recognize the nature of the convulsive disturbances which their first pancreatic extracts induced at times in dogs. Dr. Seale Harris of Birmingham, seeing this phenomenon on a visit to Toronto in 1923, was led to the deduction that similar symptoms occasionally observed in patients not diabetic and not receiving insulin might be related to spontaneous overproduction of insulin. He found low blood sugar levels in such patients and came to the conclusion—without, however, presenting any proof therefor—that he was dealing here with what he called "hyperinsulinism" or "dysinsulinism." It was our good fortune to be able to provide proof positive that such a condition, hyperinsulinism, the antithesis of diabetes, could occur.

On October 29, 1926, a man was brought directly to St. Mary's Hospital in an emergency. He was seen there first by Florence Smith, our dietitian. He seemed to her to be in "shock" from an overdose of insulin, and straightway she sent for me. I was lecturing to the diabetic patients in the sun parlor nearby. I, too, thought the man had taken too much insulin. We drew blood without delay. The value for sugar was very low, but, before this had been reported back, we had given dextrose intravenously and had observed rapid restoration to full consciousness, a response with which we had become familiar. Then we learned, to our surprise, that the man had never taken insulin. There had been several episodes like the one we had observed, and it was for this that he had come to the Clinic.

An elaborate investigation followed, and finally we convinced ourselves that we were faced with an unusual disease. The patient was a surgeon, and he himself insisted on an abdominal operation. We were more than willing. We were having to give him dextrose intravenously at frequent intervals to prevent convulsions and unconsciousness. Furthermore, his liver was enlarged, and he had some epigastric pain. Dr. Will Mayo was called in consultation. He was doubtful, having seen too many patients presenting unusual symptoms for whom surgical exploration had been useless. At last, however, he agreed to have a look. I was at his elbow when he reached the pancreas. It contained a tumor, and at once he said, "This is something different from anything that I have ever seen before." It was carcinoma, but a different kind of carcinoma than is usually encountered in the pancreas. Nodules in the liver and adjacent lymph nodes were obvious metastases, so no further surgical treatment could be done. The microscopic appearance of a specimen of the tumor was that of pancreatic islet tissue.

The patient died a few weeks later. By that time we had gathered a mass of information about this "new" disease. Finally, at necropsy we clinched the diagnosis by finding that extracts of the metastatic lesions in the liver behaved like insulin when injected into rabbits (13). Many other cases of this new disease, the antithesis of pancreatic diabetes, have been found since then, here and elsewhere. In many of these later cases the tumor of the pancreatic islets proved to be benign, so that, after surgical removal of the tumor, the patient was restored to health.

HYPERPARATHYROIDISM

In this period at St. Mary's Hospital it was also our good fortune to be among the first to recognize another "new disease." Mandl, in Vienna, in 1926 had reported the finding of a tumor of parathyroid origin and had noted the great benefit to the accompanying abnormalities of the skeleton that followed removal of the tumor. A similar case was found by Gold in the clinic of Von Eiselsberg. The third case in which this disease was clearly recognized and the first to be reported as hyperparathyroidism was that of Barr and his associates, of St. Louis. Their report was made at a meeting late in 1928 in St. Louis.

In attendance there were Rowntree and Frank Allan, who, when they returned, asked me to consider the possibility of this diagnosis in a case under study then with Dr. Power. The patient had been transferred to us by Dr. Melvin S. Henderson for calcium and phosphate balances. Many features resembled those encountered by Barr and his associates: notably, the type of rarefaction of the bones, tumors of the bone, and elevation of the calcium level and depression of the phosphorus level of the blood. Furthermore, the patient had a tumor of the neck. This had been thought to be an adenoma of the thyroid, and so it was; but on the opposite side of the neck, when the operation was performed by Dr. Frederick W.

Rankin, was a parathyroid tumor. The studies with this patient were reported in 1929 (14).

The experiences gained from this investigation led to further study of parathyroid overfunction. The final proof that generalized osteitis fibrosa, which we decided was the skeletal abnormality associated with these parathyroid tumors and resulted from excess of parathyroid hormone, was provided by my pupil Dr. Joseph Johnson when I was at the University of Chicago. Similar data were provided independently by Jaffe and Bodansky of New York City. The disease was reproduced in white rats and puppies by injections of parathyroid extracts, which had been obtained by Collip of Toronto in 1924 and soon thereafter had been made available commercially as parathormone. In the animals, with properly adjusted doses of this extract, decalcification of bone occurred, with the fibrous replacement, giant-cell tumors, and cysts characteristic of the clinical disorder. In two human volunteers who received the extract, one of them Dr. Johnson himself, abnormalities of the blood characteristic of the disease resulted, and hypotonia and muscular and mental fatigue, also characteristic, were observed. (15).

ANOTHER "NEW" DISEASE HYPEREPINEPHRINISM

It was also in the period when the Rowntree group was conducting the medical services at St. Mary's Hospital that Dr. Charlie, during laparotomy for a patient with paroxysmal hypertension, found a chromaffin tumor, the removal of which was followed by the disappearance of the patient's periodic episodes of tachycardia and hypertension (16). In the year that followed, Dr. Maurice C. Pincoffs, professor of medicine at the University of Maryland, encountered an almost identical situation, in which his surgical colleague, Dr. Arthur M. Shipley, removed an adrenomedullary tumor and brought about complete relief of the patient's symptoms. In their case, epinephrine was isolated from the tumor. These, I believe, were the first two patients with this disease to be treated successfully by operation.

Some time after that, the diabetic service was called in consultation because sugar had been found in the urine of such a patient. On this occasion I was in attendance at the operation and was able to secure half the tumor. I took this personally to Dr. Edward C. Kendall, who was then processing hundreds of pounds of beef adrenal glands in his earlier attempts to isolate adrenocortical hormones. I recall my excitement when, two days later, I went to him for his report on our tumor. He handed me a small test tube one-quarter full of white crystalline epinephrine obtained from the half-tumor. It was enough to kill a company of soldiers!

DISEASES OF THE THYROID WITH DIABETES

My collaboration with Dr. Boothby began with the metabolic study in the Olmsted Hospital, which was followed soon thereafter by our joint experiments with insulin, and continued, with one problem after another, until the retirement of Dr. Boothby in 1948. Our relationship, both professional and social, was always cordial and, like Rochambeau and Washington, "we worked together, as brothers should, in harmonious friendship."[1] Dr. Boothby came to the Clinic in 1916 from Harvey Cushing's service in Boston at the solicitation of Dr. H. S. Plummer, and, as head of a section of metabolism, he introduced the procedure for determining the basal metabolic rate. He brought with him as an assistant Irene Sandiford, who was followed in 1920 by her sister, Kathleen. Both Sandifords left in 1930, Irene (then Dr.) to take over the basal metabolic rate determinations as an assistant professor of biochemistry in the Department of Medicine at the University of Chicago, and Kathleen to marry Dr. James H. Saint, of Newcastle-on-Tyne, England.

An interest in the effect of the activity of the thyroid on the metabolism of carbohydrates and diabetes stemmed from my early studies in Chicago under Dr. R. T. Woodyatt. A precision instrument was devised by him with which fluids could be injected continuously at timed rates, and we were determining the amounts of dextrose and other sugars excreted by dogs when the inflow of sugar into a vein was maintained for periods at given amounts per minute. Thus the rate of utilization of the sugars could be measured with accuracy, as well as the rate which just sufficed to provoke glycosuria. The latter we regarded as a much more significant measurement of tolerance—of dextrose, for example—than any oral tests of tolerance proposed.

One day, in the midst of such a procedure, Dr. E. C. Kendall appeared with a sample of the crystalline thyroxin which he had recently isolated in his laboratory at the Mayo Clinic. It was supposed that the injection would increase the rate of utilization of glucose, but an experiment re-

1. The quotation is from a letter of Washington to Rochambeau engraved on the base of a statue of Rochambeau in Lafayette Park, Washington, D.C.

vealed the opposite: the rate was lowered, as was the tolerance. In the meantime, in experiments on normal human volunteers, we had found the tolerance to dextrose—that is, the highest rate of injection that could be employed without provoking glycosuria—to be between 0.8 and 0.9 gm. each hour for each kilogram of body weight. When we then turned to patients who had evident hyperthyroidism, we found the tolerance lowered from 0.8 to 0.6 or less.

Later studies with Boothby in Rochester revealed that, while tolerance to dextrose was lowered by thyroxin, the respiratory quotient after dextrose was administered rose even more abruptly than is normal, and from this we could deduce that the lowered tolerance to dextrose of hyperthyroid patients was not indicative of true diabetes mellitus. The two diseases may, however, accompany each other (17).

Other observations were of practical as well as theoretic significance. Thus mild or even obscure diabetes would be aggravated intensely by the development of hyperthyroidism, so that diabetic acidosis could result. The requirement of insulin for patients with uncomplicated diabetes could regularly be increased by the giving of thyroid extract; on the other hand, measures that lowered the metabolic rate—such as thyroidectomy or, in diabetes complicated by exophthalmic goiter, the giving of iodine in sufficient doses—regularly lowered the dose of insulin required.

DIABETIC COMPLICATIONS

Insulin was lengthening the lives of diabetic patients and soon began to throw into greater relief the more chronic complications of diabetes, notably those relating to abnormalities of the circulation. Referred to previously in connection with the earliest activities of the diabetic service were observations made with Dr. Henry P. Wagener on diabetic retinopathy. In the report of a later study of this subject, made with Dr. Wagener and Dr. Thomas J. Dry (18), appeared a comment which in my opinion deserves more attention than has been given it: namely, that lesions like those observed in the retinas of diabetic patients may also occur in other peripheral vessels and thus account for the high incidence of atherosclerosis, nephropathy, and neuropathy among diabetic patients.

TEACHING

The apprentice type of teaching had been the bulwark of the educational facility of the Mayo Foundation, but a certain amount of more formal instruction was introduced early. In the 1920's this consisted generally of seminars. At St. Mary's Hospital we held several seminars each week. One, on the diabetic service, was devoted mostly to biochemistry and the fundamentals of metabolism. Another was a general medical clinic in which we joined with Drs. Rowntree, Keith, Brown, and McVicar.

All the senior members of the Mayo Clinic staff were asked from time to time to take part in the examination of those fellows who had completed their requirements for the advanced degrees given by the University of Minnesota. At that time these were held in Rochester and were rather sketchy. It was only later, when better roads made transportation easier, that all such examinations were held on the campus of the university and were participated in by members of the faculty there as well as by our members.

SCIENTIFIC SOCIETIES

Young men with an inclination toward clinical investigation, like other scientists, desire to belong to the leading national societies in the scientific fields. The *ne plus ultra* in our field was membership in the Association of American Physicians and its loosely linked body of younger investigators, the American Society for Clinical Investigation. The latter was known as the "Young Turks," after the accomplishments of the followers of Kemal Pasha Atatürk, whose revolutionary activities in Turkey were then attracting the admiration of the Western world. Dr. Rowntree was untiring in his efforts to secure memberships in them for the senior members of his "group." Within a very short time Fitz, Keith, and I came in; others followed. Dr. Rowntree also enabled us to become members of the Central Interurban Clinical Club, a smaller group which met twice yearly in one or another of the universities of the Middle West. Later with the backing of that body and with assistance from Dr. Frank Billings of Chicago, he organized the Central Society for Clinical Research, of which the Central Interurban Clinical Club formed the founder membership. Dr. Rowntree likewise was the motivating spirit in the founding of the Minnesota Society of Internal Medicine. In addition, partly at Dr. Rowntree's urging, several of us became members of one or more of the national societies for the basic sciences. In time I belonged to three of them: the American Physiological Society, the American Society for Experimental Pathology, and the American Institute of Nutrition. The last named was organized in the later 1920's for the rapidly increasing number of physiologists, biochemists, and physicians who had joint interests in nutrition. Dr. Graham Lusk, professor of physiology, and Dr. Eugene DuBois, professor of medicine of the Cornell Medical School in New York City, were active in its establishment. I held both these men in very high regard and always saw them when I traveled in the East. In consequence, perhaps, I found myself a charter member of that institute, a connection that I later prized most highly.

Also demanding recognition in this essay—and this seems to be as good a spot as any, although out of order chronologically—is the American Diabetes Association. It was organized by Dr. Cecil Striker in 1941, and several of those with service on the metabolic sections of the Clinic have been members of its council—Drs. Allan, Pollack, Sprague, Yater, and I. Dr. Sprague was president in 1954. He was preceded by Dr. Allan. I was elected president at the celebration of the twenty-fifth anniversary of the discovery of insulin. Among those attending the meeting in Toronto then (1946) were Dr. E. P. Joslin, honorary president of the association from its establishment; Dr. B. A. Houssay, of Buenos Aires; Dr. H. C. Hagedorn, of Copenhagen; Dr. R. D. Lawrence, of London, who organized the British Diabetes Association, through which he did much for the safety of the diabetic children of England during the "blitz"; and Dr. C. H. Best.

My address at the momentous meeting in Toronto (19), after expressing jubilation over the discovery of insulin twenty-five years before, placed emphasis on what remained to be done before the diabetic person could enjoy as much health and as long a life as others and closed by quoting Banting. "It is not within the power of the properly constructed mind," he had said, "to be satisfied. Progress would cease otherwise."

At the banquet in the evening of the first day of the meeting (October 18), the chancellor of the University of Toronto called attention to the appropriateness of the day. It was the day of St. Luke the physician.

PRIMER FOR DIABETIC PATIENTS

The nine editions of the little book *A Primer for Diabetic Patients* (20), the first written in 1921, the last in 1950, provide a panorama of diabetic therapy in that interval. The first printing was based on mimeographed instruction sheets prepared in 1920 for the diabetic patients. We were then following the generally accepted treatment of that time, which was based on the research of Dr. Frederick M. Allen at the Rockefeller Institute in New York. It involved an initial period of starvation and the effort afterward to maintain control of glycosuria by a very rigidly restricted diet and periodic fast days. The second edition (1923) introduced insulin and diets made more liberal in fat. The pre-insulin diets were continued because of the cost of insulin—5 cents a unit then—and because of a disinclination to give more of this new drug than was absolutely necessary, since it was not yet known whether ill effects would result from the continued use of insulin. As the years went by, greater and greater liberality was permitted, until, in the later editions of the book, the diets recommended, although still controlled as to composition, provided almost as much protein and carbohydrate as would be contained in the well-selected diets of normal persons.

The sixth edition of the *Primer* (1937) introduced protamine insulin, developed by Professor Hagedorn of Copenhagen. Also, in a discussion of what causes diabetes, mention first appeared of the part played by the hormones of the thyroid gland, the adrenal glands (only epinephrine was considered), and the pituitary body. Studies of the thyroid gland in diabetes were referred to above. Houssay's work in Buenos Aires, which showed that ablation of the pituitary body ameliorated diabetes, had just come to general attention, and Young's production of diabetes in dogs by massive injections of pituitary extract had been reported still more recently. Reference to their studies and to the later work of Long and Lukens and that of Dr. Edward C. Kendall and others on the hormones of the adrenal cortex appeared in the seventh, eighth, and ninth editions.

With so many engaged in diabetic work, all of them contributing in one way or another to the development of our procedure for treating diabetic patients, it early became impossible to distribute properly the royalties from the sale of the *Primer*. These assumed considerable proportions and, because the book was in very fact a distillate of the experience of all of us, I decided after 1937 that the fairest way to deal with royalties would be to use them for the exclusive benefit of the diabetic patients. A fund was thus created which was named the Mary Foley Fund.

In the spring of 1929 came an invitation to become the chairman of the Department of Medicine of the University of Chicago. I had refused two similar invitations earlier, the first from the State University of Iowa, the other from Washington University in St. Louis. Since student days my ambition had been to occupy such a post, but Dr. Will had talked me out of going to Iowa and St. Louis. His mastery was phenomenal. He could persuade most of us, nearly always cheerfully, to do what he thought best.

The offer from Chicago was, however, more compelling. He recognized the difference and gave his blessing to it. The University of Chicago was my Alma Mater. My home from the age of twelve years had been adjacent to the campus. My father was the head of opthalmology at Rush Medical College, which, because of its affiliation with the University of Chicago, made him a member of the senate of the university. Furthermore, my father, as a friend of the first president, William Rainey Harper, and of Harper's successor, President Judson, long had had a lively interest in the university's affairs. Among my former teachers on the faculty were men with whom I had been intimate and whom I admired greatly—notably Robert Russell Bensley, Anton Carlson, Gideon Wells, Ludvig Hektoen, Rollin Woodyatt, and Frank Billings. Dr. Billings had had much to do with the establishment of the then recently opened clinic and hospital on the university campus. Also, he, with Dr. Bertram Sippy, had established teaching residencies at the Presbyterian Hospital in Chicago, and he had called me from war-torn Europe in 1914 to be one of their first two residents. My answer to the Chicago offer simply had to be affirmative.

A staff dinner was arranged to speed me on my way. It was given in the Kahler dining room, with the tables arranged to form the letter *W*. Most of the members of the Clinic staff were there—in black ties in those days. The head table capped the *W*, and seated at it were Dr. Charlie, Dr. L. B. Wilson, Dr. Henry Plummer, Dr. Rowntree, and the departer. Dr. Will was out of town, but he sent a telegram. Very pleasant things were said by all, but Dr. Plummer in his talk addressed me as "Leonard Rowntree." The first time it passed unnoticed; the second time it caused a titter of amusement; the third time a roar of tumultuous guffaws. Henry's disaffection for the Rowntree program at St. Mary's Hospital was widely known. Moreover, it was shared by those members of the Clinic staff who still were unconvinced about the wisdom of the Clinic's affiliation with the University of Minnesota. Hence almost everyone was aware that, in this incident, Henry's ego was breaking through the censor of his superego. I don't believe he wanted me to go, because his welcome, when I returned in 1931, was very cordial. In any case, the story became a classic among teachers of psychiatry.

Hard hit by the depression in the autumn of 1929 was the Rowntree program at St. Mary's Hospital, which included a medical department of a type already well developed in many American universities. We thus had laboratories for research in the operating ampitheater of the former surgical pavilion and other laboratories for work involving animals in a remodeled barn on the hospital grounds. Most of this was scrapped. By a decision of the Board of Governors, all chemistry was centralized in a Section of Biochemistry downtown, and all investigations which involved the use of larger animals were restricted to the Institute for Experimental Medicine. The latter, blasphemously called "the dog farm," had previously been established southwest and three miles out of town on one of Dr. Charlie's farms.

Dr. S. Franklin Adams and Dr. William P. Finney, associates on the diabetic service at the time of my departure, were detached, and Dr. Frank N. Allan, promoted from a first assistant to an associate, was placed in charge of diabetes. The others of the Rowntree group were scattered among several other sections of the Clinic. This was a terrific blow to Dr. Rowntree. He went elsewhere for treatment of polyarthritis, which developed at the time, and finally resigned. Later he became director of an institute for research in Philadelphia.

In the fall of 1931 I was asked by Dr. Will to fill the place left vacant by Dr. Rowntree's resignation. I was loath to do so on several counts but had not found the position at Chicago entirely to my liking. Finally, I decided that Dr. Will was right and that I belonged in Rochester. I could not expect to follow Dr. Rowntree's former program. Its weakness lay in imperfect integration with the activities of the Clinic as a whole. I could contribute to instruction in internal medicine and promote investigation in the areas of medicine in which I had acquired special skill. Moreover, life in Rochester could be as pleasant as it had been in the twenties. This it proved to be.

Activities of the 1930's and 1940's

ORGANIZATION

Experience acquired in Chicago and developments in endocrinology led me to the view that the activities of the goiter services, headed then by Dr. Henry S. Plummer and Dr. William A. Plummer, and those of the diabetic service ought to be combined. By this means, one closely knit group would be responsible for diseases of metabolism, endocrinology, and nutrition, which by that time had become closely interwoven. I discussed this fully with Dr. Henry Plummer, and his agreement influenced my decision to return to Rochester. Dr. Will Mayo wanted me to assume the chairmanship of the combined services, but this I at once declined, for several reasons. The first was that Dr. Henry Plummer was senior to me on all counts and the chairmanship of the sections devoted to metabolism was logically his. The second was that if I were to function as effectively as I wanted to as chief of the department of medicine of the Mayo Foundation and, in addition, was to have the time I wanted for research, I could not assume responsibility for the routine business of these sections.

The consultation offices of the sections of Drs. Henry and Will Plummer were located in suites of rooms off Desk North 10 of the 1928 clinic building, and it was arranged that each of them would provide a room or two for work with diabetic patients and also that each should assign one or more of his associates to work in diabetes and such other diseases of metabolism as might come within our joint area of interest.

Dr. Frank N. Allan left soon after my return, to assume a senior consultantship on the staff of the Lahey Clinic, Boston, and Drs. Kepler and Rynearson were selected to spend part-time in the hospitals with me to acquaint themselves with the treatment of diabetes. Then they assumed a share of the responsibility for the care of diabetic patients. In addition, each of us spent part-time at North 10 in general diagnosis and to answer calls for consultations. Much later Drs. R. G. Sprague and F. R. Keating, Jr., took part in these activities and subsequently others. This plan worked out well, despite an early informality.

In actual fact, the formal combination of the sections did not appear on paper until after Dr. Henry Plummer's death. Later, in 1947, Dr. Samuel F. Haines became chairman of the sections, with Dr. Will Plummer and, later, Dr. Rynearson heading one and Dr. Haines and, later, Dr. Sprague heading the second. The diabetic service then became a responsibility of the entire group. However, joint meetings of the diagnostic sections and metabolic services were held from the early 1930's on, both in the sections for the instruction of the fellows and in Dr. M. H. Power's laboratory, where at weekly luncheons investigation was reviewed. Attendance at the luncheons was restricted to members of the permanent staff of the sections and to colleagues in the basic-science laboratories. Dr. M. H. Power and Dr. H. L. Mason from biochemistry; Dr. C. F. Code, Dr. G. M. Higgins, and Dr. A. Albert from physiology; and Dr. W. A. Bennett from pathology were very regular attendants in the 1940's, contributing enormously to the value of these conferences and to the scientific supervision of investigations then in hand.

METABOLISM THERAPY

As the depression reached its height, many of the diabetic patients were loath to add hospital bills to their clinic charges. Therefore, it became expedient to provide outpatient care for those whose diabetes was uncomplicated. We sent these people for their meals and dietary instruction to the Rochester Diet Kitchen and taught them the use of insulin in the offices at North 10. This plan was facilitated by attaching Miss Foley to the North 10 staff. A room there was equipped for her, and after 1933 she assumed responsibility for the individual instruction in diet planning, testing urine, and use of insulin.

By 1936, however, the practice of the Clinic, which had fallen off sharply in the height of the depression, had increased enough to make it necessary to move this therapeutic work from North 10 to the Curie. The location was advantageous, above the Rochester Diet Kitchen. We called the establishment the Section of Metabolism Therapy, and the desk became MT.

The outpatient care of the diabetic patients, although forced upon us by necessity, proved to be a blessing. It enabled us to see these patients frequently and to give them more effective training than was possible in a hospital. As soon as diabetes was detected at the Clinic, the patient, if he had no complications which required care in bed, was referred for treatment to MT (Metabolism Therapy). There he would be seen at once by Miss Foley or an assistant. Training began without delay, so arranged that it would integrate with the completion of his examination in the Clinic. He was taught to test for sugar in the urine on the day of his arrival at MT, was given insulin if insulin was required, and a prescription for a diet was planned to meet his individual requirements. He was served this diet at the Diet Kitchen. The next day he was taught how to take his insulin himself, and after that for several days he reported every morning with a record of his urine tests, one made before each meal and one at night. He injected himself with insulin under supervision. At appointed hours he received instruction in his diet planning and insulin adjustment. Each day there was a lecture to the group of patients currently receiving care. The subject matter of these lectures was the content of a printed manual which was altered as procedures changed.

In the afternoons the physician in charge at MT, seated at a table and flanked by one or more of the assistants, would see these patients, one at a time, to review individual problems and make decisions as to insulin adjustment and other treatment. This passing-in-review provided an opportunity for teaching the assistants and the occasional nurse assigned to MT for instruction.

TEACHING

In 1930 Dr. Hugh Cabot, the distinguished urologist and surgeon of Harvard University and subsequently dean of the medical school at the University of Michigan, was appointed a consultant in the section of urology and a professor of surgery in the Mayo Foundation. The inadequate performance of many of the fellows during their examinations for advanced degrees prompted Dr. Cabot to introduce, in urology and surgery, a degree of formality in instruction that had been lacking theretofore. I was led by his example to establish a similar procedure for the department of medicine and, beginning in 1933, review courses were held in each of the three years of the medical fellowship. The Seniors met with me and appropriate invitees from the basic-sciences groups for review of the physiology and biochemistry of morbid processes.

My group was small enough at first so that we could gather at my home. There we could sit around the fire one evening every week for our discussions and beer and pretzels. This was the Mark Hopkins type of pedagogy. The topic had been assigned beforehand, and one of the fellows had been designated to cover the more important aspects of its background. Then all took a hand in its elaboration. The Wilder family owned a great Dane in those days. His name was Thor, after Thorstein Veblen, the philosopher of "conspicuous waste." Thor was an example of it! He almost ate us out of house and home, in addition to getting handouts from almost all the butchers in the village. At these evening seminars Thor would lie under the piano and, if the essayist was long-winded, would protest with an atrocious yawn. That quickly overcame any speaker who offended.

Later, as this group became too large for accommodation in my home, we held our meetings elsewhere, and, when the Mayo Foundation House became available, we held them at a great round table there.

Likewise, once every week all the medical services participated in a general clinic at St. Mary's Hospital. Patients were shown, the diagnosis in each case was questioned, and treatment was discussed. Also, every diagnostic section of the Clinic was urged to institute a sectional seminar.

Finally, following the example set by surgery—to provide the fellows with some experience in oral examinations before they were subjected to their ordeal at the University of Minnesota—every candidate was examined orally in the Mayo Foundation offices by a committee from the Clinic staff; participating usually were two or three clinicians and a representative or two from the basic-science laboratories in which the study for the minor sequence had been undertaken.

The value of these exercises was in time reflected not only by improvement in performances at examinations but also in increased efficiency on the Clinic floor and in the hospitals.

THE GRADUATE COMMITTEE AND MAYO FOUNDATION

The graduate teaching at the Clinic had been organized by the dean of the graduate school of the university, Professor Guy Stanton Ford, and the director of the Mayo Foundation for Medical Education and Research, Dr. Louis B. Wilson. Before this, Dr. Wilson had been professor of pathology at the university. In 1938 Professor Ford was succeeded in the deanship of the graduate school by Professor Theodore Blegen. Dr. Wilson, on his retirement in 1937, was succeeded in the directorship of the Mayo Foundation by Dr. Donald C. Balfour, who was followed by Dr. Victor Johnson in 1947. He, with Mrs. Johnson (Dr. Adelaide Johnson), had studied under me at the University of Chicago.

These men were all devoted to the teaching program at the Mayo Clinic. Integration with the University of Minnesota was accomplished through a graduate committee of the university whose members were appointed by the president—an equal number from Rochester and Minneapolis. The graduate committee was responsible for recommending appointments to and promotions in the faculty at Rochester, which included almost all the permanent professional appointees of the Mayo Clinic staff. It was also responsible for the examination of all candidates for advanced degrees in the specialties of medicine and surgery, whether presented from Rochester or from Minneapolis. The committee as a whole met once each quarter, usually at the university, and the chairman was the dean of the graduate school. In addition, the Rochester members, on whom fell the major part of the responsibilities in Rochester, held weekly meetings in the Mayo Foundation office. The chairman of these meetings was the director of the Mayo Foundation.

As chief of the department of medicine of the Mayo Foundation, I automatically became a member of the graduate committee. This added a number of activities in addition to those pertaining to the department: attendance at the committee meetings, consideration of questions of policy which arose there, and personal interviews with applicants for fellowships.

I recently found this note in a diary that I kept then: "Dec. 11, 1940 . . . reviewing applications for fellowships in medicine for July or October. There are 90 of them, 25 first class and another 20 acceptable. Their number at long last has come to equal that for surgery and the first-class men exceed the surgeons. Ed. Allen, the new Governor for Minnesota in the American College of Physicians, tells me that among the approved applications for membership in the College, ten per cent are from our graduates. This was heartening."

The preceding comment on interviews with applicants for fellowships calls to mind an applicant in medicine who was interning with my son Tom at the University of Maryland Hospital. He had failed to find me anywhere until he stepped into an elevator and saw a replica of Tom. Without hesitation he addressed me as Dr. Wilder. Tom, although a fellow in surgery, served for a quarter in the North 10 offices. That was in 1943, when I was in the War Food Administration and away. The following year Tom left for service in the Navy. I had returned, and one day when I stepped into an examining room at North 10, I was greeted by the patient there with the exclamation: "Why Dr. Wilder, how you've aged!" "C'est la guerre," was my reply. I did think at that time that it would be convenient to have a genuine double. There was so very much to do in those war years.

Hagedorn's protamine insulin was introduced in 1935. This was a protamine obtained from fish sperm in physical combination with insulin. On injection, a slow release of insulin occurred such that the effect of a single dose of insulin was prolonged. Later extra zinc was added, which further prolonged the action of the insulin and provided increased stability. A small amount of protamine insulin was received from Dr. Hagedorn in January, 1936, and soon thereafter supplies of it were provided regularly from the Eli Lilly Company. Drs. R. G. Sprague and Benjamin B. Blum were assistants on the service at that time, and with them and Dr. A. E. Osterberg, Dr. Edwin J. Kepler and I at once began extensive studies with it (21).

Also on the service in the spring and summer quarters of 1936 was Lydia Nelson, a dietitian who had registered for a fellowship in dietetics. Like Dr. Sprague, she was diabetic, and he and she were among the first to receive the new insulin at our hands.

The annual convention of the American Medical Association was held in Kansas City, May 11–15, 1936, and Dr. Joslin invited me to join him in displaying there an exhibit on diabetes. I agreed and took with me, not only as assistants but as exhibits A and B, Dr. Sprague and Miss Nelson. So far as anybody knew about us, everything went smoothly. However, on the second evening Miss Nelson, in great alarm, reported to me that Dr. Sprague was lost. We found him later, wandering in the streets distractedly in a delayed reaction from protamine insulin. No further trouble was encountered in Kansas City, but on the drive home Miss Nelson, too long without food, was unable to write her name in the registry of the hotel where we were stopping for the night. This promised to be scandalous, but a glass of orange juice re-established the proprieties and suspicion soon was laid—not, however, without great respect for our own pronouncement in the article referred to just above. It happened to appear in print that very day, May 16, 1936: ". . . that although protamine insulin, in many cases, makes possible effective management of diabetes with only one administration of insulin a day, and with less insistence on rigid control of the diet, its careless use or disregard of the diet is attended with danger."

ADDISON'S DISEASE

Almost as dramatic as the change in the outlook in diabetes which followed the discovery of insulin has been that made possible for patients with adrenal insufficiency by current hormonal medication. The study and treatment of patients with Addison's disease was undertaken in the 1920's by Dr. Rowntree. However, a review of this experience in 103 cases which he published with Dr. Albert M. Snell closed on a note of pessimism. All types of treatment tried had been ineffective. Life could be maintained only in cases in which the disease was mild, and even then infection or any other complication carried with it extreme danger. That was in 1929.

A year and a few months later Drs. Rowntree and Carl H. Greene were able to describe the successful restoration of a patient in the so-called crisis of Addison's disease by means of an extract of adrenal glands prepared in Professor Wilbur W. Swingle's laboratory at Princeton University (22).

Dr. Kendall's work on adrenocortical extractions began in the late 1920's and in 1932, administering extracts made by him, Drs. Greene, Walters, and Rowntree could report on a major surgical operation performed successfully in a case of Addison's disease. Hope was thus aroused that effective substitution therapy was at hand for this disease. Discouragement was to follow. The bulkiness of the injections, the pain associated with them, and, above all, the cost created handicaps to satisfactory treatment of the chronic stages of the disease; after three years of experience, Dr. Snell reported that only sixteen of forty-six patients had lived more than a year after treatment with the extract had begun. Only seven had survived to the time of his writing.

It was in 1933 that Dr. Snell, having transferred his interest to gastroenterology, asked us to assume responsibility for the care of Addison's disease. We were glad to do so because, as I said above, we had hoped eventually to bring other endocrine diseases into the tent that housed metabolism. On the other hand, we were not without some apprehension, because the number of patients with Addison's disease had become substantial, and each one of them presented a serious therapeutic problem. We soon had a baker's dozen of these patients in the hospital at one time, and I recollect with some amusement that my son Russell, when he was on the service as a first assistant, whimsically questioned whether the superb experience he was obtaining treating Addison's disease could later make a living for him. Russ had recently completed some excellent research on the rate of hepatic glycogenolysis for his Ph.D. degree. The work was directed by Dr. Jesse L. Bollman.

It was fortunate for us that a major contribution to the chronic treatment of Addison's disease was made soon after we took over this responsibility. In 1935 Dr. Robert F. Loeb, at Columbia University, described the changes of sodium and chloride in the plasma in the presence of adrenocortical insufficiency and pointed out the benefit of increasing the salt content of the diets of patients with Addison's disease. His observations were at once confirmed by others, among them Dr. William D. Allers, of Dr. Kendall's group. Dr. Allers added the important information that survival in adrenalectomized dogs receiving sodium chloride could be extended further if account were taken of the fact that more base was lost than acid and if base in the form of sodium bicarbonate were administered (23). Dr. Allers' observation was illustrated for us by a case of Addison's disease in which the patient not only had a craving for salt—not unusual in this condition—which she satisfied by using extra salt, but also had a "chronic sour stomach," which she relieved with baking soda. The woman had maintained her weight and strength for five years or more without the benefit of adrenal extract.

Hence our treatment was then modified with advantage to include the daily administration of 10 gm. of sodium chloride and 5 gm. of sodium citrate. Soon thereafter Allers, H. W. Nilson, and Kendall made another valuable discovery (24). This was that restriction of potassium intake further facilitated the maintenance of adrenalectomized dogs receiving salt and sodium citrate but not hormone and that by this means the sodium and potassium of the plasma could be maintained at normal levels. This additional information was at once applied to the care of the patients in the hospital, and the advantages thereof could be reported at the April, 1937, meeting of the Association of American Physicians (25). There were numerous authors of this paper: Wilder, Kendall, Snell, Kepler, Rynearson, and Mildred Adams. It stands as a very good example of the benefit to be obtained from close association of workers in the basic sciences with clinicians who are trained in scientific procedure and who have facilities for clinical investigation.

We found in this investigation that patients with Addison's disease who were receiving sodium chloride and sodium citrate could be maintained when given diets providing more than 2 gm. of potassium only if they received adrenocortical extracts; but when the intake of potassium was restricted to less than 2 gm. daily, very little or no hormone at all was required.

Limiting the intake of potassium, together with the giving of extra salt and sodium citrate and holding cortical extract in reserve for times of complications, had so improved our treatment of chronic Addison's disease that Drs. Rynearson, Snell, and Eric Hausner could report (26) that twenty-four of forty-three patients treated between 1933 and 1937 were alive and in better condition than had been the seven survivors out of forty-six patients reviewed by Snell in 1934.

Results in the treatment of Addison's disease continued to be good until the summer of 1939. For more than a year we had had no hospital deaths, although some thirty patients had been admitted in this period, many of them in Addisonian crisis. Then we received and started to use the crystalline preparation of desoxycorticosterone, which Steiger and Reichstein had prepared by synthesis in Switzerland. The patients who received this preparation responded well at first. They became stronger and much more energetic. Also, for the first time, their blood pressures rose to normal. Soon, however, we encountered edema, which persisted in some cases even when the giving of extra sodium was discontinued.

Then death knocked at the door. The first two patients to succumb had been admitted in severe, possibly hopeless, crisis. The third death was that of a woman in whom edema had developed before she arrived. She died suddenly, as if in heart failure, and the heart at necropsy was dilated. The fourth to die was a woman who did well at first after a subcutaneous implant of a pellet of desoxycorticosterone but in whom an increased venous pressure and heart failure developed later. Finally, two women and one man, all receiving the new drug, died at home soon after their dismissal from the hospital—one in convulsions, possibly from hypoglycemia; the other two suddenly as if from heart failure.

That was a bad summer, but, before the end of it, we had discovered that desoxycorticosterone not only obviates the necessity of restricting potassium and giving extra sodium but actually makes that practice dangerous. A patient who was doing well on the regime and also receiving the new drug underwent the Cutler-Power-Wilder test for suspected Addison's disease (27). He responded like a normal person, suffering no loss of sodium and exhibiting no symptoms. This aroused the suspicion that more potassium is required when desoxycorticosterone is used. Study showed that the new synthetic agent provokes retention of salt and water, leading to increased venous pressure and edema when the intake of potassium is restricted and that the giving of more potassium will prevent these developments; in other words, a dietary intake of potassium of 4 gm. or more, which had proved to be dangerous for the patient unsupported by adrenocortical extracts, is indispensable for the patient who is given desoxycorticosterone.

In the meantime, Dr. Kendall had discovered that desoxycorticosterone, powerful as it proved to be in regulating the disturbed salt and water balance of Addison's disease, is lacking in that power of the adrenal cortex to maintain a continuous supply of glucose to the tissues during periods of fasting. In contrast, it was found that this power was possessed by certain crystalline products, notably Dr. Kendall's compounds E and F, later known as "cortisone" and "hydrocortisone," which he had isolated in minute amounts from adrenocortical extracts. When cortisone became available for clinical application, administration of it or of hydrocortisone, together with a small amount of desoxycorticosterone acetate, provided the very satisfactory treatment of Addison's disease which we have today. It should be noted that Dr. Sprague's experience in the use of cortisone in Addison's disease made possible his important contribution to the study by Dr. Philip S. Hench and his associates of the effects of cortisone in the treatment of arthritis (28).

Dr. Sprague's work at the Institute of Experimental Medicine was carried out for his thesis for the degree of Doctor of Philosophy in medicine. His subject was the "Role of the Adrenal Cortex in Carbohydrate Metabolism," and from January, 1938, to April, 1939, he was engaged in this research. It was done under the direction of Dr. Frank C. Mann, but with my supervision and that of Dr. Kendall. My help, I fear, was negligible. It consisted mainly, I believe, in bequeathing Dr. Sprague a beaver coat. The winter of 1938–39 was very cold, and Dr. Sprague was traveling to the institute, three miles out of town, in an open car. I had had the coat for fifteen years. It had been a lovely garment, with mink cuffs and collar, received in trade for an antiquated Packard that Dr. H. E. Robertson and I had wrecked and left behind in a little town in northern Minnesota. The fur had been trapped locally, and it served its purpose well, particularly at the end, in preserving Randall Sprague for his later outstanding accomplishments.

ADDISON'S DISEASE WITH DIABETES

Sprague, Kepler, Keating, and Power reported on three cases of coexisting Addison's disease and diabetes that they had studied carefully (29). This was shortly after Dr. Kendall had been able to provide for clinical investigation small amounts of compounds A and E, isolated from adrenal extract. Their observations on the effect of these two hormones were made with the patients fasting and the "salt-and-water" deficiency of their Addison's disease controlled with desoxycorticosterone or salt or both. Two of the patients were women with severe Addison's disease and potentially severe diabetes. They required very small doses of insulin until the use of compound E (cortisone) was started; then, unless the dose of insulin was increased sharply, ketosis and intense glycosuria developed. Compound A was much less active in this respect, and desoxycorticosterone was without significant effect.

THE ADRENOCORTICAL SYNDROME

Among the problems which aroused the interest of the metabolic sections in the 1930's and 1940's, one of special fascination was related to *overfunction* of the cortical cells of the adrenal glands. Among the first of the many cases of this disorder to come to our attention were four reported by Dr. E. J. Kepler in a symposium given before the staff (30). This was shortly after the publication by Harvey Cushing of his observation of patients in whom tumors of the basophilic cells of the anterior lobe of the pituitary gland were associated with the polyglandular syndrome that came to be known as "Cushing's disease." The salient feature of the syndrome described by Cushing and later well summarized by Kepler in a posthumous publication (31), were ". . . a distinctive habitus characterized by a wasting of muscle and by obesity or abnormal distribution of fat, a combination which makes the trunk, face, and neck appear obese and the extremities thin; hirsutism; hypertension; osteoporosis; diabetes, either latent or frank; ecchymosis; and amenorrhea or impotence. Generally, the skin is thin, and purplish striation occurs. Sometimes there is erythema, nearly always lymphopenia. The concentration of plasma potassium frequently is reduced, and at times hypochloremic alkalosis is present, with or without elevation of plasma sodium. The amount of urinary 17-ketosteroids and corticosteroids may be increased moderately or greatly." Kepler was among the first to regard this symptom complex as adrenocortical in immediate origin.

Dr. Kepler's death in October, 1947, at the early age of fifty-three years, was mourned by all of us. Those close to him had great affection for him as well as admiration. His scientific life was one of those that flower late but remarkably effectively. His papers before the age of forty were few and, one excepted, were written as a junior author with others, but after 1934 they increased in number and significance, covering many topics and evidencing deep thinking and originality. His studies led him widely into endocrinology and were a stimulus to the later work of many. Of great importance was his contribution, made with Dr. Waltman Walters, to the ultimately successful surgical treatment of the adrenocortical syndrome (31).

NUTRITION

In recent years the problems presented by the nutritional quality of the diet have been receiving from physicians something of the recognition they deserve. In the 1930's, although knowledge of nutrition was increasing rapidly in the laboratories of biochemistry and physiology, the medical profession as a whole gave the subject scant attention. Only two groups of physicians showed an interest in nutrition: the specialists in pediatrics and those concerned with diseases involving abnormalities of metabolism. I refer here not to dietetics proper, because diets of many varieties have been used empirically for this or that disease for centuries, but rather to the scientific aspects of nutrition and to recognition of the fact that all diets, whether for the sick or for the well, must provide a certain minimum of each of many nutrients to fill the requirements not only for recovery from disease but for the maintenance of health. This I made the subject of the chairman's address at the 1931 meeting of the Section on Pharmacology and Therapeutics of the American Medical Association (32). In my address I pleaded "for the thoughtful attention of the members of the profession to this important field of therapeutics, for greater intellectual application on the part of practitioners to the quantitative features of dietetics, and for a greater amount of instruction in nutrition by medical schools." This became my theme song for the balance of my professional career.

As an editor of the *Archives of Internal Medicine*, I proposed printing in each issue a review of recent contributions in the several general fields of medicine and assumed responsibility myself for an annual review devoted to nutrition and metabolism. The reviews were well received, and the labor devoted to their preparation rewarded me by lightening the task of preparing my longer text on diabetes (33) and providing a broad background for war tasks to come in Washington, D.C., with the National Research Council's Food and Nutrition Board.

In December, 1938, at a meeting of the Council on Foods and Nutrition of the American Medical Association, of which council I was a member, I proposed encouraging the addition of thiamin to white flour. I had previously discussed the possibility of this with Dr. R. R. Williams, who, I learned, had made a similar proposal, without effect, to governmental agencies in England. I also had discussed the subject with James Ford Bell, then chairman of the Board of General Mills, Inc., and had learned from him that he and their consulting chemist, Dr. Alonzo Taylor, had given thought to such procedure. The favorable action to my suggestion taken by the aforesaid council of the American Medical Association and announced in August, 1939, served to stimulate production of a restored flour by General Mills, Inc., and likewise to guide subsequent actions in the matter of enrichment of flour and white bread taken by the Food and Nutrition Board of the National Research Council, the Food and Drug Administration of the federal government, the National Nutrition Conference called by the President to meet in May, 1941, and the War Food Administration, organized in 1942.

Thanks to the wholehearted co-operation of almost all the larger flour mills and commercial bakers, white flour and white bread, enriched with thiamin, riboflavin, niacin, and iron to meet official standards, soon became widespread. Ultimately, twenty-six of the forty-eight states passed laws requiring it, while in the other states enrichment continued to be done extensively on a voluntary basis. The benefit can hardly be disputed. It could best be demonstrated by what amounted to a controlled, large-scale experiment made in Newfoundland, where malnutrition had long been severe.

In 1944 the Ministry of Health of Newfoundland ordered enrichment of imported flour. There was no flour milling on the island, so this meant that all white flour there became enriched. A group of experts in nutrition, of which I was the senior member, was invited by the Ministry to make a nutrition survey of the population before the order for enrichment took effect. We were a month at it. A representative sample of the people was examined, and all abnormalities were recorded. Four years later, nearly the same group of experts examined approximately the same sample of the population and again recorded what they found (34). The contrast was of great significance. A marked decrease had occurred in the prevalence of lesions such as cheilosis, angular stomatitis, and magenta coloration of the tongue, attributed to deficiency of riboflavin. There were less redness, swelling, and abnormality of the papillae of the tongue, such as are observed in deficiency of nicotinic acid. Complaints of dyspnea and constipation were fewer, and the alertness of the people had increased strikingly, which I, on the basis of experiments conducted in Rochester, was certain could be credited to correction of deficiency of thiamin.

NEW FACILITIES AT ST. MARY'S HOSPITAL

In the later years of the 1930's plans were undertaken for an additional medical pavilion at St. Mary's Hospital. This was an extension westward of the surgical pavilion opened in 1922. We of the metabolic services were deeply interested. The upper floors of the tower between the new medical and the surgical pavilion were set aside for laboratories. Rooms of one, two, or six beds for our patients were on the third floor, and space was provided on the third floor of the tower for a metabolic unit. We called this a "Nutrition Unit," hoping that the name would carry a connotation which would be more acceptable to the patients than "metabolic." It comprised two wards, one of two beds and one of three, with a metabolic kitchen and a roomy laboratory. The administration of the tower facilities, including this nutrition unit and the employment of the special nurses, dietitians, and helpers for it, was by the Mayo Clinic. Plans for the unit were drawn with the aid of Dr. Eugene F. DuBois, who had organized the first such unit at Bellevue Hospital in New York City and later planned a similar but improved facility for Cornell University in the New York Hospital. Dr. DuBois had been a sailor all his life, and the guiding principle for a metabolic unit, he insisted, was to plan it like a yacht so that the helmsman would have all the sails within his range of vision all the time. In other words, the person in the metabolic kitchen should be able to overlook all that went on in the wards.

The time of completion of the new medical pavilion coincided with the time I was called upon for war activities in Washington, D.C. I was away from Rochester much of the time after that June of 1940 and thus was never able to enjoy fully the opportunity, longed for over the years, to carry on investigations in metabolism under conditions that approached what I considered ideal. On the other hand, I could take satisfaction—and I did—in the excellent work done in the Nutrition Unit by Drs. Rynearson, Sprague, and Keating and their associates and other colleagues.

THE MAYO CLINIC DIET MANUAL

The Committee on Dietetics was placed under my continuing chairmanship after 1931. Mary Foley was appointed to serve regularly as its secretary. She was followed in 1942 by Miss Hortense Allen.

The function of the Committee on Dietetics was limited at first to supervision of the dietary procedure of the several hospitals and to reviewing and advising action by the Mayo Clinic's executive committee in the matter of printing all diet lists, pamphlets, and the like intended for distribution to patients. Such material originated in one or another of the Clinic sections. By the middle 1940's the number of special diets had become so large and the procedure of the several hospital services varied to such an extent that it became a matter of necessity to review all these procedures in an attempt to arrive at some degree of uniformity.

Sister Mary Victor had previously assembled and described the diets then in use on the medical and surgical services of St. Mary's Hospital. She had had these published by the hospital but, rather than have the text re-edited, it seemed wise to her and the committee to develop a manual that would cover procedure in all the hospitals. This was a big undertaking. The physician-members of the committee were Dr. Mandred W. Comfort, Dr. Byron E. Hall, Dr. George B. Logan, Dr. R. M. Shick, and Dr. Guy W. Daugherty. Deliberations by the full committee were frequent. They were pleasant occasions, held as they were in the evening at St. Mary's Hospital, where the sisters regularly provided us with a bit of coffee and appropriate nutrition.

As agreement for each new diet was obtained, the diet would be mimeographed and distributed both to the physicians interested and to the diet department of each of the hospitals. A period of trial use followed, and revision was then made as seemed desirable. In the end, the text, reviewed and edited by M. Katharine Smith of the Section of Publications, was published in book form (35).

Epilogue—Subsequent Activities and Inactivities

As stated at the beginning, this essay represents an abridgment of longer Memoirs prepared for the Library of the Mayo Clinic. The necessary condensation results, regrettably, in omission of names and accomplishments of many pupils, assistants, and colleagues mentioned in the longer text.

On retiring from the Clinic in December, 1950, I became director of a new institute of the research arm of the U.S. Public Health Service, the National Institutes of Health. These institutes are located close to Washington, D.C., at Bethesda, Maryland. There I remained until July, 1953. Then, on the advice of my physicians, I returned to my home in Rochester, where I now reside in relative inactivity. I remain a consultant to the National Institute of Arthritis and Metabolic Diseases and visit at Bethesda from time to time. Also, in 1956, I became the president of the National Vitamin Research Foundation, which necessitated enjoyable and enlightening periodic engagements in New York. Otherwise, much reading, especially in the long-neglected humanities, some writing, and the company of a dear and talented wife and many friends fill my days most pleasantly.

The Memoirs of which this is an abridgment closed with a quotation from an old French poet, Joachim du Bellay: "Hereux qui, comme Ulysse, a fait un beau voyage." "Hereux" I translate as "blessed." Not the least of many blessings is to have lived in this period of astonishing developments in the medical sciences—and for that, but even more for all the kindnesses received upon this voyage, I am very truly thankful.

REFERENCES

1. R. M. Wilder and Carol Beeler. Am. J. Physiol., **55**:287, 1921.
2. H. P. Wagener and R. M. Wilder. J.A.M.A., **76**:515, 1921.
3. R. M. Wilder, W. M. Boothby, and Carol Beeler. J. Biol. Chem., **52**:311, 1922.
4. R. M. Wilder and C. E. Baker. Clinic Bull., Vol. 2, Nos. 307 and 308, July 27 and 28, 1921.
5. W. M. Boothby and R. M. Wilder. M. Clin. North America, **7**:53, 1923.
6. R. M. Wilder. M. Clin. North America, **7**:1, 1923.
7. S. F. Adams. M. Clin. North America, **7**:13, 1923.
8. C. J. Barborka. M. Clin. North America, **7**:25, 1923.

9. H. W. Johnson and E. H. Rynearson. Proc. Staff Meet. Mayo Clin., **26**:329, 1951.
10. R. M. Wilder, E. Parsons, and L. M. Randall. M. Clin. North America, **10**:679, 1926.
11. L. M. Randall and E. H. Rynearson. J.A.M.A., **107**:919, 1936.
12. R. M. Wilder and F. N. Allan. J.A.M.A., **94**:147, 1930.
13. R. M. Wilder *et al.* J.A.M.A., **89**:348, 1927.
14. R. M. Wilder. Endocrinology, **13**:231, 1929.
15. R. M. Wilder and J. L. Johnson. Am. J.M. Sc., **182**:800, 1931.
16. C. H. Mayo. J.A.M.A., **89**:1047, 1927.
17. R. M. Wilder. Arch. Int. Med., **38**:736, 1926.
18. H. P. Wagener, T. J. Dry, and R. M. Wilder. New England J. Med., **211**:1131, 1934.
19. R. M. Wilder. Proc. Am. Diabetic Assoc., **6**:109, 1946.
20. ———. A primer for diabetic patients. Philadelphia and London: W. B. Saunders Co., 1950.
21. R. M. Wilder *et al.* J.A.M.A., **106**:1701, 1936.
22. L. G. Rowntree and C. H. Greene. J.A.M.A., **96**:231, 1931.
23. W. D. Allers. Proc. Staff Meet. Mayo Clin., **10**:406, 1935.
24. W. D. Allers, H. W. Nilson, and E. C. Kendall. Proc. Staff Meet. Mayo Clin., **11**:283, 1936.
25. R. M. Wilder *et al.* Arch. Int. Med., **59**:367, 1937.
26. E. H. Rynearson, A. M. Snell, and E. P. Hausner. Ztschr. klin. Med., **134**:11, 1938.
27. H. H. Cutler, W. H. Power, and R. M. Wilder. J.A.M.A., **111**:117, 1938.
28. P. S. Hench *et al.* Arch. Int. Med., **85**:545, 1950.
29. R. G. Sprague *et al.* J. Clin. Invest., **26**:1198, 1947.
30. E. J. Kepler *et al.* Proc. Staff Meet. Mayo Clin., **8**:97, 1933.
31. E. J. Kepler. Ann. New York Acad. Sc., **50**:657, 1949.
32. R. M. Wilder. J.A.M.A., **97**:435, 1931.
33. ———. Clinical diabetes mellitus and hyperinsulinism. Philadelphia and London: W. B. Saunders Co., 1940.
34. W. R. Akroyd *et al.* Canad. M.A.J., **60**:329, 1949.
35. M. Katharine Smith (ed.). Mayo Clinic diet manual. Philadelphia: W. B. Saunders Co., 1949.